BEHOLD
THE PIT

CHRISTIANITY AND PSYCHOSOCIAL ISSUES

ERIC PARKER

ONESTONE
BIBLICAL RESOURCES

Scripture quotations taken from the New American Standard Bible (NASB),
Copyright 1960, 1962, 1963, 1968, 1971, 1972, 1973, 1975, 1977, 1995
by the Lockman Foundation
Used by permission. www.Lockman.org

The author has made minor stylistic modifications to Bible verses
including italicizing, reduction of redundant quotation marks, and
occasional elimination of poetic formatting.

The author is not a medical professional and nothing written herein
should take the place of professional medical advice.

The author's inclusion or referral of an organization is not an endorsement of
all for which that organization stands. The same is true of citations
from books and other reference works.

Design by Stephen Sebree / Moonlight Graphic Works

Published by One Stone Press
979 Lovers Lane
Bowling Green, KY 42103

Printed in the United States of America

ISBN: 978-1-941422-59-5

ONE STONE
BIBLICAL RESOURCES

Dedication

I lovingly dedicate this book to my father, Stanley Parker, who unexpectedly passed away during its composition. He was only able to read a few chapters from the rough draft, but he shared his support and praised my efforts as all good dads do. Without him, I would not be the man I am today.

Table of Contents

Acknowledgements

Friends and loved ones play an integral role in supporting us as we strive to achieve our goals. I am surrounded by support; voices of encouragement have allowed me to see this project through. If the Lord wills, this puts me halfway through the *Behold* Apologetics and Evidences series, for which I have a long-range vision. I know that with God's help and the continued support of my family, friends, and brethren, this is an attainable goal with many benefits to Christians.

To my friend Caitlin Miles, I am indebted for your editorial input. Your notes and comments in the editing process helped direct me toward a more precise expression of the jumbled thoughts in my head. You are a skilled writer, and your passion for poetry has served as a constant source of inspiration to me. Thank you, dear friend, for your love and devotion.

To my designer Steve Sebree of Moonlight Graphic Works, I am indebted to you for your ability to transform research and words into a beautiful format. You see things differently than many in the world, and you have the ability to provide artistic vision and aesthetic beauty to much-needed information. You did this with *Behold the Builder,* and you have done so in this work. God bless you for your skills, and God bless us in the love that exists between our families.

To the many enlisted in reading through the rough drafts for each chapter, I am thankful for your participation in this work. I would like to note a few especially. Olivia, my beloved wife, you faithfully stand by my side and have a vital role in any success that I attain. Andrew Ulmer, my fellow worker in the gospel, I thank you for your thoughts throughout the writing process. Marvin Whittaker and Louie Taylor, some of my best friends, I thank you for helping me to think more deeply about the needs of others.

Finally, to the many Christians who shared their experiences to make this book more relatable, I am thankful in a unique way for you. Your willingness to share your struggles has opened doors that you could not have imagined. I hope that in doing this, you found some benefit as well. I am greatly indebted to your ability to speak from personal experience. May God reward you for your toil.

Preface

Christians must rise to their generation's needs and apply the gospel to those needs in sincerity, love, and truth. There can be little doubt that the age we find ourselves in revolves around matters in the psychosocial realm. This book seeks to address several of these critical needs through helpful research, sound biblical principles, and loving discussion. For that reason, this book serves a key apologetic purpose. Defending the faith necessitates sound doctrine, and it also requires disciples to meet our audience in the place where they are. As such, this book is written to Christians to facilitate constructive dialogue with those outside of the church demanding answers for today's prevalent issues. This book is also composed to persuade Christians to be active in attending to psychosocial needs in the ways that God expects, demands, and authorizes. Finally, this book will respond to those who have left the church, or who are struggling with a perceived inattentiveness of the church toward the needs of real people in need.

The book is developed with a quarter-system teaching cycle in mind, with twelve chapters covering a wide range of matters. The thirteenth week may accommodate a gospel meeting, allow for a review week, or allow for the longer chapter on addictions to be split over two weeks. An individual or group may deem it necessary to spend longer on each chapter as they see appropriate to their respective needs and interests. Some chapters focus more heavily on statistics and data, others on experiences of Christians, and still others on theological and biblical underpinnings. Each chapter provides thought questions to facilitate further meditation and ensure understanding. As you read, please take the necessary time to read the footnotes, as there is essential information included in these comments and more opportunities to grow via the cited works. This book is an intermediate starting point to whet the appetite of God's people to reach out and grow more in the grace and knowledge of our Lord and Savior Jesus Christ (2 Peter 3:18). To God be the glory!

CHAPTER 1

An Introduction to Christianity and Psychosocial Issues

"He brought me up out of the pit of destruction, out of the miry clay; And He set my feet upon a rock making my footsteps firm."

Psalm 40:2

The need for instruction in each facet of God's revealed purposes is perennial. As one generation passes and a new one takes up the mantle, shifts in society and worldviews create newfound struggles the previous generation had typically not borne, or, at the very least, different manifestations of the same core struggles man has always combatted (Ecclesiastes 1:9). Sadly, an earlier generation's efforts to address its own real and pressing issues often serve to create a void that leads to the inception of new troubles. This reflection is not to lay blame on any particular generation, but simply to highlight the pendulum effect of time and the ever-active chess moves of the Adversary. Just as one issue is dealt with and one fire put out, he ignites a new fire. Given this most dangerous match, we would do well to heed the advice of the Holy Spirit:

"Finally, be strong in the Lord and in the strength of His might. Put on the full armor of God, so that you will be able to stand firm against the schemes of the devil. For our struggle is not against flesh and blood, but against the rulers, against the powers, against the world forces of this darkness, against the spiritual forces of wickedness in the heavenly places. Therefore, take up the full armor of God, so that you will be able to resist in the evil day, and having done everything, to stand firm. Stand firm therefore, having girded your loins with truth, and having put on the breastplate of righteousness, and having shod your feet with the preparation of the gospel of peace; in addition to all, taking up the shield of faith with which you will be able to extinguish all the flaming arrows of the evil

one. And take the helmet of salvation, and the sword of the Spirit, which is the word of God. With all prayer and petition pray at all times in the Spirit, and with this in view, be on the alert with all perseverance and petition for all the saints" (Ephesians 6:10-18)

The goal of this resource will be to take the Scriptures and apply them to the pressing issues of the current generation. As such, I hope to help individuals imitate what was said of David—that he served the purpose of God in his own generation and then went to eternal rest (Acts 13:36). There can be little doubt that the primary movement of societal thought has turned to psychosocial issues. I sincerely believe Christians must be equipped to go toe-to-toe in this realm if we are to gain any traction for the gospel of Jesus Christ. This book will serve an apologetic and evangelistic purpose towards those outside of the church, communicate love and compassion for those within the church who deal with these struggles, and show Christians that concern for others' plights in these areas is commendable and vital. The pit can and must be overcome!

"I waited patiently for the Lord; And He inclined to me, and heard my cry. He brought me up out of the pit of destruction, out of the miry clay; and He set my feet upon a rock making my footsteps firm. And He put a new song in my mouth, a song of praise to our God; Many will see and fear, And will trust in the Lord." (Psalm 40:1-3)

What Are "Psychosocial Issues"?

Of course, you may find yourself in the position of not being familiar with the term "psychosocial," and that's okay! Psychosocial is a way of referring to those areas that deal with both the individual mind and the interaction of the individual mind with other minds. In other words, it is where psychology and sociology find their marriage. So, when we refer to psychosocial issues, reference is being made to those actions, activities, thought processes, and states of mind wherein psychological and social disharmony are found. As we approach these matters, we will examine and apply scriptural principles to understand the proper role and function of Christians in these areas.

Naturally, an exhaustive listing of such matters would evade us; however, this book will address some of the matters at the forefront of our society's conversations. These will include such general issues as: fractures in the home, fractures in intimate relationships, fractures in families, and fractures in the mind. We will specifically consider: depression, anxiety, addictions (esp. alcohol, drugs, pornography, and gambling), abortion, adoption and fostering, human trafficking, homosexuality, transgenderism, racism, and homelessness.

Two Polarizing Issues: Apathy and the Social Justice Warrior

Sadly, Satan has a knack for creating disharmony before a proper address is given. Rather than being *"quick to listen, slow to speak, and slow to anger"* (James 1:19), we are prone to respond before we hear, exhibiting folly and finding shame (cf. Proverbs 18:13). We run the opposite risk when we give attention without taking heed in wisdom—*"The first to plead his case seems right, until another comes and examines him"* (Proverbs 18:17). In the case of psychosocial matters, this is especially true. On the one hand, some casually dismiss psychosocial issues with a wave of the hand, even becoming agitated and annoyed by those who feel a passionate spiritual responsibility and/or battle with psychosocial issues in some way themselves. On the other hand, the "social justice warrior" faces the temptation of not being able to have a single conversation without jumping on a hobby horse and berating others for their alleged inattentiveness to psychosocial issues. These discordant positions often polarize more deeply over time, ineffective conversation becomes the norm, and fractures in the body of Christ form. All the while, those in physical need, as well as those in spiritual need, are overlooked and neglected, and the bride for which Christ died is clothed in robes of arrogance, pomposity, and division. Those in the pit stay in the pit, and those outside of the pit hurl themselves into it. How sad!

Is there a way to overcome these issues and achieve agreement? If we desire to enter the gates of Heaven, we must find a way! There is no room for gaps in the mortar between the precious stones of the church. More important than whether believers can find agreement is that agreement is found in a God-glorifying and God-sanctioned way. If the Scriptures instruct disciples to be passionate about psychosocial troubles, that settles it. If the Scriptures do not give attention to psychosocial issues, then that settles it. Answering this first will then lead to a proper conversation on how Christians must proceed in unity.

Do the Scriptures Give Attention to Psychosocial Issues?

Though brief in the grand scheme of bound volumes, the Scriptures possess a depth and scope unrivaled by all others. Several thousand years of Bible history provide timeless moral and ethical examples and considerations for believers' edification. While Scriptures specific to each issue are included in their respective chapters, let's consider some passages that reveal God's expectation for His people to care for those in need. As we do this, keep in mind that these expectations are in full agreement with the Lord's care and provision for the afflicted (cf. Exodus 34:6-7; Deuteronomy 10:18; Psalms 68:5; 146; 2 Corinthians 1:3-5).

Instructions and Examples in the Old Testament

God's character was to be displayed in His people; they were to be a peculiar people for His own possession and a kingdom of priests (Exodus 19:5-6; cf. 1 Peter 2:1-12). Systematic benevolence and concern were built into the Law of Moses in a plethora of ways to ensure the afflicted would not be marginalized, neglected, and forgotten. A few key passages serve to illustrate the Law's provisions:

"Now when you reap the harvest of your land, you shall not reap to the very corners of your field, nor shall you gather the gleanings of your harvest. Nor shall you glean your vineyard, nor shall you gather the fallen fruit of your vineyard; you shall leave them for the needy and for the stranger. I am the Lord your God. You shall not steal, nor deal falsely, nor lie to one another. You shall not swear falsely by My name, so as to profane the name of your God; I am the Lord. You shall not oppress your neighbor, nor rob him. The wages of a hired man are not to remain with you all night until morning. You shall not curse a deaf man, nor place a stumbling block before the blind, but you shall revere your God; I am the Lord. You shall do no injustice in judgment; you shall not be partial to the poor nor defer to the great, but you are to judge your neighbor fairly. You shall not go about as a slanderer among your people, and you are not to act against the life of your neighbor; I am the Lord. You shall not hate your fellow countryman in your heart; you may surely reprove your neighbor, but shall not incur sin because of him. You shall not take vengeance, nor bear any grudge against the sons of your people, but you shall love your neighbor as yourself; I am the Lord...You shall rise up before the gray-headed and honor the aged, and you shall revere your God; I am the Lord. When a stranger resides with you in your land, you shall not do him wrong. The stranger who resides with you shall be to you as the native among you, and you shall love him as yourself, for you were aliens in the land of Egypt; I am the Lord your God. You shall do no wrong in judgment, in measurement of weight, or capacity. You shall have just balances, just weights, a just ephah, and a just hin; I am the Lord your God, Who brought you out from the land of Egypt. You shall thus observe all My statutes and all My ordinances and do them; I am the Lord." (Leviticus 19:9-18, 32-37; cf. Deuteronomy 24:19-22)

"At the end of every seven years you shall grant a remission of debts. This is the manner of remission: every creditor shall release what he has loaned to his neighbor; he shall not exact it of his neighbor and his brother, because

*the Lord's remission has been proclaimed. From a foreigner you may ex-
act it, but your hand shall release whatever of yours is with your brother.
However, there will be no poor among you, since the Lord will surely bless
you in the land which the Lord your God is giving you as an inheritance
to possess, if only you listen obediently to the voice of the Lord your God,
to observe carefully all this commandment which I am commanding you
today. For the Lord your God will bless you as He has promised you, and
you will lend to many nations, but you will not borrow; and you will rule
over many nations, but they will not rule over you. If there is a poor man
with you, one of your brothers, in any of your towns in your land which
the Lord your God is giving you, you shall not harden your heart, nor close
your hand from your poor brother; but you shall freely open your hand
to him, and shall generously lend him sufficient for his need in whatever
he lacks. Beware that there is no base thought in your heart, saying, 'The
seventh year, the year of remission, is near,' and your eye is hostile toward
your poor brother, and you give him nothing; then he may cry to the Lord
against you, and it will be a sin in you. You shall generously give to him,
and your heart shall not be grieved when you give to him, because for this
thing the Lord your God will bless you in all your work and in all your
undertakings. For the poor will never cease to be in the land; therefore, I
command you, saying, 'You shall freely open your hand to your brother,
to your needy and poor in your land.' If your kinsman, a Hebrew man or
woman, is sold to you, then he shall serve you six years, but in the seventh
year you shall set him free. When you set him free, you shall not send him
away empty-handed. You shall furnish him liberally from your flock and
from your threshing floor and from your wine vat; you shall give to him as
the Lord your God has blessed you."* (Deuteronomy 15:1-14)

God's wrath and indignation were ignited when these terms of the covenant were neglected or repudiated, and the prophets repeatedly drew attention
to failures in this respect. Examples include:

*"Woe to those who enact evil statutes
And to those who constantly record unjust decisions,
So as to deprive the needy of justice
And rob the poor of My people of their rights,
So that widows may be their spoil
And that they may plunder the orphans."* (Isaiah 10:1-2; cf. Jeremiah
5:28; 7:6)

"'Woe to him who builds his house without righteousness
And his upper rooms without justice,
Who uses his neighbor's services without pay
And does not give him his wages,
Who says, 'I will build myself a roomy house
With spacious upper rooms,
And cut out its windows,
Paneling it with cedar and painting it bright red.'
Do you become a king because you are competing in cedar?
Did not your father eat and drink
And do justice and righteousness?
Then it was well with him.
He pled the cause of the afflicted and needy;
Then it was well.
Is not that what it means to know Me?'
Declares the Lord.
'But your eyes and your heart
Are intent only upon your own dishonest gain,
And on shedding innocent blood
And on practicing oppression and extortion.'

Therefore, thus says the Lord in regard to Jehoiakim the son of Josiah, king of Judah,

'They will not lament for him:
'Alas, my brother!' or, 'Alas, sister!'
They will not lament for him:
'Alas for the master!' or, 'Alas for his splendor!'
He will be buried with a donkey's burial,
Dragged off and thrown out beyond the gates of Jerusalem.'" (Jeremiah 22:13-19)

"Thus says the Lord,
'For three transgressions of Israel and for four
I will not revoke its punishment,
Because they sell the righteous for money
And the needy for a pair of sandals.
These who pant after the very dust of the earth on the head of the helpless
Also turn aside the way of the humble;
And a man and his father resort to the same girl
In order to profane My holy name.'" (Amos 2:6-7)

"They hate him who reproves in the gate,
And they abhor him who speaks with integrity.
Therefore, because you impose heavy rent on the poor
And exact a tribute of grain from them,
Though you have built houses of well-hewn stone,
Yet you will not live in them;
You have planted pleasant vineyards, yet you will not drink their wine.
For I know your transgressions are many and your sins are great,
You who distress the righteous and accept bribes
And turn aside the poor in the gate.
Therefore, at such a time the prudent person keeps silent, for it is an evil
time.

Seek good and not evil, that you may live;
And thus may the Lord God of hosts be with you,
Just as you have said!
Hate evil, love good,
And establish justice in the gate!
Perhaps the Lord God of hosts
May be gracious to the remnant of Joseph." (Amos 5:10-15)

"Hear this, you who trample the needy, to do away with the humble of the
land, saying,

'When will the new moon be over,
So that we may sell grain,
And the sabbath, that we may open the wheat market,
To make the bushel smaller and the shekel bigger,
And to cheat with dishonest scales,
So as to buy the helpless for money
And the needy for a pair of sandals,
And that we may sell the refuse of the wheat?'" (Amos 8:4-6)

The Law and the Prophets were not the only sections of the Old Testament that focused on care for the burdened. The Old Testament Wisdom Literature heavily emphasizes this theme as well. The exceeding value of this is that Christians can look to such passages without dismissing them as being restricted to the Law of Moses. Selections from Proverbs are illustrative:

"There is one who scatters, and yet increases all the more,
And there is one who withholds what is justly due, and yet it results only
in want.
The generous man will be prosperous,
And he who waters will himself be watered." (11:24-25; cf. 19:17)

"He who oppresses the poor taunts his Maker,
But he who is gracious to the needy honors Him." (14:31; cf. 14:21; 17:5)

"He who mocks the poor taunts his Maker;
He who rejoices at calamity will not go unpunished." (17:5)

"He who shuts his ear to the cry of the poor
Will also cry himself and not be answered." (21:13)

"The rich and the poor have a common bond,
The Lord is the maker of them all." (22:2; cf. 29:13)

"He who is generous will be blessed,
For he gives some of his food to the poor." (22:9)

"He who increases his wealth by interest and usury
Gathers it for him who is gracious to the poor." (28:8)

"He who gives to the poor will never want,
But he who shuts his eyes will have many curses." (28:27)

"The righteous is concerned for the rights of the poor,
The wicked does not understand such concern." (29:7)

"Open your mouth for the mute,
For the rights of all the unfortunate.
Open your mouth, judge righteously,
And defend the rights of the afflicted and needy." (31:8-9)

"[The virtuous woman] extends her hand to the poor,
And she stretches out her hands to the needy." (31:20)

Instructions and Examples in the New Testament

God's care for the physically, emotionally, psychologically, and socially needy carries over into the New Testament. Jesus repeatedly attends to the rejected and forgotten of society (e.g., Mark 10:46-52; 12:41-44; Luke 7:11-17; John 9). He frequently demonstrates compassion and sympathy (e.g., Matthew 9:36-37; 15:32ff; 20:34; Mark 1:41) and extols the value of loving one's neighbor, whoever that is, as oneself (e.g., Luke 10:25-37; 16:19-31).

The compassionate character of Immanuel (i.e., "God with us") serves as the ideal goal for Christians in their spiritual development. The actions of the early disciples emulate Jesus' kindness (e.g., Acts 3-4; 19:11-12). In fact, benevolence toward the destitute was one of the key emphases of the early church (cf. Galatians 2:10), serving as an illustration of true repentance (cf. Luke 3:11; Daniel 4:27). Such compassionate deeds corroborate the markers of true religion outlined in the New Testament:

"So then, while we have opportunity, let us do good to all people, and especially to those who are of the household of the faith." (Galatians 6:10)

"If anyone thinks himself to be religious, and yet does not bridle his tongue but deceives his own heart, this man's religion is worthless. Pure and undefiled religion in the sight of our God and Father is this: to visit orphans and widows in their distress, and to keep oneself unstained by the world." (James 1:26-27)

"What use is it, my brethren, if someone says he has faith but he has no works? Can that faith save him? If a brother or sister is without clothing and in need of daily food, and one of you says to them, 'Go in peace, be warmed and be filled,' and yet you do not give them what is necessary for their body, what use is that? Even so faith, if it has no works, is dead, being by itself. But someone may well say, 'You have faith and I have works; show me your faith without the works, and I will show you my faith by my works.' You believe that God is one. You do well; the demons also believe, and shudder. But are you willing to recognize, you foolish fellow, that faith without works is useless? Was not Abraham our father justified by works when he offered up Isaac his son on the altar? You see that faith was working with his works, and as a result of the works, faith was perfected; and the Scripture was fulfilled which says, 'And Abraham believed God, and it was reckoned to him as righteousness,' and he was called the friend of God. You see that a man is justified by works and not by faith alone. In the same way, was not Rahab the harlot also justified by works when she

received the messengers and sent them out by another way? For just as the body without the spirit is dead, so also faith without works is dead." (James 2:14-26)

Moreover, the magnanimity Christians can express to those weighed down by psychosocial matters matches God's expectation for believers to be zealous for good deeds (cf. Ephesians 2:10; Titus 2:7, 11-14; 3:8, 14; Hebrews 10:24-25; James 3:13; 1 Peter 2:12). In the Day of Judgment, compassion becomes a litmus test for authentic discipleship:

"But when the Son of Man comes in His glory, and all the angels with Him, then He will sit on His glorious throne. All the nations will be gathered before Him; and He will separate them from one another, as the shepherd separates the sheep from the goats; and He will put the sheep on His right, and the goats on the left.

Then the King will say to those on His right, 'Come, you who are blessed of My Father, inherit the kingdom prepared for you from the foundation of the world. For I was hungry, and you gave Me something to eat; I was thirsty, and you gave Me something to drink; I was a stranger, and you invited Me in; naked, and you clothed Me; I was sick, and you visited Me; I was in prison, and you came to Me.' Then the righteous will answer Him, 'Lord, when did we see You hungry, and feed You, or thirsty, and give You something to drink? And when did we see You a stranger, and invite You in, or naked, and clothe You? When did we see You sick, or in prison, and come to You?' The King will answer and say to them, 'Truly I say to you, to the extent that you did it to one of these brothers of Mine, even the least of them, you did it to Me.'

Then He will also say to those on His left, 'Depart from Me, accursed ones, into the eternal fire which has been prepared for the devil and his angels; for I was hungry, and you gave Me nothing to eat; I was thirsty, and you gave Me nothing to drink; I was a stranger, and you did not invite Me in; naked, and you did not clothe Me; sick, and in prison, and you did not visit Me.' Then they themselves also will answer, 'Lord, when did we see You hungry, or thirsty, or a stranger, or naked, or sick, or in prison, and did not take care of You?' Then He will answer them, 'Truly I say to you, to the extent that you did not do it to one of the least of these, you did not do it to Me.' These will go away into eternal punishment, but the righteous into eternal life." (Matthew 25:31-46)

Institutionalism Versus Non-Institutionalism

There is no doubt God wants His people to prioritize the spiritual over the physical. Likewise, God desires for His people to be diligent in their demonstrations of love in the world. The critical question is how these may simultaneously, and appropriately, be done.

In 1 Timothy 5, instructions are laid out for the care of widows within the church. Of note are the limitations in the scope of collective benevolence from the church's treasury. Not only is benevolence limited to believing widows, but there is a series of stipulations limiting even this collaborative work of the church. Prescription is given for widows who do not meet these criteria; specifically, family members are to fulfill their duties of honor outside of the collective church's resources so that the church would not be burdened (5:16). On first reading, this seems harsh and stifled in compassion; however, the church's finances are limited in amount and authorization (compare the limited use of the funds in Acts 11 and 20-21 for believers in Jerusalem and Judea). Consider also the church's limitations in light of such a huge need, for the poor will always be among us (cf. Mark 14:7). God's wisdom differentiates between what the church may do collectively and what responsibilities remain in the realm of the private individual. God's intent is that true needs are met in the most effective way.

To illustrate the wisdom of this divine order, let us consider the care of orphans and widows, the scriptural test for religiosity (cf. James 1:26-27). In an institutional conception of the church, a congregation collects funds that are then dispersed to orphan homes, rehabilitation centers, retirement homes, sponsoring churches, or other organizations that oversee the care of widows and orphans. This structure places multiple degrees of separation between the people in need and those attempting to provide for that need. These degrees of separation can result in a variety of monetary issues, including embezzlement, fraud, theft, etc. Of specific relation to the church, this system can result in over-extension of a congregation's resources marginalizing evangelism and edification, and create a vast gulf between believers and those in need, thus inhibiting the actual availability and flow of resources that end up getting to orphans and widows. With a non-institutional conception of the church, these dangers are minimized, and believers can more actively actualize the responsibilities laid out in James 1:26-27 and Galatians 6:10, a reality we will discuss further in Chapter 7. Funding is also more likely to be provided for the church's collective and individual responsibilities, circumventing many opportunities for Satan to insert his influence into the process.

There is wisdom in God's order, but only if the church, as a collective and as private individuals, is fulfilling its responsibilities in its distinct capacities.

As an important caveat, the organization of Christians outside of the scope of the church (e.g., charities, benefits, fundraisers, etc.) to attend to needs may not only be useful, but may also be wise and helpful. The issue is in properly understanding God's provisions and expectations for the private individual Christian and the collective body of Christians.[1]

The Evangelistic and Apologetic Value of Good Deeds

Consistency is a beacon of light in a dark and dying world. Not only that, but inconsistency is a ground of accusation for those hostile to the truths of the gospel (cf. 2 Samuel 12:14; 2 Peter 2:2). When a person verbally espouses a relationship with Christ, preaching a message of love, forgiveness, grace, mercy, and compassion, and then in their manner of life are apathetic or hateful to the plight of those in affliction, nonbelievers' assumptions and doubts regarding the gospel are confirmed in their minds. Of course, these perceptions do not accurately reflect the gospel, but rather the sin which the gospel aims to resolve! Regardless, this discrepancy poses obstacles for these inconsistent persons and for those who strive for constancy in the gospel. This spirit is absolutely condemned in the Scriptures:

> "Then Jesus spoke to the crowds and to His disciples, saying: 'The scribes and the Pharisees have seated themselves in the chair of Moses; therefore, all that they tell you, do and observe, but do not do according to their deeds; for they say things and do not do them. They tie up heavy burdens and lay them on men's shoulders, but they themselves are unwilling to move them with so much as a finger. But they do all their deeds to be noticed by men" (Matthew 23:1-5a)

> "Woe to you, scribes and Pharisees, hypocrites! For you tithe mint and dill and cumin, and have neglected the weightier provisions of the law: justice and mercy and faithfulness; but these are the things you should have done without neglecting the others. You blind guides, who strain out a gnat and swallow a camel!

> Woe to you, scribes and Pharisees, hypocrites! For you clean the outside of the cup and of the dish, but inside they are full of robbery and self-indul-

---

[1] For a beneficial and sound treatment of the differences between the responsibilities of the collective church and the private individual, see: Moyer, Doy. *Mind Your King*. CreateSpace, 2016. See also: *The Simple Pattern: A Straight-Forward Explanation of Institutionalism & Related Issues*, edited by Jim Deason. ECI Publishing, 2012.

gence. You blind Pharisee, first clean the inside of the cup and of the dish, so that the outside of it may become clean also.

Woe to you, scribes and Pharisees, hypocrites! For you are like white-washed tombs which on the outside appear beautiful, but inside they are full of dead men's bones and all uncleanness. So, you, too, outwardly appear righteous to men, but inwardly you are full of hypocrisy and lawlessness." (Matthew 23:23-28)

"But if you bear the name 'Jew' and rely upon the Law and boast in God, and know His will and approve the things that are essential, being instructed out of the Law, and are confident that you yourself are a guide to the blind, a light to those who are in darkness, a corrector of the foolish, a teacher of the immature, having in the Law the embodiment of knowledge and of the truth, you, therefore, who teach another, do you not teach yourself? You who preach that one shall not steal, do you steal? You who say that one should not commit adultery, do you commit adultery? You who abhor idols, do you rob temples? You who boast in the Law, through your breaking the Law, do you dishonor God? For 'the name of God is blasphemed among the Gentiles because of you,' just as it is written." (Romans 2:17-24)

"But when Cephas came to Antioch, I opposed him to his face, because he stood condemned. For prior to the coming of certain men from James, he used to eat with the Gentiles; but when they came, he began to withdraw and hold himself aloof, fearing the party of the circumcision. The rest of the Jews joined him in hypocrisy, with the result that even Barnabas was carried away by their hypocrisy. But when I saw that they were not straightforward about the truth of the gospel, I said to Cephas in the presence of all, 'If you, being a Jew, live like the Gentiles and not like the Jews, how is it that you compel the Gentiles to live like Jews?'" (Galatians 2:11-14)

"They profess to know God, but by their deeds they deny Him, being detestable and disobedient and worthless for any good deed." (Titus 1:16)

"Therefore, putting aside all filthiness and all that remains of wickedness, in humility receive the word implanted, which is able to save your souls. But prove yourselves doers of the word, and not merely hearers who delude themselves. For if anyone is a hearer of the word and not a doer, he is like a man who looks at his natural face in a mirror; for once he has looked at *himself and gone away, he has immediately forgotten what kind of person he was. But one who looks intently at the perfect law, the law of liberty, and abides by it, not having become a forgetful hearer but an effectual doer, this man will be blessed in what he does...What use is it, my brethren, if someone says he has faith but he has no works? Can that faith save him? If a brother or sister is without clothing and in need of daily food, and one of you says to them, 'Go in peace, be warmed and be filled,' and yet you do not give them what is necessary for their body, what use is that? Even so faith, if it has no works, is dead, being by itself."* (James 1:21-25; 2:14-17)

More than just avoiding grounds of accusation, active participation and interest in our age's psychosocial issues show people of the world and our fellow Christians that the gospel is indeed good news. This concern, in turn, reveals substantial positive changes in the lives of its adherents.[2] People lost in the world need to see the positive transformation of Jesus in His followers, and they need to see the light of His love magnified in word and deed in a world shrouded in darkness (cf. John 13:34-35). When those in the world see this, the gospel is positively fragrant. This is especially the case in metropolitan areas near coastal cities as the needful of society in these areas take a more prominent role in legislation, support by charities, and widespread discussion.[3]

In sum, as expressed in response to psychosocial struggles, good deeds will serve to share the gospel of Jesus Christ in a way that answers the call of our current age. In compassion and sympathy, concern and love, Christians broadcast the message of salvation worldwide to those who do not know salvation (Matthew 28:18-20; Mark 16:15-16). Furthermore, these good deeds towards pressing needs serve an apologetic purpose, which Christians are to faithfully observe (cf. Philippians 1:16; 1 Peter 3:15).

A Closing Word on Passion

God's people are passionate. They are passionate in their marriages; they are passionate in their families; they are passionate in their work; they are passionate in their congregations. A lack of passion can be symptomatic of dis-

---

[2] Though he does not distinguish collective and private responsibilities and is denominational, Timothy Keller helpfully examines the growing interest in psychosocial issues among espoused Christians in his book *The Reason for God: Belief in an Age of Skepticism*.

[3] For one researcher's examination of the relationship between population density and conceptions of systematized benevolence, see: https://www.facebook.com/ShannonWelch/posts/10158317586703617.

tance from Christ. So, when a believer becomes passionate about a just and noble cause, they should be highly and positively esteemed! They should not be disregarded, dismissed, and dissuaded from their passion. While passion can take the form of lust for the physical, desire itself is not evil!

The chief goal for Christians is to be passionate for the spiritual needs of a dark and dying world; it is noble to participate in this aspect of the good and acceptable and perfect will of God (Romans 12:1-2). First and foremost, preach the gospel to the world for the salvation of souls; the one who does this finds blessing in his or her endeavor (cf. Proverbs 11:28-30). Second, broadcast compassion and love to affirm the value of this gospel. Passion in both these areas opens doorways for the gospel to spread among the multitudes. Be passionate to aid the mentally afflicted, the addicted, the immoral, the prostitutes, and the sinners—Jesus certainly was! (cf. Matthew 9:10-11; 11:19; 21:31-32; Mark 2:15-16; Luke 15:1)

Thought Questions

1) What emotions arose as you read this chapter and how did this information affect you?

_____

_____

2) Describe the relationship that exists between the Christian and psychosocial issues.

_____

_____

3) What dangers lie in being a "social justice warrior"?

_____

_____

4) What dangers can arise in apathy toward psychosocial issues?

_____

_____

5) In what ways can passion for psychosocial matters positively impact one's discipleship?

_____

_____

6) What are some of your favorite Old Testament passages that speak about believers and psychosocial issues?

_____

_____

7) What are some of your favorite New Testament passages that speak about believers and psychosocial issues?

_____

_____

CHAPTER 2

Depression

I t was the third consecutive day she was in bed. It was the second time this month that she had missed Sunday worship services. She wanted to be there; she knew she should be there. Her children kept asking her what was wrong. How could she explain it? A month ago, her oldest found her with a bottle of sleeping pills in her bedroom, about to make the worst decision she could ever make. That moment was etched in her memory and sent her spiraling even more, though she had held off that night. She hated herself. She hated life. She hated feeling like this. She wanted change; she craved change. She wanted help, but she had not found it. She wanted her spiritual brothers and sisters to understand, but she also did not want to feel judged or misunderstood. She was depressed, and she knew it. She struggled like millions of others, and she was a Christian. She serves to illustrate the heart and soul of this chapter.

When we consider the most pressing psychosocial issues for the church, we must understand that fractures in the home inevitably lead to fractures in psychological states, which in turn create fractures in society and the church. One of the most prominent of these fractures is depression. Depression is a real, widespread mental illness with numerous spiritual connections. The fact is that many outside and inside of the church strive to cope with depression every day. It is a sad reality that, if avoided or ignored, will only worsen, and God forbid that Christians would engage in such an evil behavior as to deny the mental anguish of their spiritual brother or sister. Instead, let us focus our attention on equipping ourselves and others to discuss this reality from an informed standpoint that will prove effective because the church must address this issue. May God be glorified as His people manage all areas from the pattern of His inspired Word (Psalm 119:160; 2 Timothy 3:16-17).

What Is Depression?

The American Psychological Association (APA) uses a systematic manual to diagnose mental illness known as the *Diagnostic and Statistical Manual of Mental Disorders.* The current fifth edition of that manual is the DSM-5. The basic guidelines from the DSM-5 will help us to define depression to facilitate our response to this disorder of the mind.[4]

The DSM-5 generally defines depression by stating:
"Depression, otherwise known as major depressive disorder or clinical depression, is a common and serious mood disorder. Those who suffer from depression experience persistent feelings of sadness and hopelessness and lose interest in activities they once enjoyed. Aside from the emotional problems caused by depression, individuals can also present with a physical symptom such as chronic pain or digestive issues. To be diagnosed with depression, symptoms must be present at least two weeks."[5]

The manual specifies the following: *"The individual must be experiencing five or more symptoms during the same two-week period and at least one of the symptoms should be either (1) depressed mood or (2) loss of interest or pleasure"* and then proceeds to list the criteria:

- *Depressed mood most of the day, nearly every day.*
- *Markedly diminished interest or pleasure in all, or almost all, activities most of the day, nearly every day.*
- *Significant weight loss when not dieting or weight gain, or decrease or increase in appetite nearly every day.*
- *A slowing down of thought and a reduction of physical movement (observable by others, not merely subjective feelings of restlessness or being slowed down).*
- *Fatigue or loss of energy nearly every day.*
- *Feelings of worthlessness or excessive or inappropriate guilt nearly every day.*
- *Diminished ability to think or concentrate, or indecisiveness, nearly every day.*

---

[4] The World Health Organization (WHO) uses similar criteria in their manual, known as the *International Classification of Diseases*, which is now in the eleventh edition (ICD-11).

[5] *Diagnostic and Statistical Manual of Mental Disorders: DSM-5.* American Psychiatric Association, 2017.

- *Recurrent thoughts of death, recurrent suicidal ideation without a specific plan, or a suicide attempt or a specific plan for committing it.*

To these standards, we offer several additional observations. First, there are a plethora of different forms and manifestations of depression (e.g., Postpartum, Major, Atypical, Psychotic, Seasonal Affective, Dysthymia, etc.), which offer additional or nuanced criteria.[6] Mental illness rarely, if ever, fits neatly into a box. Also, depression and anxiety are two sides to the same coin, as we will explain further in Chapter 3. In addition to the criteria above, depressed individuals can present with irritability, brooding, obsessive rumination, anxiety, phobias, excessive worry over physical health, and complaints of pain often with no physiological cause (i.e., somatic symptom disorder). For a formal diagnosis, there must be, by definition, clinically significant distress or impairment in social, occupational, or other important areas of functioning. According to statistics from the World Health Organization (WHO) and the National Institute of Mental Health (NIMH), depression affects at least 322 million people worldwide and 16-17 million people every year in the United States.[7][8] Based on reporting, there is a gender component here as well, as women are more likely to be diagnosed than men. Major depressive disorder is associated with high mortality, mainly because of suicide, drug use, and reckless behavior. This amounts to a yearly average of over a million deaths!

While many struggle with chronic disorders of the mind, I sincerely believe that each person has experienced a degree of situational depression, or Adjustment Disorder.[9] This is not the same as chronic depression, but it does help those who do not have it to begin to empathize with those who do. This shared pain also provides an opportunity for Christians to open up with one another, building toward mutual edification. Such is God's plan for those who deal with affliction:

---

[6] For a helpful article on some of these differences, see: Koskie, Brandi. "Depression: Facts, Statistics, and You." *Healthline*, Healthline Media, 3 June 2020, www.healthline.com/health/depression/facts-statistics-infographic#Types-of-depression.

[7] Depression and Other Common Mental Disorders: Global Health Estimates. Geneva: World Health Organization; 2017. CC BY-NC-SA 3.0 IGO.

[8] "Major Depression." National Institute of Mental Health, US Department of Health and Human Services, Feb. 2019, www.nimh.nih.gov/health/statistics/major-depression.shtml.

[9] The extensive difficulties of the COVID-19 pandemic in 2020 highlight this reality. For one such research study showing this, see: Roy Perlis, et al. "The State of the Nation: A 50-State COVID-19 Survey, Report #23: Depression Among Young Adults," *The COVID-19 Consortium for Understanding the Public's Policy Preferences Across States,* November 9, 2020, v.1.

"Blessed be the God and Father of our Lord Jesus Christ, the Father of mercies and God of all comfort, who comforts us in all our affliction so that we will be able to comfort those who are in any affliction with the comfort with which we ourselves are comforted by God. For just as the sufferings of Christ are ours in abundance, so also our comfort is abundant through Christ" (2 Corinthians 1:3-5).

Indeed, Christians might better serve each other by bearing one another's burdens in such a sober area of life (cf. Galatians 6:2).

God's People Struggle with Depression

So, what about Christians? Do Christians struggle with depression, or is it just a problem of "the world"? Is it a matter of low or high spirituality? With the fact that 25% of people meet the criteria for a depressive episode in their lives, it statistically stands to reason that God's people struggle with depression. Such a self-evident truth is illustrated in the inspired record of God. As the psalmist lamented:

"Answer me quickly, LORD, my spirit fails;
Do not hide your face from me,
Or I will be the same as those who go down to the pit.
Let me hear Your faithfulness in the morning,
For I trust in You;
Teach me the way in which I should walk;
For to you I lift up my soul" (Psalm 143:7-8).

Building on this truth from God's Word and common-sense statistics, I solicited further evidence via input from Christians to see if this was indeed verifiable in the real world. The response was, simply put, overwhelming. Listen to the following real testimonies gathered from all across demographic lines within the church: men, women, college-educated, military, young, old, wealthy, and poor.

"Depression comes out of the blue. You see no hope, happiness, or future. You don't want to talk to anyone, and if you are out in public, you make no eye contact. You are very quiet and withdrawn. You feel like you are in a deep dark well and you can't get out! You also are very tired and would

like nothing better than to stay in bed all day (that makes it worse, so just get up)."

"I am no expert, but have dealt with depression the majority of my life. It is one of the very cunning, baffling, insidious, and powerfully evil methods that Satan uses against people to destroy them."

"When I was in college, about two-thirds of my friend group struggled with some form of anxiety, depression, suicidal tendencies, etc. I think it's more pervasive than we care to admit. Probably the worst thing someone said to me was that people who are depressed are selfish and if they weren't as self-absorbed, they'd be okay. It absolutely broke me. My self-harm and depression have always been triggered by feeling like I'm failing others. If I could say one thing to Christians struggling with this, it would be that Scripture tells us to seek wisdom. Counseling and therapy are wisdom. It makes us masters of our own minds again. And helps us be the most effective Christians we can."

"I struggle with depression caused by various reasons more than I like to admit. The crazy thing about it is, it's often the catalyst to anger, guilt, and shame for me. As a man it makes me feel weak and like I am self-pitying which causes the emotions of anger, guilt and shame. As a Christian it can make me feel unappreciative for what God has blessed me with which feeds a sense of failure causing me to get inside my head and pick myself apart. The challenge for me is talking about it. I struggle with expressing how I feel because throughout life I've had to learn how to turn things on and off to protect myself and others around me, resulting in a man who has trouble expressing himself in a healthy way at times. Romans 8:26-27 comforts me because as much as I like to talk, I struggle to find the words when I'm feeling low. I'm thankful for God's love, mercy and grace but I don't always feel worthy of it."

What a humbling assortment of testimonies from real Christians who struggle with depression! Also important to keep in mind is that the calamities of life can also increase these experiences and the aforementioned diagnostic rates. When the patriarch Job suffered incomparable loss, he lamented, *"Man, who is born of woman, is short-lived and full of turmoil. Like a flower he comes out and withers. He also flees like a shadow and does not remain"* (Job 14:1-2). And was it not Jesus Who preached, *"Each day has enough trouble of its own"*? (Matthew 6:34) During the particularly difficult year of 2020, one Christian candidly shared the following: *"Has anyone else felt like this lately? I didn't mind quarantine much at first. But lately I'm starting to feel the way people were talking about early on during lockdown. Isolated, worried, a little paranoid, lacking friends, unmotivated, the days blurring together, etc."* She was not the only one! One study done by the CDC shows remarkably high increases in depression and anxiety during the Coronavirus surge.[10] In addition to this study and others, suicide hotlines saw significant increases during these tumultuous months, up to 75x higher rates in major metropolitan areas![11]

What Does the Bible Say About Depression?

The Bible is filled with all manner of thoughts, observations, and instructions on life across various genres. As such, the Bible discusses depression in a variety of contexts. God's inspired Word reflects on the spiritual and metaphysical origin of mental disorder. In the Garden of Eden, all was perfect (Genesis 1:31; 2; 3). When humanity chose to sin, open access to perfection was cut off because sin separated man from God (cf. Isaiah 59:1-2)—being cut off brought corruption and death, including degeneration of the human mind (Romans 8:18-25; 2 Corinthians 4:4; 10:5; 11:3; Ephesians 6:10-18; 1 John 5:19). This is scientifically attested to by a massive meta-analysis study where a review of 444 studies showed that a religious or spiritual intervention for depressed individuals resulted in improvement 61% of the time. Only 6% of the time did it increase depressive symptoms. This analysis overwhelmingly shows that depression has a spiritual connection and metaphysical component.[12]

In addition to these spiritual origins, there are ongoing spiritual factors that can aggravate disorders of the mind, particularly depression and anxiety. Proverbs 12:25 discusses this explicitly: *"Anxiety in a person's heart weighs it down, but a good word makes it glad."* So how does Satan weigh down the heart of human souls? He afflicts us socially and emotionally through loneliness, isolation, bullying, pride, partiality, guilt, remorse, and the like. He compounds these stresses by tempting us to use "fixes," which in reality intensify

---

[10] Czeisler MÉ , Lane RI, Petrosky E, et al. Mental Health, Substance Use, and Suicidal Ideation During the COVID-19 Pandemic — United States, June 24–30, 2020. MMWR Morb Mortal Wkly Rep 2020;69:1049–1057. DOI: http://dx.doi.org/10.15585/mmwr.mm6932a1

[11] Sweeney, Don. "Some Areas of the Country See Increase in Suicide Related-Calls as Coronavirus Spreads." Sacbee, The Sacramento Bee, 25 Mar. 2020, www.sacbee.com/news/coronavirus/article241493126.html.

[12] Bonelli, Raphael, et al. *"Religious and Spiritual Factors in Depression: Review and Integration of the Research." Depression Research and Treatment* vol. 2012 (2012): 962860. doi:10.1155/2012/962860.

or perpetuate depression. The Devil encourages drugs, alcohol, licentiousness, promiscuity, theft, gambling, etc. to provide temporary relief but no enduring satisfaction. Moses' example in overcoming this temptation is inspiring:

> "By faith Moses, when he had grown up, refused to be called the son of Pharaoh's daughter, choosing rather to endure ill-treatment with the people of God than to enjoy the temporary pleasures of sin, considering the reproach of Christ greater riches than the treasures of Egypt; for he was looking to the reward" (Hebrews 11:24-26).

Having established these foundational factors, let us now proceed to consider biblical examples of those who seem to have struggled with depression, both situational and chronic.

Old Testament examples of depression are multitudinous. No doubt, Job would have met the diagnostic criteria for depression. The text openly shares Job's response to years of Satanic challenges:

> "Why did I not die at birth,
> Come out of the womb and expire?" (3:11)

> "I am not at ease, nor am I quiet,
> And I am not at rest, but turmoil comes." (3:26)

> "I loathe my own life;
> I will give full vent to my complaint;
> I will speak in the bitterness of my soul." (10:1)

> "Terrors are turned against me;
> They pursue my honor as the wind,
> And my prosperity has passed away like a cloud.
> And now my soul is poured out within me;
> Days of affliction have seized me.
> At night it pierces my bones within me,
> And my gnawing pains take no rest.
> By a great force my garment is distorted;
> It binds me about as the collar of my coat.
> He has cast me into the mire,
> And I have become like dust and ashes.
> I cry out to You for help, but You do not answer me;
> I stand up, and You turn Your attention against me.
> You have become cruel to me;

With the might of Your hand You persecute me.
You lift me up to the wind and cause me to ride;
And You dissolve me in a storm.
For I know that You will bring me to death
And to the house of meeting for all living.
Yet does not one in a heap of ruins stretch out his hand,
Or in his disaster therefore cry out for help?
Have I not wept for the one whose life is hard?
Was not my soul grieved for the needy?
When I expected good, then evil came;
When I waited for light, then darkness came." (30:15-26)

Similar to Job's situational struggles, 1 Kings 19 speaks of Elijah's experiential depression. King David struggled (e.g., 2 Samuel 12:15-23; 18:19-33). Jonah struggled with depression resulting from his sinful response to God's compassion (Jonah 4). Jeremiah, "The Weeping Prophet," also struggled with depression throughout his decades-long ministry (e.g., 15:10, 18; 20:14, 18).

New Testament examples of depression are not as frequent, but some interesting case studies are worth considering. Judas Iscariot suffered a mental crisis resulting from the guilt and shame of his treatment of the Lord, perhaps exacerbated by his pilfering from the collective funds used by the apostles (John 12:6; Matthew 27:3-5; Acts 1:18-20). If we are willing to set aside the common incorrect assumption that depression makes one somehow less godly, we might also consider the Lord Himself, Who across years expressed difficulty with the struggles of life and was even prophetically identified by this:

"He was despised and forsaken of men, a man of sorrows and acquainted with grief; and like one from whom men hide their face He was despised, and we did not esteem Him." (Isaiah 53:3)

"But I have a baptism to undergo, and how distressed I am until it is accomplished!" (Luke 12:50)

"Now My soul has become troubled; and what shall I say, 'Father, save Me from this hour'? But for this purpose I came to this hour." (John 12:27)

"And He took with Him Peter and James and John, and began to be very distressed and troubled. And He said to them, 'My soul is deeply grieved to the point of death; remain here and keep watch.' And He went a little beyond them, and fell to the ground and began to pray that if it were possible, the hour might pass Him by. And He was saying, 'Abba! Father! All

things are possible for You; remove this cup from Me; yet not what I will, but what You will" (Mark 14:33-36)

"And being in agony He was praying very fervently; and His sweat became like drops of blood, falling down upon the ground." (Luke 22:44)

Shouldn't we also consider the apostle Paul who labored with many toils, among which were afflictions of the flesh and the mind? (2 Corinthians 4-5; 11-12)

The Bible does not promise an earthly cure-all for life's afflictions, much less depression. However, the Bible does affirm that a strong relationship with God and His people can equip one with valuable resources to cope with depression on this side of eternity and to look forward to full deliverance on the other side. Jesus speaks to this when He offers His invitation in Matthew 11:28-30: *"Come to Me, all who are weary and heavy-laden, and I will give you rest. Take My yoke upon you and learn from Me, for I am gentle and humble in heart, and you will find rest for your souls. For My yoke is easy and My burden is light."* Solace to the tormented mind is in Christ's hope (Psalm 42:11; 2 Corinthians 1:10; Colossians 1:5-6, 23, 27; 1 Timothy 1:1). Christians can be confident that God is near to His people and find balm for the soul in that security (Psalms 34:18; 50:15; 2 Corinthians 7:6a). Moreover, God is not alone in His comforts, as He offers a spiritual family to those who feel isolated and overwhelmed by loads too heavy to bear (Psalm 68:6; 1 Timothy 3:15).

God has designed the body and the mind (Psalm 139:13-16), yet sin has brought corruption (Romans 8:19-22). Even so, there are certain aspects of your body that God has designed to combat depression. These built-in, designed protocols include an arsenal of hormones and neurotransmitters that can be naturally stimulated through nutrition, exercise, rest, and love. Furthermore, through His Word, God's instruction provides a system by which accountability, camaraderie, and reciprocal sharing of woes and trials can mutually edify and share the individual's load. God has also given gifts, knowledge, and talents to people both within and outside the church who are skilled to effectively address depression, situational, chronic, or otherwise (Romans 12:4-8; 1 Corinthians 12:27-28; 1 Peter 4:10-11).

How Can Christians Effectively Address Depression?

Depression is a sad and widespread actuality. Fractures in the home, fractures in the world, and fractures within the soul and mind ensure that depression will be around until the Lord returns with His mighty angels and destroys these elements with intense heat (2 Thessalonians 1:7-9; 2 Peter 3). This

psychosocial matter necessitates that Christians be prepared for constructive dialogue and helpful deeds to assist those who struggle with depression, both inside and outside the church.[13] All believers would be prudent not to ignore or underestimate the destruction wrought by depression. All disciples need to encourage openness, giving a platform for those who struggle to share their experience. Other helpful areas where believers can show vigilance and steadfastness include: governing one's speech (James 1:19; 3:1ff), showing compassion, sympathy, and empathy when possible, educating oneself to understand some of the basic facts regarding depression introduced above, and learning about resources available in your immediate area. Above all, listen to those suffering from depression by creating a safe space for others, setting aside preconceived personal or societal notions or biases. Listening to learn will be one of the most comforting acts for the person suffering, and it will also be instructive for the listener.

For those personally struggling with depression, here are some grounding thoughts, advice, and encouragement. First, your identity is found in being a child of God, not in a diagnostic label. You are not lesser or greater for having this disorder. Also, it's okay to need and seek help; this most certainly does not make you less of a Christian. The humility of recognizing your need and asking for help demonstrates healthy discipleship! Second, familiarize yourself with treatment options. Try to develop an action plan that uses God-given methods for treatment rather than the humanistic ones. The primary appli-

---

[13] The APA has a helpful compendium of resources, scholarly and layman articles, and information on their website https://www.apa.org/.

cation of prayer and meditation on God's Word may be aided by therapeutic techniques such as psychoanalysis, behavioral activation, cognitive behavioral therapy, interpersonal psychotherapy, homeopathy, and medication. These theological and mainstream methods will be augmented through consistent and wholesome nutrition, exercise, rest, etc. Your perspective on treatment should be guided by the reason(s) for the onset of your depression, including such factors as biology, environment, trauma, or spiritual life. Third, always pray fervently to the Lord regarding this thorn in your mind. God hears prayer, and prayer is effective (Matthew 7:7-8; James 5:16). Fourth, know that you are not alone!

Here are some helpful reminders for the family members of those struggling with depression. You may struggle as a result of your loved one's battle. You are loved and have the support you need if you will be receptive to accept it. Your strain is not the same as your loved one's burden, but they are related. Be willing to share their burden, and share your burden, with others with whom you can be confident. For as the Holy Spirit pointed out, Christians are to *"rejoice with those who rejoice, and weep with those who weep. Be of the same mind toward one another; do not be haughty in mind, but associate with the lowly. Do not be wise in your own estimation"* (Romans 12:15-16). In the process of sharing another's load, strive not to take remarks and actions personally, especially when your loved one lashes out from the pit. This is easier said than done, but oh so needed! As in all areas of challenging discipleship, persevere in being sympathetic and in encouraging proper treatment protocols.

Here are some constructive guidelines and safeguards for those seeking to share the gospel with someone struggling with depression. Your evangelistic approach will have to consider the person with whom you are trying to share the gospel. Do not ever lie or misrepresent the gospel, pretending that every difficulty in life will magically disappear as soon as one obeys the gospel. Rather than prove helpful, this sets a person up for greater difficulty with their depression. However, Christianity does offer hope and healing. It provides support for people and a God Who understands the human mind's complexity because He designed it. He also understands the depth to which sin has ensnared the mind, and promises resolution. Like our corruptible flesh, our minds can put on the incorruptible (2 Corinthians 4-5).

A Concluding Thought

Depression is a corruption of the human mind resulting from sin being in the world. It may degenerate further, be effectively managed, or fully resolve depending on one's openness to seek treatment and spiritual healing. It will continue to be a genuine struggle in this world as a psychosocial issue as long as sin is active. Nevertheless, there is the hope of redemptive healing through Christ. I want to affirm the value of God's people in their understanding and the hope of spiritual regeneration. I want to encourage you to talk to a spiritually-minded person educated in such areas. Do this for your benefit. Do this for the benefit of your family. Do this for the benefit of your spiritual brothers and sisters. Know that God freely offers forgiveness from sins, one of the most taxing weights on the human mind. Let us all immediately take care of this weight first and vow to address the rest in time, not because we are weak, but because we are strengthened in Christ (Philippians 4:13). In so doing, we will revolutionize the church, and the church will become a beacon and light in our society, providing hope and deliverance, joy and peace. Next, let's turn our attention to "the other side of the coin."

Thought Questions

1) What emotions arose as you read this chapter and how did this information affect you?

_____

_____

_____

2) What information or statistic was the most surprising or impactful for you?

_____

_____

_____

3) Can God's people struggle with depression?

_____

_____

_____

4) Which Christian's account of their struggle with depression touched you? How so?

_____

_____

_____

5) Can you think of other biblical examples who may have struggled with depression?

_____

_____

_____

6) Contrast a helpful and an unhelpful way of interacting with someone who copes with depression.

_____

_____

_____

7) Will you pray this week for those who are struggling with depression?

_____

_____

_____

CHAPTER 3

One weekend in college, while driving home to visit my parents, I remember accelerating to over 100 MPH on I-75 N in my 1996 Jeep Grand Cherokee. I set the cruise control and stood up through the sunroof. It was late at night, and I did not care if a deer ran out, if my tire blew out, or if one of another hundred deadly possibilities occurred. I did not care if I died; part of me wanted to die. It was not the first time I was recklessly willing to throw my life away. I had come to one of the lowest points of my life that night. For years, I had seen volatility in my home and tried to help hold my family together. All the while, I tried to maintain a job, do well in school, be involved in church, gain and keep scholarships, support friends, be an athlete, and be a good person. I simply could not handle the pressure anymore. The anxieties of my life had a death grip on me.

Thankfully, I had enough remaining sense to sit back down and finish the drive, but that night was a turning point for me in recognizing that everything I was feeling was not at all normal. I had come face to face with my own anxiety disorder. Since then, I have come a long way, but I still struggle with things from time to time, if I am honest. So, to help me and to help others, I want to spend this chapter discussing what so many, both outside and inside of the church, deal with every day regarding anxiety. We will define what anxiety disorders are, illustrate how Christians do indeed struggle with anxiety, review what the Bible says about anxiety, and discuss steps Christians can implement to address this disorder of the mind and spirit. Throughout these thoughts, please keep in mind the close association between anxiety and depression, as mentioned in the last chapter.

What Is Anxiety?

While each person faces anxiety on a daily level, the DSM-5 generally designates an anxiety disorder by using the following criteria:[14]

- *Excessive anxiety and worry (apprehensive expectation), occurring more days than not for at least six months, about a number of events or activities (such as work or school performance).*
- *The person finds it difficult to control the worry.*
- *The anxiety and worry are associated with three or more of the following six symptoms (with at least some symptoms present for more days than not for the past six months): restlessness or feeling keyed up or on edge, being easily fatigued, difficulty concentrating or mind going blank, irritability, muscle tension, and sleep disturbance.*
- *The disturbance is not better explained by another mental disorder.*
- *The anxiety, worry, or physical symptoms cause clinically significant distress or impairment in social, occupational, or other important functioning areas.*
- *The disturbance is not attributable to the physiological effects of a substance (e.g., a drug of abuse, a medication) or another medical condition (e.g., hyperthyroidism).*

Clinically, anxiety disorders can result from chemical and neurotransmitter imbalances in the body and brain and from overwhelming stress in life such as abuse, work, and conflict. Spiritually, we might add that anxiety disorders can also come from unconfessed or past sin (e.g., Psalm 38:18), but the presence of an anxiety disorder does not necessitate this.[15] Additionally, there are many different forms and manifestations of anxiety disorders that present with varying symptoms. Some common anxiety disorders include Generalized Anxiety Disorder (GAD), Separation Anxiety, Panic Disorder, Obsessive-Compulsive Disorder (OCD), and even phobias. Each of these legitimate anxiety disorders has unique challenges and respond differently to diverse treatment protocols. Some hormonal imbalances, environmental toxins, and medical issues may present with the symptoms of anxiety disorders but these are all categorically

---

[14] *Diagnostic and Statistical Manual of Mental Disorders: DSM-5.* American Psychiatric Association, 2017.

[15] This point is pivotal in understanding anxiety disorders. The presence of an anxiety disorder does not automatically make a Christian devoid of spiritual maturity or holiness. I have observed much mislabeling, bullying, and gossiping in this area, and it is shameful conduct wholly unbecoming of disciples of Jesus (James 3:10).

distinguished by medical personnel. With these multi-faceted variations and considerations, diagnosis and prognosis complexities are voluminous.

Another complicating factor is that depression and anxiety are two sides to the same coin. Often, the diagnostic criteria for each overlap; some mental disorders contain both (e.g., Bipolar Disorder). Some studies show that 50% of those diagnosed with one condition are diagnosed with the other as well.[16] Generally speaking, there are distinctions in how anxiety manifests itself apart from depression. Depression tends to present with sluggish thoughts and movements; anxiety tends to present with racing thoughts and actions. Depression tends to produce stagnation in the present; anxiety tends to manufacture concern over the future. As with depression, those with anxiety disorders may exhibit a great deal of self-sabotage and self-harm. Furthermore, anxiety disorders are associated with high mortality, primarily because of suicide, drug use, and generally risky behaviors.

Sadly, while mental illness is becoming more destigmatized, some take advantage of this movement and who, as a trend, romanticize, dramatize, or falsely present as having anxiety and depression, using genuine disorders to excuse controllable behavior or falsely justify illicit behavior. Though we should be careful not to accuse people of faking an illness such as this, as anxiety is a very real issue, the reality is that some misuse, mislabel, and take advantage of such struggles for personal gain. Such faddish pretenders hinder effective communication about life with legitimate anxiety and concretize false conceptions about anxiety.

Anxiety as a Psychosocial Issue

The frequency with which anxiety disorders occur and the damage they cause is nearly incalculable. According to the National Institute of Mental Health (NIMH), they are the most widely diagnosed mental disorders in the United States.[17] According to this same NIMH data, as well as data from the World Health Organization (WHO)[18] and the Anxiety and Depression Asso-

---

[16] DeVane, C. Lindsey, et al. "Anxiety Disorders in the 21st Century: Status, Challenges, Opportunities, and Comorbidity with Depression." *AJMC*, 30 Oct. 2005, www.ajmc.com/view/oct05-2158ps344-s353.

[17] "Any Anxiety Disorder." *National Institute of Mental Health*, US Department of Health and Human Services, Nov. 2017, www.nimh.nih.gov/health/statistics/any-anxiety-disorder.shtml.

[18] Depression and Other Common Mental Disorders: Global Health Estimates. Geneva: World Health Organization; 2017. License: CC BY-NC-SA 3.0 IGO.

ciation of America (ADAA)[19], anxiety disorders affect an estimated 1 in 13 people in the world, 1 in 8 people annually in the US, 1 in 4 teenagers, and 1 in 8 children. Except for OCD and PTSD, women are twice as likely to be diagnosed.[20] To further illustrate the impact of these disorders, consider two more thoughts: one for practical comparison and one for economic consideration. First, the average person spends approximately 55 minutes a day worrying, whereas those with GAD report an average of 300 minutes worrying per day. Second, anxiety exacerbates all medical issues, particularly chronic health problems. As a result, anxiety disorders cost the US more than $42 billion per year, amounting to 30% of the US mental health bill. Shockingly, this total is only the result of a meager 30% of diagnosed individuals seeking help and 10% actually receiving effective treatment![21]

Another concern is that people often seek, resort, or default to addressing their anxiety via chemical relief with little or entirely without consideration of the consequences and possible side effects. Altogether, 65% of Americans take medicines daily, with 43% taking mood-altering prescriptions daily. In the context of mental health, Paxil and Zoloft consistently rank in the top ten prescribed medications in the US.[22] These two medications bring in around $5-6 billion annually. In addition to, or in place of, these prescriptions, many may seek out comfort through the use of illicit substances, including marijuana, ecstasy, and various other recreational drugs. Millions more commit themselves to alcoholism to try and deal with the stress. I will address such approaches and their failures in Chapter 4.

What does this information mean? It means that anxiety is a global psychosocial problem. Anxiety, worry, and stress are killing us psychologically, socially, and spiritually! Some are dying rapidly; some are gradually atrophying. Anxiety destructively affects industrial output, academics, and international

---

[19] "Facts & Statistics." *Anxiety and Depression Association of America, ADAA,* adaa.org/about-adaa/press-room/facts-statistics.

[20] This may be a quantifiable demonstration of what the Holy Spirit tells us in 1 Peter 3:7 – *"You husbands in the same way, live with your wives in an understanding way, as with someone weaker, since she is a woman; and show her honor as a fellow heir of the grace of life, so that your prayers will not be hindered."*

[21] "The Economic Burden of Anxiety Disorders," a study commissioned by ADAA in *The Journal of Clinical Psychiatry,* 60(7), July 1999.

[22] These two medications are Selective Serotonin Reuptake Inhibitors (SSRIs) and are used to treat both anxiety and depression disorders. Other medication classes used for mental health include Selective Serotonin and Norepinephrine Reuptake Inhibitors (SNRIs), Norepinephrine-Dopamine Reuptake Inhibitors (NDRIs), and Benzodiazepines.

affairs. Because of anxiety, our society and the church are stifled and prevented from reaching their potential. Anxiety mangles relationships with family, friends, coworkers, and self. Anxiety destroys the body, the mind, and the soul. One writer put it this way:

> "...modern science underscores Jesus' teaching by insisting that worry actually shortens life, causes ulcers, and makes one hard to live with! Some worrying husbands growl all over the house whether it has a den or not; some fretting wives, instead of being given a bouquet and called 'Rose,' are given the sobriquet 'Snapdragon.'"[23]

Not only does anxiety have these and other collective psychosocial impacts, but anxiety also has a colossal effect on our personal spiritual lives. Anxiety may lead us to question our faith and whether God is present and near. Anxiety can distance us from God, cloud our ability to see Him, and hinder our desire to draw close to Him. As such, there is no room for apathy or negligence toward anxiety! The evidence shows that anxiety disorders are on the rise as millions are now fitting the diagnostic criteria due to the events of 2020, ever-increasing demands on workload, and skyrocketing stresses in the family. Many are currently struggling with what others have been besieged with for years and now battle more intensely. With this on the rise outside and inside of the church, Christians are learning to empathize with those who already struggle. Such increased empathy is crucial in providing an opportunity for disciples to humbly speak freely with one another and be honest regarding our struggles with the anxieties of life (cf. Job 14:1-2; Matthew 6:34b; Galatians 6:2).

Christians Struggle with Anxiety Disorders

Is anxiety a widespread issue with Christians? To answer this question, I solicited feedback from Christians around the world. As with the testimonies shared about depression, this feedback crosses standard demographic parameters. Here is a meager fraction of their input.

> "I think levels of anxiety have recently increased, but there are different types and some increase depending on situations in life, whereas others do not. My anxieties aren't just based on how bad or good the current events in the world are. It might make them worse but even if things are going well in the world I still believe I will have anxiety. I feel anxious in groups

---

[23] Eddleman, H. Leo. *Teachings of Jesus: in Matthew 5-7*. Books of Life Publishers, 1975, 115.

of people or if I talk to people, but sometimes I am fine. I will feel panicky for no reason and fear is there on repeat."

"I think the vast majority of people at some point have endured some degree of anxiety. It's quite common as disorders go. So, it makes sense that a large portion of Christians have to deal with it on a persistent basis, though honestly I am extremely hesitant to bring it up. My experience can be best described by comparing anxiety to the tide. At times it is low, no problems at all. Periodically it will rise due to various reasons, or sometimes for no reason at all. Even when it is high though, there are things you can do to protect yourself from it. Then, at the worst times, the tide will rise over the flood wall and it feels like it consumes you. It can feel as though some horrible harm is about to happen to either you or your loved ones, but you don't know what it is or when it will happen. This ominous fear becomes exhausting and causes physical fatigue, panic attacks, and a desire to completely withdraw from any interaction with another. If I could say one thing to someone struggling with this, it would be that you do not deserve to suffer like this for your entire life. Your friends and family want you to be at peace. All we ask is that you try to receive help. We don't expect perfection. We will try and support you, but just try and see if it helps."

"I think anxiety might be more common among those in the church than most realize; I just think people aren't talking about it. I mean, I'm not a person that's really talking about. I talked to someone I went to pharmacy school with about church once, and she said she stopped going because 'church and God and all the rules made her anxious.' She felt that she would never actually be good enough, so she quit. She said she's felt a lot better ever since. I hated hearing that from her, but if she felt that way I can imagine that others in the church could feel that way and are embarrassed to admit it. Most of the time I just feel like I'm doing something wrong when my mind gets stuck in one of its 'something's wrong, something's wrong, something's wrong, something's wrong' loops. Jesus told his disciples not to worry about their lives. It says in Matthew 6 not to worry about tomorrow because tomorrow has its own troubles. If I know that God is in control and that God will take care of me, am I not doing something wrong when I feel this way? Because really, there's nothing explicitly wrong with my life. So, what am I worried about?"

"Anxiety can be both a real medical problem and a problem to which God has the solution. It makes perfect sense that the God Who created the body has the answers for healing it. I think God has the answers for preventing it, too, in many cases, though. Starting with how parents raise their children, treating our body like a temple of the Holy Spirit, not succumbing to use of drugs and alcohol to deal with trauma – and the list goes on. Go to the Lord and beg for a blessing. Any other starting point will leave you running in circles. Rely on brethren? Will they let you down? Probably, but when we follow God's path, the blessings will come. Give your brethren a chance to not let you suffer alone."

"I think when I was a kid, I didn't even realize that the way I was thinking was something anyone else struggled with. In fact, I think on some level, I thought that my OCD coping mechanisms were normal and everyone else was just better at it, or I was an exceptionally bad person. But after I opened up and got help, I realized that it was actually quite common and was definitely not a normal way to think/behave. I don't think people realize that anxiety-driven compulsions can be based in a religious practice. Satan is tricky that way, and he delights in twisting God's Word to mean something that it doesn't. For examples: you just had a bad thought—better pray right now or you'll go to Hell. Grace is mentioned, sure, but if people know what you did, they'd hate you. Better be extra good. Result? Attempt at rigid unwavering control of every waking moment of your brain without any forgiveness or grace for yourself. Which turns into complete exhaustion and lack of productivity. The most hurtful things that have been said to me were actually things that were Scripture-based, but twisted to fuel Satan's lies to me instead of fighting them. They were from people who meant well but did not know what I was struggling with and unintentionally added ammunition to the devil's pile. Until you are aware that those anxieties are lies, often you take truth and misapply it to support the anxiety process rather than supporting a healthy process. I don't think that means we should fear to encourage each other with God's words, but I do think we should stop throwing pat Scriptures at our brethren and walking away feeling like we did something good. If you do that without taking the time to get to know someone and understand their problems and thought processes, you can actually do harm. It's like talking without listening and expecting your words to be helpful. It's not because God's Word is wrong or insufficient – it's because Satan is so good at what he does. Seeking help is not weird, weak, trendy, or somehow indicative that you're failing. It is strong. Paul says to lay aside every weight that keeps us from running the race. I can promise you anxiety is a weight that is keeping you from your full potential as a Christian. There is no 'one time' magic bullet for this problem. I fight it every day, sometimes unnoticeably even to myself, sometimes it's an all-out war. Therapy gives you the weapons you need to fight that war with the devil. Because let's be honest, that's who you're fighting with. You better believe he's using every weapon in his arsenal. Therapy adds more weapons to yours. It's not weakness, you're arming yourself for war. I have never had to take prescriptions, but I've been in therapy three times. And I'd go again if it gets bad again. The solution is not the same for everyone, but whether medication is needed or not, I strongly recommend going to a reputable licensed therapist. They are the equivalent of taking your brain to the gym to build the mental muscles you'll need for the bat-tle. It's something I'm passionate about, because it has scarred my life so deeply, but with God's grace I'm overcoming."

"I am an advocate for getting help. There is no shame at all in seeing an issue and addressing it as needed, even if that help isn't strictly 'go to church, trust God more, read your Bible'. Of course, those things should be foundational. But would we not encourage a brother who struggles with alcoholism to seek rehab or AA? Why would we not equally rally behind a brother who is seeking help with their inability to stop worrying? There is never shame in seeking help and growing, there is only glory. Only make sure God is your center; you are sure to succeed!"

Such candid admissions reveal that Christians are in desperate need of three central areas of development: bearing one another's burdens (Galatians 6:2), confessing our difficulties (James 5:16), and using common adversities to empower us to comfort one another as God comforts us (2 Corinthians 1:3-5).

What Does the Bible Say About Anxiety?

King Solomon memorably expressed that "there is nothing new under the sun" in the Book of Ecclesiastes (1:9). Anxiety is not a novel construct devel-oped by sociologists or any particular generation. Anxiety disorders have ex-isted since the advent of sin in Eden (Genesis 3). When Adam and Eve chose to sin, they became isolated and that isolation from God brought corruption and death, including the breakdown of the human mind (Romans 8:18-25; 2 Corinthians 4:4; 10:5; 11:3; Ephesians 6:10-18; 1 John 5:19). Throughout God's canon, there is little doubt that God's people—strong religious people—strug-gled with situational and even chronic anxiety disorders.

Through months and maybe even years of herculean difficulties, the pa-triarch Job displayed the criteria for depression and for anxiety as well. This should not be surprising, for Satan plagues the mind as well as the flesh. Take a few moments to note Job's anxious lamentation in chapter 3:

"Let the day perish on which I was to be born,
And the night which said, 'A boy is conceived.'
May that day be darkness;
Let not God above care for it,
Nor light shine on it.
Let darkness and black gloom claim it;
Let a cloud settle on it;
Let the blackness of the day terrify it.
As for that night, let darkness seize it;
Let it not rejoice among the days of the year;
Let it not come into the number of the months.
Behold, let that night be barren;
Let no joyful shout enter it.
Let those curse it who curse the day,
Who are prepared to rouse Leviathan.
Let the stars of its twilight be darkened;
Let it wait for light but have none,
And let it not see the breaking dawn;
Because it did not shut the opening of my mother's womb,
Or hide trouble from my eyes.

Why did I not die at birth,
Come forth from the womb and expire?
Why did the knees receive me,
And why the breasts, that I should suck?
For now I would have lain down and been quiet;
I would have slept then, I would have been at rest,
With kings and with counselors of the earth,
Who rebuilt ruins for themselves;
Or with princes who had gold,
Who were filling their houses with silver.
Or like a miscarriage which is discarded, I would not be,
As infants that never saw light.
There the wicked cease from raging,
And there the weary are at rest.
The prisoners are at ease together;
They do not hear the voice of the taskmaster.
The small and the great are there,
And the slave is free from his master.

Why is light given to him who suffers,
And life to the bitter of soul,
Who long for death, but there is none,
And dig for it more than for hidden treasures,
Who rejoice greatly,
And exult when they find the grave?
Why is light given to a man whose way is hidden,
And whom God has hedged in?
For my groaning comes at the sight of my food,
And my cries pour out like water.
For what I fear comes upon me,
And what I dread befalls me.
I am not at ease, nor am I quiet,
And I am not at rest, but turmoil comes."

Job was not the only Bible character to struggle. Even a cursory reading of 2 Samuel, 1 Chronicles, and Psalms reveals that God's chosen king David regularly struggled with anxiety, sometimes as a result of his own choices (e.g., Bathsheba and Uriah) and occasionally due to the choices of others (e.g., Saul's murderous jealousy and Absalom's revolt).

God's elect prophets struggled as well:

"Where am I to get meat to give to all this people? For they weep before me, saying, 'Give us meat that we may eat!' I alone am not able to carry all this people, because it is too burdensome for me. So if You are going to deal thus with me, please kill me at once, if I have found favor in Your sight, and do not let me see my wretchedness." (Moses in Numbers 11:13-15)

"But he himself went a day's journey into the wilderness, and came and sat down under a juniper tree; and he requested for himself that he might die, and said, 'It is enough; now, O Lord, take my life, for I am not better than my fathers.'" (Elijah in 1 Kings 19:1-4)

"But it greatly displeased Jonah and he became angry. He prayed to the Lord and said, 'Please Lord, was not this what I said while I was still in my own country? Therefore in order to forestall this I fled to Tarshish, for I knew that You are a gracious and compassionate God, slow to anger and abundant in lovingkindness, and one who relents concerning calamity. Therefore now, O Lord, please take my life from me, for death is better to me than life.' The Lord said, 'Do you have good reason to be angry?'" (Jonah 4:1-4)

"Cursed be the man who brought the news to my father, saying,
'A baby boy has been born to you!'
And made him very happy.
But let that man be like the cities
Which the Lord overthrew without relenting,
And let him hear an outcry in the morning
And a shout of alarm at noon;
Because he did not kill me before birth,
So that my mother would have been my grave,
And her womb ever pregnant.
Why did I ever come forth from the womb
To look on trouble and sorrow,
So that my days have been spent in shame?" (Jeremiah 20:15-18)

Satan can and does attack on levels we do not typically think about: DNA, our thoughts and cognitions, our medical and mental state, even environmental, agricultural, and chemical toxins! Satan uses social media, paired with the globalization and digitalization of information, to bombard us with an over-abundance of matters to worry about and fight over that we are not individually equipped to process. We are brought face-to-face with the horrors and corruptions of people all over the world, every moment of every day. Satan further tears us at the spiritual seams by tempting us with activities offering temporary relief, but no true satisfaction (e.g., drugs, alcohol, sleeping around, theft, gambling, etc.; cf. Proverbs 14:12; 16:25; Hebrews 11:25). This further complicates the battle to manage anxieties.

Despite such obstacles, God repeatedly condemns anxiety and expects us to avoid it as far as is in our control by entrusting our thoughts, feelings, and worries to Him, and by having confidence that He cares for us (e.g., Psalm 55:22; Matthew 6:25-34; Philippians 4:6-7; 1 Peter 5:6-7; et al.). However, we must understand these instructions in the light of foundational biblical principles, specifically regarding sin being willful lawlessness and the extent to which sin has deeply impacted this world. Even with the plethora of warnings against anxiety and the Devil's exposed schemes, we still struggle, by our own choices, by the choices of others, and because of the corruption of this world, which is passing away and destined for destruction. This ongoing campaign is one of the chief reasons for God's gift of the Bible, which gives guideposts and examples to inspire us to keep fighting.

How Can Christians Effectively Address Anxiety?

With such catastrophic impacts, anxiety seems an indomitable foe. How could one begin to reverse such destruction? Where should we start? We start with not walking past the person in need, physically, socially, or conversationally. In the Day of Judgment, I fear many espousing Christians will be exposed as priests and Levites who bypassed the man in need (cf. Luke 10:25-37). Negligence and apathy are as sinful as violence (James 4:17). Acknowledging this starting point, let's get more specific.

Godly people must invite open and constructive discourse about more than just trivial matters and instead engage in challenging and humbling conversations. To do this, here are a few tips:

- Do not ever stigmatize mental disorders.
- Open up with others about your struggles. You would be surprised how you initiating the conversation will give someone the courage to open up about themselves.
- Learn about what kinds of anxiety disorders there are, how to combat them, and available treatment options.
- Be understanding of the different reasons for anxiety disorders, and learn how to converse about these causes.
- Know your limitations.[24]
- Persevere in sympathy, empathy, prayer, patience, encouragement, and evangelism
- Know the simple but powerful value of a good word – *"Anxiety in a person's heart weighs it down, but a good word makes it glad"* (Proverbs 12:25).

If you personally struggle with an anxiety disorder, you are not any less spiritually valuable or dedicated than someone else who does not. You are also not alone; anxiety disorders are one of the most common ailments in the world, and the church does not exist in a vacuum away from that fact! Refresh yourself on what we cited above from God's Word. Know that anxiety disorders are very treatable, but sadly less than half seek treatment (cf. Jeremiah 15:18; 17:14). Seeking help is not a sign of feebleness; rather, it can redirect you to more tremendous potential in the Lord. Know there are an abundance

---

[24] Much appreciation to Art Adams, Executive Director for Leaving the Pit Behind, a non-profit 501c3 Mental Health and Addiction Services organization that makes high-quality, low-cost healthcare accessible to Christians, who provided this sound counsel. Their website is https:www.leavingthepitbehind.org.

of options for treatment: individual or group therapy, cognitive exercises, homeopathy, physical exercise, nutrition counseling, medication, etc. Before moving forward with any of these options, thorough research is imperative. This can be especially true regarding pursuing medicinal treatment because if used negligently, one can end up in far worse condition or, in some extreme cases, can end up dying as the result of conditions like Serotonin Syndrome.[25] God has given people gifts, knowledge, and talents within the church who are professionally equipped to effectively address anxiety (Romans 12:4-8; 1 Corinthians 12:27-28; 1 Peter 4:10-11).[26] Within the worldwide body of Christ, resources are abundant: therapists, counselors, physicians, homeopaths, nutrition educators, personal trainers, pharmacists, nurses, and others who want to serve! (cf. Ecclesiastes 4:9-12) These options and these people, with God, prayer, Bible study, and accountability in the church as foundations, can and will get you on track to the road to growth, better-combating anxiety, or, in some cases, becoming the master of it. When we replace "I" with "We," "Illness" can become "Wellness"! Without this partnership first and foremost, any and all treatments and therapies will be inadequate, for *"unless the LORD builds the house, they labor in vain who build it"* (Psalm 127:1a).

Allow me to interject some personal advice that has immeasurably aided my journey. Pouring your already anxious mind into demanding and constructive work, projects, hobbies, or goals can allow you to channel the fast-paced thoughts you already have. This book is the product of my own channeling. Business guru Lee Iacocca suggests this same idea when he states, *"In times of great stress or adversity, it's always best to keep busy, to plow your anger and your energy into something positive."* President Barack Obama likewise adds, *"The best way to not feel hopeless is to get up and do something. Don't wait for good things to happen to you. If you go out and make some good things happen, you will fill the world with hope, you will fill yourself with hope."*

For all Christians seeking to effectively address anxiety, know what is coming into your home, body, and mind. Too many are negligent and, as a result, invite disaster into their own lives. Being informed and intentional in your research and in your life can provide greater power over what you can control as far as triggers, toxins, and other sources that cause or aggravate anxiety (cf. 1 Corinthians 3:16-17; 6:19-20). Learn more about your body. Learn about how activities involving the natural stimulation of serotonin, dopamine,

---

[25] Here especially, I am indebted to pharmacist Rachel Morrison's professional assistance.

[26] One Christian, Julie Adams, started The Still Waters Counseling and is using her personal and professional experiences to aid others struggling with grief, depression, anxiety, and a host of other challenges. The website for her counseling service is www.stillwaterslife.com.

and oxytocin can offset and flush the body of cortisol and adrenaline, stress hormones that contribute to anxiety. These are systems designed by God (cf. Psalm 139:13-16) to help you combat stress, worry, and anxiety and, if you are able to employ them in the fight, they can help tremendously!

A Closing Thought

Like depression, anxiety is a corruption of the human mind resulting from sin's dominance in the world. Situationally-based, biologically-based, and sin-based anxiety disorders may degenerate further or have the option of being effectively managed depending on one's openness to seek treatment and spiritual healing. Anxiety, stress, and worry will continue to be very real struggles in this world as long as sin is in this world until God destroys this world as He has promised (1 John 2:17). Allow God to ease the suffering of your mind as much as is possible by casting all your anxieties on Him and being confident in His care for you (1 Peter 5:7). Such trust and confidence will provide God's peace (Philippians 4:6-7), which will find ultimate fulfillment and expression in Heaven. Commenting on Matthew 6:25-34, a wise warrior of the faith fittingly described our campaign and God's care in this fashion:

> *"The Lord's concern over our worrying ways is ultimate. He is not merely offering prudent counsel; He is issuing a command upon which our relationship to the kingdom of God hinges. Facing this fact honestly can serve at times to fill us with despair. We are so disposed to chronic fearfulness and, as much as we come to hate it, our struggle with our fears seems always to be more of a long, plodding war of attrition than a quick, decisive engagement...It will help us if we realize that the freedom from fear to which Jesus calls us is a lesson we master over time, by long practice—by reminding ourselves again and again of what the cross says about the unchanging faithfulness of our Father's love and by prayerfully taking our burdened thoughts to Him."*[27]

---

[27] Earnhart, Paul. *Invitation to a Spiritual Revolution: Studies in the Sermon on the Mount.* Gary Fisher, 1999, 122.

Thought Questions

1) What emotions arose as you read this chapter and how did this information affect you?

_____

_____

2) What is the difference between everyday anxiety that someone might feel and a full-fledged anxiety disorder?

_____

_____

3) Is anxiety sinful? Explain.

_____

_____

4) Which Christian's account of their struggle with anxiety touched you? How so?

_____

_____

5) How can Christians correctly and incorrectly use Scripture in addressing anxiety?

_____

_____

6) What are some controllable and uncontrollable triggers for anxiety?

_____

_____

7) What will you do this week to positively influence those struggling with anxiety?

_____

_____

CHAPTER 4

Addictions

Addictions are one of the most insidious challenges facing the world to-day. Many have become shackled by Satan in these diabolical devotions and, through his slavery, have had their lives destroyed. It is imperative to realize Satan's tactics with addictions are not confined to those outside of the church; he is also quite effective in using addictions to infiltrate churches and destroy believers. Satan is active in addiction; he seeks to enslave any soul by any means necessary!

The church faces the challenge of addressing addictions among its membership with a message of hope and deliverance, while also serving as a beacon to those outside of the church lost in sin, sometimes including addiction. In preaching a message of change and repentance, the church needs to offer compassion and mercy while also being careful not to enable or permit impermissible behaviors. This is an arduous responsibility, but our Lord faced challenging cases, and so must His people.

Addiction as a Psychosocial Issue

Webster's Dictionary defines "addiction" as:

"the compulsive need for and use of a habit-forming substance charac-terized by tolerance and well-defined physiological symptoms upon with-drawal; persistent compulsive use of a substance that is known by the user to be harmful; to devote or surrender oneself to something habitually or obsessively."

The DSM-5 details many addictive disorders: compulsive gambling and internet gaming, eating disorders, substance addiction, pornography addiction, and others. Society often will accommodatively delineate two primary forms of addiction—substance and process—that we will use to guide and narrow our discussion. Regarding the latter, we will discuss two examples, pornography and gambling.

Substance Addictions

High-profile celebrities like Matthew Perry of *Friends* and Cory Monteith of *Glee* illustrate the powerful allure of alcohol and drug addiction. Perry serves to demonstrate the victory that is possible in recovery; Monteith, who fatally overdosed, shows the ultimate disaster addiction can bring.[28] Tom Hardy, the actor playing "Bane" in *The Dark Knight Rises,* candidly said regarding his drug addiction, *"I would have sold my mother for a crack rock."* No doubt, the stories of other celebrities like Miley Cyrus, Lindsay Lohan, Zac Efron, Robert Downey Jr., Robin Williams, Oprah, and Judy Garland and their addictions also flash before the eyes.

The extent of drug addiction in the United States is overwhelming. According to the *American Addiction Centers,* in data taken from 2017:[29]

- *19.7 million American adults (aged 12 and older) battle a substance use disorder. This includes 1 in 25 adolescents (aged 12-17), 1 in 7 young adults (aged 18-25), and 1 in 25 adults (aged 26+).*
- *Men are nearly twice as likely to have a substance addiction.*
- *American Indians and Alaska Natives (aged 12 and older) have the highest dependence and substance abuse rate, at 12.8%. Whites have a 7.7% rate of substance abuse. About 6.8% of African Americans struggle with substance use disorders, while the percentage of Hispanics or Latinos who suffer from substance use disorders is 6.6%. Approximately 4.6% of Native Hawaiians and Pacific Islanders suffer from substance use disorders. Asian Americans have the lowest rate of substance use disorders at 3.8%.*
- *About 38% of adults battle an illicit drug use disorder.*

[28] Matthew Perry's journey is recounted in the cover story of *People* magazine from July 15, 2013. Cory Monteith's tragic end is recounted in the July 29th, 2013 cover story of *US Weekly.*

[29] "Addiction Statistics: Drug & Substance Abuse Statistics." *American Addiction Centers,* 11 Jan. 2021, https://www.americanaddictioncenters.org/rehab-guide/addiction-statistics.

- *Almost 74% of adults suffering from a substance use disorder have also struggled with an alcohol use disorder. 1 in 8 adults struggle with alcohol and drug use disorders simultaneously.*
- *8.5 million American adults suffer from both a mental health disorder and a substance use disorder, or co-occurring disorders.*
- *Drug abuse and addiction cost American society more than $740 billion annually in lost workplace productivity, healthcare expenses, and crime-related costs.*

Substance addiction not only appears in the ivory palaces of the worldly elite, or even just among the pagan masses, it also occurs in the Lord's church.[30] Listen to this brother in Christ and his journey out of alcoholism:

"I started drinking beer when I was around twenty years old. I progressed to whiskey and vodka until I was 39.

My family has a history of alcoholism. I also had a traumatic childhood with physical and psychological abuse. My mother attempted suicide numerous times as I was growing up. When I was five years old, I found her after she had shot herself (she survived). When I started my career in the family business, I worked away from home regularly. Staying in a hotel 200 nights a year leaves a lot of alone time. I ended up losing my job and getting a divorce. My drinking only intensified after this.

I tried to stop many times over those years and even went to rehab twice. Losing my family and my job still wasn't enough to get my attention to take quitting seriously. From July 2012 until November 2013, all I did was drink. On November 6th, 2013, I was admitted into the local hospital. I went into a hepatic coma for around 30 days. I now have cirrhosis of the liver. The doctors told me that I would die if I started drinking again. Death has been a pretty big deterrent for me! I just celebrated seven years of sobriety.

---

[30] Our aim is not necessarily to dispute what constitutes drunkenness but rather to deal with the problem of alcohol addiction as it stands. The standard examination of what the Bible says regarding alcohol and intoxication is: Patton, William. *Bible Wines: Laws of Fermentation and Wines of the Ancients.* Schmul Publishing Co., 2005.

I would tell someone struggling with alcoholism to be completely honest with yourself about your habit. If others around you are questioning your consumption, then it's time to pay attention. The alcoholic is typically the last one to truly recognize that they have a problem. Addiction and dishonesty are generally a package deal. This not only means that you're deceiving others, but you're also lying to yourself about your problem.

I believe the church has a responsibility to anyone struggling with any addiction. It starts at the individual level, though. Relationships need to be cultivated where we feel as though we can tell our brother or sister when we are struggling. We should also be close enough with our brother or sister to recognize when there may be a problem with them. Having said that, addiction has always been taboo in the church. When it comes to issues with drugs or alcohol, the church has a tendency to 'shoot their wounded' rather than show grace, patience, and love that nurture the weak and sick back to health."

Pornography[31]

Seemingly hidden from the cultural narrative, pornography creeps into the lives of many and devours them from an early age. Statistics from the Barna Group and Covenant Eyes help illustrate the scale and impact of this addiction, and, according to their findings, even the religious do not escape unscathed. According to their research, here is how some of the numbers break down:[32]

- *Over 40 million Americans are regular visitors to porn sites. The average visit lasts 6 minutes and 29 seconds.*
- *There are around 42 million porn websites, which totals approximately 370 million pages of porn.*
- *The porn industry's annual revenue is more than the NFL, NBA, and*

---

[31] There are many helpful resources to read in order to understand more about sexual and pornography addiction. Hardin, Jason. *Hard Core: Defeating Sexual Temptation with a Superior Satisfaction.* DeWard Pub. Co., 2010. Arterburn, Stephen, et al. *Every Man's Battle: Winning the War on Sexual Temptation One Victory at a Time.* WaterBrook, 2020. Carnes, Patrick. *Don't Call It Love: Recovery from Sexual Addiction.* Piatkus, 1992. Carnes, Patrick. *In the Shadows of the Net.* Hazelden, 2001. Carnes, Patrick. *Out of the Shadows: Understanding Sexual Addiction.* CompCare Pub., 1983.

[32] "15 Mind-Blowing Statistics About Pornography and the Church." *Conquer Series,* 18 Sept. 2020, https://www.conquerseries.com/15-mind-blowing-statistics-about-pornography-and-the-church/.

MLB combined. It is also more than the combined revenues of ABC, CBS, and NBC.

- *47% of families in the US reported that pornography is a problem in their home and pornography use increases the marital infidelity rate by more than 300%. 56% of American divorces involve one party having an "obsessive interest" in pornographic websites.*
- *The average age that a child is first exposed to porn is 11, and 94% of children will see porn by 14. Of young Christian adults 18-24 years old, 76% actively search for porn.*
- *70% of Christian youth ministers report that they have had at least one teen come to them for help in dealing with pornography in the past 12 months.*
- *68% of church-going men and over 50% of ministers view porn frequently.*
- *59% of ministers said that married men seek their help for porn use.*
- *33% of women aged 25-and-under search for porn at least once per month.*
- *Only 13% of self-identified Christian women say they never watch porn – 87% of Christian women have watched porn.*
- *55% of married men and 25% of married women say they watch porn at least once a month.*
- *57% of ministers say porn addiction is the most damaging issue in their congregation, and 69% say porn has adversely impacted the church.*
- *Only 7% of ministers say their church has a step-by-step plan to help people struggling with pornography.*
- *The porn industry is, in numerous ways, directly linked to human trafficking.[33]*

Listen to this brother in Christ and his journey with pornography addiction:

"I remember the very first time I was exposed to porn. I was 15 years old, working my first job. I was left alone in a warehouse washing vans for a paint company when I saw a pornographic calendar on the wall for all to see. I had never seen a naked woman before, and I was mesmerized. Almost immediately, I was ashamed and guilt-ridden. I turned to walk away, but for several months afterward, I studied that calendar every time I was there. I was hooked, and if I couldn't get my hands on that calen-

---

[33] The non-profit group, Fight the New Drug, has done a fantastic job exposing this horrific connection. Their resources may be found at: https://www.fightthenewdrug.org.

dar, I found other ways to indulge my lust. I had no idea the kind of pain and suffering I was bringing upon myself, my relationships, and my future marriage. Not a day goes by now that I don't wish I could go back and never have turned around to stand face to face with what I would become a slave to for years to come.

I often speak to others about the three A's of pornographic addiction: accountability, affordability, and accessibility. This three-headed monster made it far too easy for me to make the wrong choices that sparked my enslavement to pornography for the remainder of my teens and early twenties. The sad truth is that viewing pornography today is much different from the past. In the past, if you desired to view something pornographic in nature, it would cost you your money and your pride. You would have to look someone in the face as you made the purchase and keep it hidden from others. Additionally, you used to have to jump through several hoops to view pornography. Now it's as simple as the click of a button. Within literally seconds, anyone in the world with internet access can have a screen playing pornographic videos right in front of their eyes. The internet, a tool with so much potential for good, also has the potential for so much evil – and without self-control, it can destroy your soul and the lives of those around you. Today you can even delete browser history or surf the web in incognito mode. You can 'cover your tracks' while feeding your lust. Satan convinces you that nobody will ever know, but you can only believe that for so long before you start to lose your mind living a double life.

Despair played an integral role in my victory. I was tired of destroying not only my life but the lives of those around me. When I began dating the woman who is now my wife, by God's grace, I started trying desperately to break away from my addiction. I began to see the lie that I bought into hook, line, and sinker from Satan. Pornography was not real intimacy; it was a fake and destructive imitation – and a poor one at that. If I ever wanted to experience true love or true intimacy, I needed to rid my heart and mind from this filth to do so. And I have! It has been years since I have visited a porn website, but rest assured that Satan will not give up on you! He always endeavors to find a way to tempt you. It could be a movie, a tv show, an app, a book, even an advertisement. Increasing my accountability, growing to understand the unaffordable nature of pornography addiction, and decreasing my access to porn have also been key to my victory. A phone and computer monitoring service called Covenant Eyes has helped me to do this. The constant accountability makes it so that I truly am never 'alone' with access to the internet.

If I could say anything to a person struggling with this addiction, I would offer four pieces of advice. First, STOP IT! You have no idea of the consequences that your actions will bring upon you. Calamity will come suddenly, and you will only have yourself to blame. You will destroy yourself and those around you because of your lack of discipline, and because of your incredible stupidity, you will be lost (Proverbs 5:23). This might sound cruel and harsh, but it is said with all the love in the world. The person addicted to porn does not need the 'Mr. Rogers' approach. The person caught in this addiction needs someone who will shake them loose to help them come to their senses and wake up to see the awful things they have done—someone to pull them out of the fire before it's too late! The second thing I would say is that you cannot achieve victory on your own. You will lie to yourself and say, 'I can stop anytime I want. I do not need

help. Others don't have to know, that will only make things worse.' It's too late now, and the longer you try to fix it on your own, the more pain you will cause down the road when you are found out. Darkness must be exposed (Ephesians 5) for it to be truly dealt with. Do not hate the light because your works are evil (John 3:19-21); if you honestly want to change, you need to be exposed. The third thing I would say is that you are not alone. It does not justify the severity of our actions, but often the reason many conceal their sins is that they feel like no one else could possibly understand. I know I felt that way – that no one could relate to what I had done; I felt so ashamed. Yet as I allowed myself to become more open and as I allowed the light to shine on my ugliest, darkest secrets – I discovered that there were so many more that had fallen in the same way that I had. Not only did they understand, but they had the tools to help bring me up from the pit and change my life. Do not misunderstand me; there is great shame associated with this sin, and there should be. But do not believe that no one will understand or offer you a hand up. The fourth thing I would recommend is to read Proverbs 5. When you're done, reread it. Read it every single day, and when you are tempted, read it. I will let the text do the talking! The last thing I would say is I love you, and so does Jesus. Jesus died for you, His blood dripped down His head and His body to pay the price of your selfish actions and sinful practices. Jesus wants more than anything for you to repent and turn to Him so that He might forgive you. While you cannot remove all of the consequences you will suffer because of past choices, you can start over today in a restored relationship with Jesus. You can know real intimacy with God. You can know true intimacy with a spouse. You can discover what it feels like to no longer hate yourself, being double-minded and constantly looking over your shoulder. What Jesus offers you is freedom, true freedom. Will you take it?

As for the church and individual Christians, I believe we have responsibilities. We are called to bear one another's burdens and to restore those who are caught up in transgression in a spirit of gentleness (Galatians 6:1-5). We are also called to confess our sins to one another (James 5:13-20). I have witnessed a culture of pretending in the church. People can live double lives, putting on a face that everything is great in their lives when secretly they struggle and do not allow their actions to be exposed. As a result, no one is authentic. People play the hypocrite – fooling others around them but not fooling our Lord. If we truly want to help people overcome the temptations surrounding pornography, it means we need to talk about it. It needs to be exposed for what it is, and we need to humble ourselves before others and confess our sins. It should not be a taboo subject unaddressed in a class or from the pulpit. It should be discussed, and there should be lessons given on how to equip Christians with how to prevent it and how to recover from it in their own homes. We must create a culture within the church where this is addressed, where those who are struggling are given every opportunity to receive the help they so desperately need."

Gambling

Often viewed as merely a personal choice with little to no destructive tendencies, the realities behind compulsive gambling are far different. The data is particularly enlightening:[34]

- *Over 80% of American adults gamble every year.*
- *Approximately 1-3% of the US population, or between 3.5 to 10.5 million people, struggle with gambling addiction. The scope of this*

---

[34] McCann, Adam. "Most Gambling-Addicted States." *WalletHub*, 23 Apr. 2019, https://www.wallethub.com/edu/states-most-addicted-to-gambling/20846. "The Top Most 5 Alarming Gambling Addiction Statistics." Addictions.com Leading the Way to Recovery, 5 Aug. 2019, www.addictions.com/gambling/5-alarming-gambling-addiction-statistics/.

number varies due to differing standards regarding what constitutes gambling addiction.

- *750,000 young people, aged 14-21, struggle with a gambling addiction. Those aged 20-30 exhibit the highest rates of gambling addiction.*
- *The gaming industry annually brings in approximately $261 billion. Gambling losses amount to $100 billion annually in the US. The average male addict accumulates between $55,000 and $90,000 in debt; the average female addict, $15,000.*
- *The five states with the highest overall gambling addiction rate are Nevada, South Dakota, Montana, Mississippi, and Oklahoma. The five states with the lowest gambling addiction rate are Utah, Florida, Alaska, Nebraska, and Alabama.*
- *Gambling addiction increases 23x for people with alcohol addiction.*
- *Approximately 50% of those with a gambling addiction engage in criminal activity supporting their addiction.*
- *Co-occurrence rates between gambling addiction and mental disorders like anxiety, depression, PTSD, and anti-social personality disorder are high.*

Listen to one Christian's journey out of gambling (and sexual immorality addiction as well):

"In my late teens and early twenties, I started noticing problems with lust. In my twenties, I battled off-and-on with sexual immorality and gambling. I finally hit my emotional bottom when I was 29. Prior to that, there was a significant amount of denial and resistance to accept/admit there were problems. There was often a need to escape from whatever issues were going on and escape into something that I rationalized as a solution. Entitlement was also a key excuse for me because I felt mistreated by the world.

When in the throes of addiction, my desire would begin with fantasizing, which is where the greatest high is actually achieved rather than in the activity itself. For example, in gambling, it was all about the build-up of the bet. During the bet, my mind was thinking, 'Well, this is too slow!' or 'Let me get to the next bet!' In sex, the act also could not live up to the fantasy. The high was never enough. That is the gist of the problem that the addict faces—it is never enough! In my battle against sexual lust, some of the behaviors included: soliciting prostitutes, compulsive masturbation, voyeurism, exhibitionism, and compulsive viewing of pornography. I did not understand the power of objectification until recovery. The other per-

son was not a person, but a thing to meet my desires. In gambling, I often went to casinos, illegally run games at businesses, games at people's homes, and Catholic festivals. I also played the lottery. I recall that when I was engaging in one activity, I would often want to be doing another. I was never satisfied, and many years are now a blur.

My main catalysts for my addictions were a lack of fulfilling relationships, inability to achieve my educational goals, work stress, unreasonable expectations I placed on myself, and abuse during my childhood. Only after experiencing enough heartache could I finally surrender to the fact that I had a problem. No one could admit it for me or force me into getting help. I had to want to get better. I had previously gone to meetings, therapy, and inpatient treatment, but I was doing it for all the wrong reasons, like appeasing others and biding time until I could return to the old behaviors. Once I finally surrendered and started working on myself, I was able to get sober. I have not placed a bet or engaged in sexual immorality since April 24, 2010.

I believe that people who have the ability to listen without becoming an enabler is key. Sometimes tough love is warranted because people have to fall down sometimes in order to get up. It is so important not to try and control others. If you are struggling, focus on doing the next right thing, one day, one hour, one minute at a time. Believers need to be willing to set aside time for someone if they are asking for help, and be willing to take someone to a meeting if they need transportation. And as always, if the conversation ever lends itself to the spiritual/religious, then the believer needs to be willing to talk about Christ as Lord."

Key Catalysts in the Onset of Addiction

The scientific and anecdotal data reveal a wide variety of reasons for the onset of addiction. Often, these root factors are combinatory. The presence of sin in the world combines with mental disorders, issues in the home, genetic predispositions, abuse, sociocultural factors, poor academic achievement, work stress, and/or other factors to form fractures in the hearts and souls of those who are created in the image of God. Attempts to remedy these fractures outside of a wholesome relationship with God inevitably lead many to seek fulfillment and pleasure by means hostile to the sort of healthy sobriety humans should pursue. Among the most destructive of these departures is the pursuit of satisfaction by means of addicting and intoxicating influences. The addict seeks to fill a God-shaped void, and the addiction fails to fulfill its empty promises. G.K. Chesterton drew this out when he famously said, *"Every time a man knocks on the door of a brothel he is knocking for God."* Satan entices the addict to attempt to fulfill a corrupted form of God-designed desires like acceptance, comfort, strength, intimacy, etc. Living for the action and living for the escape promise freedom but bring bondage.

Addictions can also come from hiding from God's truth and substituting one's own truth (cf. Proverbs 3:5-6; 14:12; Jeremiah 17:9). Addicts do this mainly to avoid unpleasant feelings and/or an aching conscience. For example, the addict might try to drown out feelings of shame and others' disappointment, the hope being that the high will bring release. In the form of addiction, sin claims to show the addict an escape and ultimately become one's god (i.e., idolatry). Addicts sometimes believe that if they devote themselves to something carnal, they will get good in return, but sadly they become slaves (e.g., Deuteronomy 7:24). A workaholic may be deceived into thinking the job will better provide for his family. Another may be fooled into thinking spending most of the day on social media will help them excel in life.

The Struggle of Sin Serves as an Analogy for Addiction

While addiction is never explicitly mentioned by name in the Scriptures, there is a fitting comparison to be made between the universal bondage of sin and addiction. Three key passages help establish this connection in a way that benefits those struggling with substance and process addictions, as well as those who do not battle with these addictions.

Romans 6:12-23 reads,

"Therefore do not let sin reign in your mortal body so that you obey its lusts, and do not go on presenting the members of your body to sin as instruments of unrighteousness; but present yourselves to God as those alive from the dead, and your members as instruments of righteousness to God. For sin shall not be master over you, for you are not under law but under grace. What then? Shall we sin because we are not under law but under grace? May it never be! Do you not know that when you present yourselves to someone as slaves for obedience, you are slaves of the one whom you obey, either of sin resulting in death, or of obedience resulting

in righteousness? But thanks be to God that though you were slaves of sin, you became obedient from the heart to that form of teaching to which you were committed, and having been freed from sin, you became slaves of righteousness. I am speaking in human terms because of the weakness of your flesh. For just as you presented your members as slaves to impurity and to lawlessness, resulting in further lawlessness, so now present your members as slaves to righteousness, resulting in sanctification. For when you were slaves of sin, you were free in regard to righteousness. Therefore what benefit were you then deriving from the things of which you are now ashamed? For the outcome of those things is death. But now having been freed from sin and enslaved to God, you derive your benefit, resulting in sanctification, and the outcome, eternal life. For the wages of sin is death, but the free gift of God is eternal life in Christ Jesus our Lord."

Several elements of this text sound quite similar to addiction. Sin *"enslaving"* people and *"making them obey"* shows habitual obsession, compulsion, devotion, and surrender. *"Lawlessness leading to more lawlessness"* conveys tolerance, dependence, and the tendency of addiction to perpetuate itself. The fruitlessness of this struggle illustrates harmfulness. Note that Paul, through the Holy Spirit's inspiration, speaks of this slavery in the past tense, thereby conveying a message to recovering addicts and current addicts of sin that victory is possible in Jesus!

Shortly after this passage, Paul introspectively and evocatively addresses addictive behavior again in Romans 7:13-24. The text states,

"Therefore, did that which is good become a cause of death for me? May it never be! Rather it was sin, in order that it might be shown to be sin by effecting my death through that which is good, so that through the commandment sin would become utterly sinful. For we know that the Law is spiritual, but I am of flesh, sold into bondage to sin. For what I am doing, I do not understand; for I am not practicing what I would like to do, but I am doing the very thing I hate. But if I do the very thing I do not want to do, I agree with the Law, confessing that the Law is good. So now, no longer am I the one doing it, but sin which dwells in me. For I know that nothing good dwells in me, that is, in my flesh; for the willing is present in me, but the doing of the good is not. For the good that I want, I do not do, but I practice the very evil that I do not want. But if I am doing the very thing I do not want, I am no longer the one doing it, but sin which dwells in me. I find then the principle that evil is present in me, the one who wants to do good. For I joyfully concur with the law of God in the inner man, but I see a different law in the members of my body, waging

war against the law of my mind and making me a prisoner of the law of
sin which is in my members. Wretched man that I am! Who will set me
free from the body of this death?"

This passage shows us that the law of God highlights the ugliness of sin, yet all people have sinned and fallen short of the glory of God. How many of us can say we have been there or are there now? We know what we are doing is wrong, but we are addicted to the passing pleasure (cf. 7:16, 19). Paul says that this is sin (7:17). The Holy Spirit is asserting that the weakness of all people is overcome in the new covenant, inaugurated by the blood of Jesus which teaches the righteous to live by faith (cf. Habakkuk 3:2) and not in systematic law-keeping resulting in merit-based righteousness. This message is unpacked in the rest of Romans 7 and 8, which firmly communicates a law of life and liberty, forgiveness and deliverance. Freedom is found in the gospel of God's grace and a liberating walk by faith guided by the Holy Spirit (cf. John 8:32; Galatians 5:1).

In harmony with these passages from Romans is what God led Paul to write in Galatians 5:16-24:

"But I say, walk by the Spirit, and you will not carry out the desire of the
flesh. For the flesh sets its desire against the Spirit, and the Spirit against
the flesh; for these are in opposition to one another, so that you may not do
the things that you please. But if you are led by the Spirit, you are not un-
der the Law. Now the deeds of the flesh are evident, which are: immorality,
impurity, sensuality, idolatry, sorcery, enmities, strife, jealousy, outbursts
of anger, disputes, dissensions, factions, envying, drunkenness, carousing,
and things like these, of which I forewarn you, just as I have forewarned
you, that those who practice such things will not inherit the kingdom of
God. But the fruit of the Spirit is love, joy, peace, patience, kindness, good-
ness, faithfulness, gentleness, self-control; against such things there is no
law. Now those who belong to Christ Jesus have crucified the flesh with its
passions and desires."

This passage from Galatians reveals a war perpetually fought between the flesh and the spirit (cf. Ephesians 6:10-17). There is an analogous Cherokee folk tale of an aged chief talking to a young boy. The chief tells the boy that in the heart of every man lives two fighting wolves. One wolf is righteous: full of love, kindness, joy, and peace. The other is wicked: full of hate, selfishness, anger, and envy. The boy asks the chief, "Which wolf wins the fight?" The chief smiles back at the boy and simply answers, "The wolf you feed and nurture." The choice all people have before them is either spiritual fulfillment in God's will or fleshly indulgence through bondage to sin. Because of this universal struggle, empathy can begin to develop towards those with substance and process addictions!

What Does the Bible Say About Specific Addictions?

Broadly speaking, sin is an addiction, but let's consider more specifically what the Bible has to say in principle regarding particular addictions.

The Bible on Drug Addiction

Though the Bible does not give extensive teaching on drug addiction, it does offer some counsel wherein God uniformly calls Christians to avoid drug abuse. The primary issue obscuring this teaching is that translation between languages disguises these references. Modern English versions of the Bible will often translate those passages that do apply to drug use with terms like "sorcery" or "magical arts" (Greek: *pharmakeia*, whence "pharmacy"). This word and corresponding words in Hebrew and Latin often denote occult and idolatrous practices that use pharmacological substances to enter alternate states of consciousness in an effort to engage subjects of reverence, much akin to the use of drugs today, in concept. In each usage (e.g., Galatians 5:20; Revelation 9:21; 18:23; cf. Exodus 7:11, 22; 8:18; Isaiah 47:9), the sort of manipulation brought out by drug addiction is outright condemned. Add to this the obvious health and social concerns of drug use and addiction, as well as the civil illegality of drugs regulated by the laws of God-ordained civil leaders (e.g., Romans 13:1-7; 1Peter 2:13-17), and one has even greater spiritual incentive to avoid drugs.

The Bible on Alcohol Addiction

In contrast to drugs, the Bible gives vastly more attention to the issue of alcoholism. Many of the passages condemning devotion to alcohol also serve, in principle, to speak against drug use and addiction as well. Read this powerful approbation of the alcoholic in Proverbs 23:29-35:

> *"Who has woe? Who has sorrow?*
> *Who has contentions? Who has complaining?*
> *Who has wounds without cause?*
> *Who has redness of eyes?*
> *Those who linger long over wine,*
> *Those who go to taste mixed wine.*

Do not look on the wine when it is red,
When it sparkles in the cup,
When it goes down smoothly;
At the last it bites like a serpent
And stings like a viper.
Your eyes will see strange things
And your mind will utter perverse things.
And you will be like one who lies down in the middle of the sea,
Or like one who lies down on the top of a mast.
'They struck me, but I did not become ill;
They beat me, but I did not know it.
When shall I awake?
I will seek another drink.'"

In direct contrast to this straightforward treatment of drunkenness, many have chosen to replace the biblical conception of alcohol with a worldly conception. We live in an age where indulgent drinking has become the norm for many, even espoused believers. Such persons even go so far as to post pictures of their signature drink on Instagram. Middle-aged women name-drop their favorite brand of Pinot Grigio to impress their wine-snob friends, and men chug beers and debate favored liquors (contrast 1 Timothy 3:8; Titus 2:1-8). Some churches even leverage this movement via carnal marketing campaigns with slogans like, "Give our church a shot!" featuring an edgy shot glass graphic. Such a ubiquitous culture counteracts sound biblical teaching on alcoholism.

The Bible on Pornography

The Bible speaks extensively on the value of sexual purity and the proper expression of sexuality within the confines of marriage. Three New Testament Greek terms convey the violation of God's sexual norms:

- *Porneia* (whence "porn") refers to illicit sexual intercourse with a distinct emphasis on fleshly self-indulgence and may include fornication, adultery, bestiality, homosexuality, incest, masturbation, voyeurism, and a variety of other sexual perversions (e.g., 2 Corinthians 12:21; Galatians 5:19; Colossians 3:5).

- *Akatharsia* refers to sensual uncleanness (e.g., Romans 1:24; 6:19; 2 Corinthians 12:21; Galatians 5:19; Ephesians 4:19; 5:3; Colossians 3:5; 1 Thessalonians 2:3).

- *Aselgeia* refers to lasciviousness, wantonness, filth, shameless conduct, etc. and denotes excess, licentiousness, absence of restraint, indecency (e.g., Mark 7:22; Romans 13:13; 2 Corinthians 12:21; Galatians 5:19; Ephesians 4:19; 2 Peter 2:18).

The first two of these terms appear in 1 Thessalonians 4:3-8, which views God's will as antithetical to pornographic devotion:

"For this is the will of God, your sanctification; that is, that you abstain from sexual immorality; that each of you know how to possess his own vessel in sanctification and honor, not in lustful passion, like the Gentiles who do not know God; and that no man transgress and defraud his brother in the matter because the Lord is the avenger in all these things, just as we also told you before and solemnly warned you. For God has not called us for the purpose of impurity, but in sanctification. So, he who rejects this is not rejecting man but the God Who gives His Holy Spirit to you."

Jesus also addresses the specific issue of sexual visualization and fantasizing in Matthew 5:27-30, which says:

"You have heard that it was said, 'You shall not commit adultery'; but I say to you that everyone who looks at a woman with lust for her has already committed adultery with her in his heart. If your right eye makes you stumble, tear it out and throw it from you; for it is better for you to lose one of the parts of your body, than for your whole body to be thrown into hell. If your right hand makes you stumble, cut it off and throw it from you; for it is better for you to lose one of the parts of your body, than for your whole body to go into hell."

A third passage speaks of pornography addiction's power to prevent one from entering Heaven as well as one being enabled to overcome addiction to porn through the power of sanctification. This passage is 1 Corinthians 6:9-11, which reads:

"Or do you not know that the unrighteous will not inherit the kingdom of God? Do not be deceived; neither fornicators, nor idolaters, nor adulterers, nor effeminate, nor homosexuals, nor thieves, nor the covetous, nor drunkards, nor revilers, nor swindlers, will inherit the kingdom of God. Such were some of you; but you were washed, but you were sancti-

fied, but you were justified in the name of the Lord Jesus Christ and in the Spirit of our God."

The Bible on Gambling

The Bible openly condemns the various issues underlying compulsive gambling and may even explicitly condemn gambling itself in 1 Peter 4:3. The casting of lots for the clothes of Jesus may also be an example of gambling (John 19:23-24). The reality of gambling is that any hope of gain is determined by an uncertain event that is arbitrarily decided, a risk far different than what is encountered in farming or investments. This type of risk-taking is foreign to God's approved methods of income which include sensible money-bringing activities such as labor (e.g., Ephesians 4:28; 2 Thessalonians 3:6-12; 1 Timothy 5:17-18; Colossians 4:1), bartering (e.g., Acts 4:36-37), investing (e.g., Proverbs 6:6-8; 13:16; 21:5, 20; 24:27; 27:23; Matthew 25:14-30; Luke 14:28-30), and charity (e.g., Acts 4:32; 20:35; 2 Corinthians 8-9).

One of the key issues with gambling (and all addiction) is greed and lust, which amount to idolatry. These sins are wholly condemned in places such as Colossians 3:5-6. Gambling necessarily involves a loss of monetary value for one to the profit of another. This mindset undermines the second most important commandment to love one's neighbor as oneself (Matthew 22:39), which also requires giving preference to one another (Romans 12:10). Eliminate greed from the equation, and gambling will disappear!

Another issue with compulsive gambling that the Bible condemns is the gambler's cavalier attitude regarding stewardship. The fact that the gambler consents to losing does not make it right. Our attitude toward any evil doesn't change its evil nature! Gambling is not determined by degrees whether a wager is $50, $5, or 5¢. All we have is from God, and we are stewards (James 1:17a). What does God expect us to do with what we have? (1 Corinthians 4:2, 7). One's gambling losses are an ungrateful and ungodly waste of what has been given by God. Furthermore, gambling makes money an idol (1 Timothy 6:10; Matthew 6:24).

Association in gambling is also a factor worthy of consideration (1 Corinthians 15:33). People actively engaging in gambling and promoting it are not going to be building up good morals. Gambling certainly does not increase the influence of Christians (Matthew 5:16). In fact, the nickname "Sin City" for Las Vegas shines neon lights on the true nature of gambling! The true nature of gambling is further exposed by the fact that it is so regulated by every conceivable agency. One does not see such regulations on the fruit of the Spirit!

Two Key Biblical Principles on Addiction

Sobriety

The Bible extols sobriety in a variety of ways, whether it be in reference to one's influences, or as preparation for the return of Jesus Christ. God desires the utmost sobriety in His people (cf. Romans 13:13-14; 1 Corinthians 15:34; Galatians 5:19-23; 1 Thessalonians 5:6-8; 2 Timothy 4:5; 1 Peter 1:13; 4:1-5, 7; 5:8; et al.) and people simply cannot be sober-minded if they are not healthfully sober (not merely abstinent!). We should all want to be fully cognizant and ready for the imminent return of Christ, not fuzzy, distracted, and disengaged. The only influence disciples should be under is God's (cf. Ephesians 5:18), and that influence is accomplished through prayer, Bible study, fellowship with Christians, and worship. Addictions alter judgment and lower resolve to resist temptation, thereby increasing the difficulty of practicing self-control. Addictions simply do not help us run the race that Jesus has marked out before us; instead, they serve as an encumbrance, and if something hinders my sober walk by dishonoring the lordship of Jesus Christ, I need to forsake it (Hebrews 12:1-3). Christians are called to live a life of total surrender to God and separation from the world.

God encourages sobriety in the best interest of humanity. Sobriety benefits one's family. A lack of sobriety has never made a positive difference in a family; rather, addiction unilaterally destroys families. Keep in mind the risk of passing an addiction on within a family. Moreover, consider the benefit of sobriety upon one's spiritual family. Your spiritual family benefits from your sobriety because you are not squandering your mind, talents, and resources but are fully dedicating them to the body of Christ. Non-Christians are also positively influenced by sobriety (cf. 1 Peter 4:3-5). Even the unsaved know Christians should not be devoted to addictive substances and behaviors! When the world sees Christians lost in addiction, it sends the message that Jesus is insufficient (cf. Romans 12:2). Addictions claim to numb pain and sorrow; in actuality, they multiply them. Addictions claim to bring fun and joy; in actuality, they bring regrets. Addictions claim to bring peace; in actuality, they are counterfeit and give turbulence. Addictions distract and derail you from living the victorious life for which Christ died.

Self-Control and Self-Denial

The Bible likewise extols the value of self-control, self-denial, and self-mastery. These are among the fruit that the Holy Spirit produces in the life of a believer (Galatians 5:22-23), and they are also explicitly mentioned as requirements in discipleship to Jesus (Matthew 16:24-27). Self-control is the ability to choose between glorifying God with our body, mind, and soul or settling for the temporary appeasement we receive through self-indulgence (Hebrews 11:25b). By exercising self-jurisdiction, we check our base desires and prioritize God's will in our lives. Some actively strive after this measure of self-control (e.g., 1 Corinthians 9:24-27), while others have no interest (e.g., 2 Timothy 3:1-5). Still others strive for this type of discipline in a way that sadly victimizes them in self-abasement and harsh treatment of the body (Colossians 2:18-23). God's people must healthfully exercise self-control: in body (Romans 6:12-14; 1 Peter 2:11; 1 Corinthians 6:18-20), in words (James 1:26; 3:1-12; Proverbs 12:13; 13:3; 18:21), and in heart and thoughts (Proverbs 16:32; 25:28; Matthew 5:21-22, 27-28; Mark 7:20-23). Thankfully, God provides satisfactory methods of fulfilling desires in a wholesome and honorable fashion!

The apostle Paul stood in chains before one civil leader and declared the gospel message (Acts 24:24-25). Paul presented the unadulterated gospel of Jesus Christ in a threefold format: righteousness, self-control, and the judgment to come. In an often-unrecognized way, Christianity emphasizes self-control. Self-control and addiction are real problems for all people. We all have our vices. We all struggle to keep control. We all can empathize. Without striving for self-control, one cannot lay hold of salvation! Lack of self-control will ultimately lead to addictive behaviors that will make a person a slave to sin. Christians must learn to curb desires and gain mastery over themselves. Learning to do this, with the help of Christ and His grace for when we do lose control, guides us toward more noble endeavors. It keeps us on the straight and narrow path.

How Can Christians Effectively Address Addictions?

Acknowledgment of the problems associated with addiction is pivotal in establishing a proper direction in coping with and overcoming them. This knowledge must be united to the promises of God in order to address the spiritual side of man throughout the journey. Without addressing the God-shaped void in a person's soul, no victory has lasting significance. Secondarily, a variety of uninspired resources are available for those struggling with addiction. There are books, videos, podcasts, counselors, software, and programs that can all help with accountability and understanding, and all that are in line with scriptural principles should be utilized. If you or someone you know may be struggling with an addiction, but you are not sure, look at the "Twenty Questions" inventories for the related twelve-step program to gauge the nature of the situation.

For those battling addiction, take each moment at a time. When you focus on limitless conceptions of time, sabotage is par for the course. Let each minute and each hour and each day be a success. Over time, each moment will come easier, so be careful about attempting to solve all your problems at once. Momentum is vital for lasting success because it brings increased effort, ability, stamina, and further determination. Full, internalized dedication to self-discipline is profitable before God (cf. 2 Peter 1:6). This momentum and internalized dedication, united with training, support, and love, will bring victory. One commentator might be valuable to consider here. He says,

> "There are times when we do not wish to pray; there are times when the easy way is very attractive; there are times when the right thing is the hard thing; there are times when we would like to relax our standards. But the Christian is a man under discipline. He must train himself never to relax in the life-long attempt to make his soul pure and strong."[35]

Another commentator applies the ancient regimen of athletes to this sort of dedication to offer inspiration. He says,

> "The Greek athlete was required to spend ten months in preparatory training before the contest. During this time, he had to engage in prescribed exercises and live a strictly separated life in regard to ordinary and lawful pursuits of life, and he was placed on a rigid diet. Should he break training rules, he would, in the words of the A.V. be a castaway (1 Cor. 9:27), barred from engaging in the athletic contest."[36]

Support will be key in providing enabling power over your lusts, so be open and receptive and seek out partnership(s) to make yourself stronger (Ecclesiastes 4:9-12). Self-mastery requires outside support (Psalm 141; Hebrews 12:1-3). You may decide to do this in the local congregation; you may seek out professional help with group and individual counseling; you may seek recovery through one of the twelve-step programs nationwide (e.g., Narcotics Anonymous – www.na.org; Alcoholics Anonymous – www.aa.org; Sexaholics Anonymous – www.sa.org; Gamblers Anonymous – www.gamblersanonymous.org) or a comparable program; or you may seek help at an inpatient or outpatient treatment facility. Many have found help with these resources, but

---

[35] Barclay, William. *The Letters to Timothy, Titus, and Philemon.* Westminster John Knox Press, 2003.

[36] Wuest, Kenneth Samuel. *Wuest's Word Studies from the Greek New Testament: for the English Reader.* Eerdmans, 1999.

each individual must find the resources and support best suited for them. In the fiery midst of your struggle, you can also take advantage of the Substance Abuse and Mental Health Services Administration (SAMHSA) national helpline at 1-800-662-HELP. Whatever you do, find peers who can sympathize and empathize without enabling or creating co-dependence. Focus on the ultimate spiritual goal with these peers, and God will strengthen you for success (Philippians 3:14; 1 Timothy 4:7b-10). Likewise, ensure that you avoid tempting situations and relationships. Identify your triggers and cut whatever you need to out of your life to ensure success (Proverbs 5:15-23; Lamentations 3:40-41; Matthew 18:8-9; Romans 12:9-12; 2 Timothy 2:22). Set parental controls and lose the password. Use accountability software like Covenant Eyes, X3 Watch, or Ever Accountable. Post Scripture in places that might otherwise serve to trigger you when you cannot totally eliminate negative influences from your life. As with any bad habit, we must replace the practice with something good (cf. Matthew 12:43-45). Submit to God and resist the devil, and he will flee from you! (James 4:7)

For those who do not personally struggle with substance or process addictions, show love, compassion, and grace toward those who do. Build strong relationships with others and pay attention, in love, to their difficulties. Addicts tend to exhibit telltale signs like an inability and unwillingness to accept reality, emotional insecurity, and immaturity. Be careful regarding enabling behaviors, or thoughtlessly providing situations where those tempted with addiction may partake in damaging behaviors. What you say and how you say it, what you do and when you do it, can all play a factor in sabotaging or providing deliverance for someone else. Never pose an unnecessary stumbling block in front of another, for the one who does will find opposition from the throne of God. Additionally, take care to not project manmade standards of wrong-doing on those with addictions. Pushing more shame and ridicule on someone who has fractures in their wellbeing will only impede or arrest their journey to change, or potentially send them into another tail-spin. Show faithful dedication, but do not force another into a decision they are not ready to make. Each person must be accountable for their own actions, as hard as that may be to accept. Tough love may play an essential role in the ascent of a soul from the pit, even if it requires the withdrawal of fellowship in the local congregation, which is commanded in the case of unrepentant Christians.

If you are interested in learning more about your loved one's addiction, there are copious resources available for you. For example, for each twelve-step group, there typically is a corresponding group empathetically addressing the needs of those impacted by a loved one's addiction. Examples include Al-Anon for alcohol addiction, Gam-Anon and Gam-A-Teen for gambling addiction, and Nar-Anon for narcotics addiction. The American Addiction Centers

(AAC) and the Substance Abuse and Mental Health Services Administration (SAMHSA) of the US Department of Health and Human Services (HHS) also have a host of resources available.

Closing Thoughts

Addiction is so destructive! It ruins everything it touches. The fight of all against sin builds a degree of empathy toward those who struggle each day with substance and process addictions (Romans 3:10, 23; 1 John 2:16). Ultimately, anything can be an addiction if we give ourselves over to it, yet there is hope for us all! No, there is no panacea for addiction, but there is hope for peace and fulfillment. By the grace of God, true healing can come to our souls, and He can lead us to paths of freedom. Even though Satan and our lusts are powerful, there is hope and victory. There is recovery and forgiveness. There is a true escape and true elevation out of this world. Addicts can find all of this and more in the comforting arms of Jesus Christ. He is truthful, and His decrees reinforce the value of a sober life of self-discipline and self-denial. He can deliver you if you will dedicate yourself wholly to Him and seek help.

Today you and I are standing at the brink of a major turning point. We have come to the cross to nail our addictions down, to be regenerated by the blood of Christ. When Jonah prayed for forgiveness in the belly of the great sea beast, he admitted, *"Those who cling to worthless idols, forfeit the grace that could be theirs"* (Jonah 2:8). Will you cast your sins in the fire to be destroyed forever? Will you forsake the idols in your life? Or will you forfeit the grace that could be yours?

Thought Questions

1) What emotions arose as you read this chapter and how did this information affect you?

_____

_____

_____

2) Which addiction statistics were surprising to you?

_____

_____

_____

3) What are some of the catalysts for addiction and what can be done to counteract and/or prevent these issues?

_____

_____

_____

4) In light of the universal struggle with sin, how can all Christians empathize with addicts?

_____

_____

_____

5) Discuss the role of shame and guilt in addiction.

_____

_____

_____

6) What does the Bible teach regarding sobriety, self-control, and self-denial?

_____

_____

_____

7) What will you do this week to extend compassion toward those struggling with addiction?

_____

_____

CHAPTER 5

The inventions and innovations of the post-Industrial Age have been astounding, to say the least. The Information Age has brought the internet, a highly useful tool and blessing. As the internet burgeoned, mass forms of communication also developed. Naturally, these goals merged and produced social media. Over time, social media became an integral tool on a variety of new and fantastic devices, including computers, smartphones, and tablets. At each juncture, social media became more and more dominant and, in the eyes of many, necessary. From the early days of Instant Messenger, Pleonast, and Myspace, to the indomitable era of Facebook, Twitter, Instagram, Snapchat, and Pinterest, to the conservative movement towards Parler and MeWe, each step surges forward like a missile. As more platforms continue to develop, some cannot survive, while others thrive and become staples in the daily social media diet. As of 2020, 3.6 billion people use social media, nearly half of the world's population! Experts project this number to exceed 4.41 billion by 2025![37] This worldwide figure reaches an even higher rate of nearly 70% of Americans using social media and social networking regularly, often daily.[38] Naturally, such changes have brought and continue to bring blessings and curses with them. Let's examine some of these now with the Bible in hand and

[37] Tankovska, H. "Number of Social Media Users Worldwide from 2017 to 2025." *Statista*, 28 Jan. 2021, www.statista.com/statistics/278414/number-of-worldwide-social-network-users/.

[38] "Demographics of Social Media Users and Adoption in the United States." *Pew Research Center: Internet, Science & Tech,* Pew Research Center, 5 June 2020, www.pewresearch.org/internet/fact-sheet/social-media/.

with the primary goal of well-disciplined spiritual influence in a world in dire need of the gospel of Jesus Christ!

Some of the Blessings of Social Media

Though much discourse is devoted to the threats and perils of social media, in truth, there are many benefits that have come from its inception, especially with the church. This is an important truth to acknowledge, since differing judgments often approach social media conversations with different areas of focus, causing many of these discussions to implode. The middle-ground of balance can establish a better appreciation for the entire picture, as opposed to merely focusing on one's own soapbox. Christians express positive aspects of social media this way:

> "I like how I am able to be a part of spiritually-minded groups and keep in touch with brethren. Social media enables me to keep in touch with family, friends, and brethren all over the world. I can also make great new friends!"

> "I love the ability to keep in touch with people who have moved far away. I also love all the Zoom events one can be a part of! That has helped keep me sane during the COVID pandemic. I've been feeling down lately, but through social media, people have encouraged me on here. I need all the building up I can get!"

> "I like social media's ability to facilitate: renewed friendships, keeping up with friends you aren't able to see often, being able to engage in casual, but professional groups to share knowledge, and being able to reach countless people to help encourage them and be encouraged by them!"

Through social media, connections have been made in ways traditional in-person interaction has failed to achieve. Millions of people have been able to read scriptural articles, view scriptural videos, and link to congregational websites via posts for the message of salvation. One recent study by Lifeway Research breaks down the numbers and trends:

> "Among those who use social media in 2017, 97 percent use it to inform people about coming events. Eighty-seven percent use it to interact with the congregation, while 86 percent use social media to interact with outsiders. Eighty-four percent use social media to capture memories of church

activities, while 68 percent use social media to help church members interact.

Even most small churches—those with fewer than 50 attenders—are likely to have a Facebook page (70 percent). Larger churches—those with 250 or more attenders—are more likely to also use Twitter (39 percent) and Instagram (29 percent)."[39]

That being said, these connections have in many ways been improved upon by meeting in-person to study the Scriptures. One example has been the use of the social media platform Meetup to establish contacts in the community to then meet in coffee shops and other public congregational areas to read and discuss the Scriptures. I have personally leveraged this avenue of making contacts and baptized several through this means, including a family who has adopted through Sacred Selections and one man who has become an ardent evangelist in the Lord's church! These contacts may have been nearly impossible to make without the aid of social media.

Social media has also produced new and creative ways of fellowshipping via increased communication. Many churches have used public pages and private group pages to embrace these developments. One outcome has been that fellow believers have a greater knowledge of and appreciation for prayer needs. This results in more specific prayers and greater attentiveness to the happenings of brethren's lives. Christians have learned more about their spiritual loved ones regarding their families, life events, work successes and challenges, passions, hobbies, etc. Video platform resources like Facebook Live and Zoom have even partially bridged the facelessness so typical of social media, a great benefit especially during times in which in-person interaction may be high-risk.

Social media has also opened up more pathways of inter-congregational communication and dialogue. Formerly, interactions between congregations tended to be limited to in-person annual or bi-annual interactions at gospel meetings, lectureships, revivals, VBS, and chance meetings with Christian friends. Now, one can be aware of sermons, Bible classes, opportunities, and other information relative to different congregations. One added advantage here is in the case of announcing the cancellation of services at one's own congregation due to inclement weather or building repairs. Not only can one be informed about the assembly they typically attend, but they can also be informed about other opportunities still available at other congregations.

---

[39] Smietana, Bob. "Most Churches Offer Wi-Fi but Skip Twitter." *Lifeway Research,* 9 Jan. 2018, lifewayresearch.com/2018/01/09/most-churches-offer-free-wi-fi-but-skip-twitter/.

Social Media, Psychosocial Issues, and Related Biblical Principles

Despite the many advantages of social media, it has also produced several demonstrable issues which have a markedly detrimental impact on the minds of individuals, on society at large, and on the souls of men and women. We must not overlook these challenges for the strengths of social media. Several Christians share their discouragements and frustrations regarding social media this way:

"I recognize addictive, habitual, and escapist tendencies for myself on social media. It is difficult for me emotionally at times to see how people, especially brethren, speak to each other on social media. I am, at times, tempted to respond harshly to such people."

"Social media has disadvantages. People hate on things that are just matters of opinion and then unfriend, unfollow, or don't talk to you about your thoughts. I loathe people arguing, being mean, discouraging, and bashing others on social media."

"I dislike that people post rude comments – things you would never say to someone in person. I also dislike that social media provides the ability to video embarrassing incidents of others and post it. Before social media, the only people to see embarrassing incidents were the ones present. As a professional therapist, I also see widespread addiction to social media in which people are becoming detached in personal interaction, all the while constantly seeking the approval of others online."

Social media's ability to produce innumerable relationships often lacks in providing depth to those relationships. A "like" on a picture once in a while is not nearly the same as an intimate in-person relationship. Though a friend to all people, even Jesus held several friendships close to His heart. The Apostle John, Lazarus, Mary, and Martha are all called disciples whom Jesus particularly loved (John 11:3, 5, 11, 36; 12:1-2; 13:23; 19:27-29). John, along with Peter and James, are seen to have shared a special relationship with Jesus given their integral function in key events in the Gospel narratives (e.g., the Transfiguration in Mark 9:2-3; the resurrection of Jairus' daughter in Luke 8:49-56; Jesus' prayer in Gethsemane in Matthew 26:36-38).

Another danger related to friends and followers is the lack of filtration, which can result in temptation and spiritual downfall through social media's open interaction. God's Word even specifically warns of having too many friends and followers: *"A man of too many friends comes to ruin"* (Proverbs

18:24a). The Scriptures also advise believers to beware the dangers of immoral friends and influences:

"Do not associate with a man given to anger;
Or go with a hot-tempered man,
Or you will learn his ways
And find a snare for yourself." (Proverbs 22:24-25)

"He who keeps the law is a discerning son,
But he who is a companion of gluttons humiliates his father."
(Proverbs 28:7)

"Do not be deceived: 'Bad company corrupts good morals.' Become so-
ber-minded as you ought, and stop sinning; for some have no knowledge
of God. I speak this to your shame." (1 Corinthians 15:33)

"Do not be bound together with unbelievers; for what partnership have
righteousness and lawlessness, or what fellowship has light with darkness?
Or what harmony has Christ with Belial, or what has a believer in com-
mon with an unbeliever? Or what agreement has the temple of God with
idols? For we are the temple of the living God; just as God said,

'I will dwell in them and walk among them;
And I will be their God, and they shall be My people.
Therefore, come out from their midst and be separate,' says the Lord.
'And do not touch what is unclean;
And I will welcome you.
And I will be a father to you,
And you shall be sons and daughters to Me,'
Says the Lord Almighty.

Therefore, having these promises, beloved, let us cleanse ourselves from all
defilement of flesh and spirit, perfecting holiness in the fear of God."
(2 Corinthians 6:14-7:1)

As a counterbalance, the Scriptures extol the virtue of good companions and social relations:

"I am a companion of all those who fear You,
And of those who keep Your precepts." (Psalm 119:63)

"He who walks with wise men will be wise,
But the companion of fools will suffer harm." (Proverbs 13:20)

"A friend loves at all times,
And a brother is born for adversity." (Proverbs 17:17)

"Two are better than one because they have a good return for their labor.
For if either of them falls, the one will lift up his companion. But woe to the
one who falls when there is not another to lift him up. Furthermore, if two
lie down together they keep warm, but how can one be warm alone? And
if one can overpower him who is alone, two can resist him. A cord of three
strands is not quickly torn apart." (Ecclesiastes 4:9-12)

Whether our friendships are in-person, online, or both, they have the capacity to spiritually edify us or tear us down. An additional encouragement is necessary for parents, who play an essential role in their children's spiritual development. Writer Joe Price explains,

"Do you know what your child is posting on [Facebook]? If not, find out.
You wouldn't let your child bring a stranger into your home with your
knowledge and permission. Do not let them indiscriminately bring strang-
ers into their lives on FB. Adolescent brains are not fully developed yet
to be able to completely assess actions and consequences. Don't be naïve,
don't make assumptions, but get the facts. Such knowledge is vital in order
to train your children in the way they should go (Prov. 22:6)."[40]

Therefore, choose wisely who you and your children associate with, especially on social media! Not doing so can lead to physical danger as well as spiritual shipwreck!

Social media also has a habit of causing Christians to be slow to hear, quick to speak, and quick to anger, in direct contradiction to the Lord's wisdom—*"This you know my beloved brethren. But everyone must be quick to hear, slow to speak and slow to anger; for the anger of man does not achieve the righteousness of God"* (James 1:19-20; cf. Ecclesiastes 7:8-9). Social media's instantaneous nature often reprograms the mind, disengaging self-governance and facilitating the unfiltered expression of unwise thoughts. One commentator describes this danger of social media:

"If you ridicule someone you have become arrogant and unloving. If you

---

[40] Price, Joe. "Facebook," *Truth Magazine*, volume LIV, number 12, December 2010, page 5.

post profanity and join in coarse joking you have lowered yourself to join the world in the sewer of vulgarity (Eph. 4:29; 5:3-4). If you post unfounded rumors, malicious gossip, and tale bearing you have left the land of brotherly love and crossed over into the land of bitterness and malice (Eph. 4:31-32)."[41]

The Bible repeatedly warns about the multiplication of words, especially when listening should be prioritized:

"When there are many words, transgression is unavoidable,
But he who restrains his lips is wise." (Proverbs 10:19)

"The one who guards his mouth preserves his life;
The one who opens wide his lips comes to ruin." (Proverbs 13:3; cf. 10:8; 21:23)

"He who restrains his words has knowledge,
And he who has a cool spirit is a man of understanding.
Even a fool, when he keeps silent, is considered wise;
When he closes his lips, he is considered prudent." (Proverbs 17:27)

"Either make the tree good and its fruit good, or make the tree bad and its fruit bad; for the tree is known by its fruit. You brood of vipers, how can you, being evil, speak what is good? For the mouth speaks out of that which fills the heart. The good man brings out of his good treasure what is good; and the evil man brings out of his evil treasure what is evil. But I tell you that every careless word that people speak, they shall give an accounting for it in the day of judgment. For by your words you will be justified, and by your words you will be condemned." (Matthew 12:33-37)

"For we all stumble in many ways. If anyone does not stumble in what he says, he is a perfect man, able to bridle the whole body as well. Now if we put the bits into the horses' mouths so that they will obey us, we direct their entire body as well. Look at the ships also, though they are so great and are driven by strong winds, are still directed by a very small rudder wherever the inclination of the pilot desires. So also the tongue is a small part of the body, and yet it boasts of great things.

See how great a forest is set aflame by such a small fire! And the tongue

---

[41] Ibid.

is a fire, the very world of iniquity; the tongue is set among our members as that which defiles the entire body, and sets on fire the course of our life, and is set on fire by hell. For every species of beasts and birds, of reptiles and creatures of the sea, is tamed and has been tamed by the human race. But no one can tame the tongue; it is a restless evil and full of deadly poison. With it we bless our Lord and Father, and with it we curse men, who have been made in the likeness of God; from the same mouth come both blessing and cursing. My brethren, these things ought not to be this way. Does a fountain send out from the same opening both fresh and bitter water? Can a fig tree, my brethren, produce olives, or a vine produce figs? Nor can salt water produce fresh.

Who among you is wise and understanding? Let him show by his good behavior his deeds in the gentleness of wisdom. But if you have bitter jealousy and selfish ambition in your heart, do not be arrogant and so lie against the truth. This wisdom is not that which comes down from above, but is earthly, natural, demonic. For where jealousy and selfish ambition exist, there is disorder and every evil thing. But the wisdom from above is first pure, then peaceable, gentle, reasonable, full of mercy and good fruits, unwavering, without hypocrisy. And the seed whose fruit is righteousness is sown in peace by those who make peace." (James 3:2-18)

Social media can sometimes simply devolve into a venue to share an excess of information, whether private or superfluous in nature. This has led to widespread egocentrism, where people are so self-focused and praise-seeking that they post every little detail of their lives. Thoughtless posting is also a struggle for all and has become a nasty habit for many. Trivialities often supplant meaningful communication and expression. A consequence of this is that those more meaningful spiritual truths shared via social media are veiled with a cloak of superficiality, readily dismissed as shallow in nature. This cloaking is expedited by the flagrant devotion of some of God's people to perpetually sharing and posting foolishness. The regular gush of silliness and mindless chatter on our accounts can poison the well of gospel truth, inhibiting the living water's flow among the nations. Be especially careful of gossip, backbiting, and busybody tendencies, struggles which the Scriptures repeatedly warn of:

"A perverse man spreads strife,
And a slanderer separates intimate friends." (Proverbs 16:28)

"He who conceals a transgression seeks love,
But he who repeats a matter separates intimate friends." (Proverbs 17:9)

"At the same time [undisciplined younger widows who might be supported by the church] also learn to be idle, as they go around from house to house; and not merely idle, but also gossips and busybodies, talking about things not proper to mention." (1 Timothy 5:13)

Many people struggle with outright addiction to social media. The dangers of "social media brain" are a constant subject of scientific study, especially when comparing the brain scans of social media and internet addicts to the brain scans of substance addicts. Research suggests strong relationships between social media use and decreases in sustained focus, increases in attentional-switching, changes in memory protocols, detrimental effects in offline sociality, increases in stress response and allostatic load, and addiction-like triggers and damage in brain reward centers such as the Ventral Tegmental Area (VTA).[42] To bring this into the personal realm, have you ever been scrolling through your social media account or newsfeed, 15-20 minutes pass by, and you look up wondering where the time went? This is what research is finding!

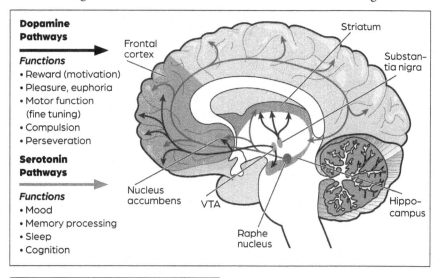

---

[42] Examples of this research include: Firth, Joseph et al. "The 'Online Brain': How the Internet May Be Changing Our Cognition." *World Psychiatry: Official Journal of the World Psychiatric Association (WPA)* vol. 18,2 (2019): 119-129. doi:10.1002/wps.20617; Gordon, Billi. "Social Media Is Harmful to Your Brain and Relationships." *Psychology Today,* Sussex Publishers, 20 Oct. 2017, www.psychologytoday.com/us/blog/obesely-speaking/201710/social-media-is-harmful-your-brain-and-relationships; Sherman, Lauren E., et al. "The Power of the Like in Adolescence: Effects of Peer Influence on Neural and Behavioral Responses to Social Media." *SAGE Journals,* 31 May 2016, journals.sagepub.com/doi/10.1177/0956797616645673. An excellent film that reviews these and other impacts is *The Social Dilemma* on Netflix.

Idleness on social media can become a massive waste of time, squandering opportunities to serve the Lord and missing out on helping our fellow people. This wastefulness is in direct contradiction to the direction given in the Scriptures regarding time management and discipline:

"Laziness casts into a deep sleep,
And an idle man will suffer hunger." (Proverbs 19:15)

"I passed by the field of the sluggard
And by the vineyard of the man lacking sense,
And behold, it was completely overgrown with thistles;
Its surface was covered with nettles,
And its stone wall was broken down.
When I saw, I reflected upon it;
I looked, and received instruction.
'A little sleep, a little slumber,
A little folding of the hands to rest,'
Then your poverty will come as a robber
And your want like an armed man." (Proverbs 24:30-34)

"She looks well to the ways of her household,
And does not eat the bread of idleness." (Proverbs 31:27, of the virtuous woman)

"For this reason it says,

'Awake, sleeper,
And arise from the dead,
And Christ will shine on you.'

Therefore be careful how you walk, not as unwise men but as wise, making the most of your time, because the days are evil. So then do not be foolish, but understand what the will of the Lord is." (Ephesians 5:14-17)

Jesus even mentions the folly of idleness in several of His parables (e.g., Matthew 20:1-16; 25:1-13, 14-30). While the world continues around a person, they may be absent in the void of social media. Consider too the devotion of such time to what is typically found on social media, postings that, more often than not, do not fit the category of scripturally-approved meditation. Contrast the drivel regularly filling social media against these passages regulating the Christian's mental devotion:

"Let the words of my mouth and the meditation of my heart
Be acceptable in Your sight,
O Lord, my rock and my Redeemer." (Psalm 19:14)

"Rejoice in the Lord always; again I will say, rejoice! Let your gentle spirit
be known to all men. The Lord is near. Be anxious for nothing, but in ev-
erything by prayer and supplication with thanksgiving let your requests be
made known to God. And the peace of God, which surpasses all compre-
hension, will guard your hearts and your minds in Christ Jesus.

Finally, brethren, whatever is true, whatever is honorable, whatever is
right, whatever is pure, whatever is lovely, whatever is of good repute, if
there is any excellence and if anything worthy of praise, dwell on these
things." (Philippians 4:4-8)

"For the grace of God has appeared, bringing salvation to all men, in-
structing us to deny ungodliness and worldly desires and to live sensibly,
righteously and godly in the present age, looking for the blessed hope and
the appearing of the glory of our great God and Savior, Christ Jesus, Who
gave Himself for us to redeem us from every lawless deed, and to purify for
Himself a people for His own possession, zealous for good deeds." (Titus
2:11-14)

How Can Christians Effectively Address Social Media Issues?

In addition to what has been previously discussed, Christians can and
should take a variety of steps in order to take advantage of the benefits and
minimize the detrimental impacts of social media.

First and foremost, exercise self-restraint in your social media usage! As
we have seen in the previous chapter on addictions, self-control and discipline
are necessary components of discipleship. Such self-imposed limitations begin
with understanding one's personal areas of temptation. Learning more about
who we are and what triggers our fleshly side can provide direction regarding
success through accountability. This internal appraisal must lead us to make
substantive changes with attainable goals and real-life practicality. For example, one might use apps that monitor device usage or set usage controls on
their devices.

Second, invest in intimate personal relationships. Do what you can to meet
with your friends, family, loved ones, and acquaintances in-person. This will
effectively marginalize mind-numbing commitment to trivialities, sift out true
friends, minimize misunderstandings through the conveyance of nonverbal

communication, etc. Moreover, invest in supplemental ways of communication in order to connect with those who are afar. Write letters, travel, and choose communication methods that transcend the issues plaguing social media.

Third, fill your time with meaningful interactions and soul-winning. If you pursue this through social media, regulate yourself; if you think you are approaching the slippery slope of ungodliness, take a step back. If you choose to do this in person, make the most of each conversation! Whatever you choose, show others that you love and care for them by sharing the hope of the gospel of Jesus Christ (1 Peter 3:15). Such dedication is never wasteful!

Fourth, if necessary, take a social media fast or excise it from your life altogether. Social media is a relatively new invention; the world existed long before Facebook and Snapchat! Fasting may be an effective way to reboot your mind, recenter your focus, and recharge your batteries. Sharing this with others, when not done as a measure of egocentric moralizing, can encourage them to do the same and hold you accountable. Fasting is repeatedly offered in the Scriptures as an effective approach in dealing with lack of focus, excessive interest in fleshly matters, or as an appeal to God for deliverance. Think of the fasting of Esther, Mordecai, and the Jewish nation who faced a holocaust at the hands of Haman (Esther 4). Consider Jesus' fasting when facing temptation for forty days and forty nights in the wilderness (Matthew 4). Recall the fasting of the early disciples leading up to crucial choices (Acts 13-14). If fasting does not work for you, consider eliminating social media from your life. One can exist and thrive outside of the realm of social media; in fact, this may be the most advantageous option for you. Jesus commended this sort of sacrifice and prioritization of the spiritual person:

> *"If your right eye makes you stumble, tear it out and throw it from you; for it is better for you to lose one of the parts of your body, than for your whole body to be thrown into hell. If your right hand makes you stumble, cut it off and throw it from you; for it is better for you to lose one of the parts of your body, than for your whole body to go into hell."* (Matthew 5:29-30; cf. 18:8-9)

Closing Thoughts

Social media is a rich blessing when used correctly, but the plain truth is that it is exceedingly difficult to avoid the problems social media use can create. Satan has a powerful grip on social media, and the temptation to think improperly and do wrong is enormous. He has corrupted this tool into his own personal platform by which to disseminate misinformation, provoke and inflame emotions, cause the uncontrollable tongue to set worldwide fires, ensnare and enslave souls in addiction, and create fissures and fractures between the church and the world, and even within the church herself.

Christians have an uphill battle if they choose to utilize social media. Ultimately, it is a personal choice how one will do so and with what platforms. Apply godly discretion and sound wisdom in what you use and how you use it. Seek guidance from current or former users before starting an account and seek forgiveness when you fall short of using that account for the glory of God. In the end, the impartial Judge of all the earth will judge all our social media activities. Will He say to you, "Well done!" or "Depart from Me"?

Thought Questions

1) What emotions arose as you read this chapter and how did this information affect you?

_____

_____

_____

2) Is involvement in social media necessary in this day and age?

_____

_____

_____

3) What are some positive ways that social media has impacted the church?

_____

_____

_____

4) What are some negative ways that social media has impacted the church?

_____

_____

_____

5) List three biblical principles that guide social media use.

_____

_____

_____

6) How can marketing on social media entrap believers and tempt them to sin?

_____

_____

_____

7) How can you better glorify God in your social media usage this week?

_____

_____

_____

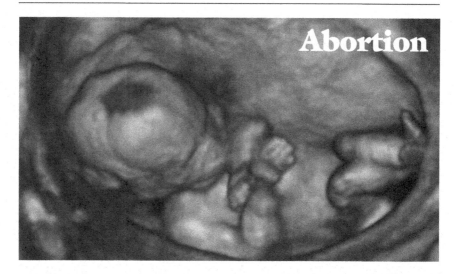

Abortion

A barbaric practice, abortion has become legal and commonplace in a world degenerating at breakneck speed. Wrong is called right, and evil is applauded (cf. Isaiah 5:20-21; Romans 1:28-32).[43] Sadly too, arguments around abortion often become a cheap political pawn; as a result, constructive discussion often evades many as emotions swelter, egos inflate, and seats are taken on opposite sides of the aisle. Opponents enter echo chambers, and typical roadblocks habitually prevent Christians in particular from being a voice for the voiceless (Proverbs 31:8-9). Mothers in need of love and compassion are bypassed and children in need of preservation are cast aside. What can a Christian do?

Despite these frustrating obstacles, Christians can have effective conversations regarding the topic of abortion. The key is to understand: what abortion is, what factors have made abortion acceptable in the minds of the world, what God has to say about abortion, and what Christians can do to effectively respond to and curtail the acceptance of abortion. When Christians master these areas, beneficial communication can and will occur.

What Is Abortion?

Abortion is defined in manifold ways, complicating discussions for Christian apologists. To help wade through these, let us consider two basic categories medically labeled as abortion.

---

[43] In the case of abortion, #shoutyourabortion and the celebration of governmental and societal institutions in New York at the passing of the Reproductive Health Act illustrate such ungodly extolling of ungodly actions.

The first category is known as "voluntary" abortion. This usage denotes the removal of an embryo or fetus from the uterus to terminate a pregnancy willfully. A variety of methods, discussed in the next section, are intentionally chosen to prematurely conclude pregnancy. To obscure the reality of this choice, medical jargon is used to callous one's emotions and cloak one's knowledge of the child one vivisects. Rather than refer to this child with relational terms otherwise used when the baby is desired, words like "embryo," "fetus," or "tissue" are employed. Even in abortion clinics, aborted babies are not referred to in relational terms but rather as "Products of Conception," (POC), which are then pieced back together in glass dishes to ensure no body parts remain inside the patient.

The second category is known as "spontaneous" abortion. The application of the term "abortion" to this second category serves to obscure the true nature of abortion and to evoke compromise in the event of difficulties during pregnancy. In reality, spontaneous abortion is a miscarriage, a wholly different situation than the intentional ending of a human life in the womb. To miscarry is a trauma devoid of maternal control or responsibility, assuming the mother did not contribute to a hostile womb environment for the child through her lifestyle choices. A life is lost, for seen (e.g., ectopic pregnancy) or unforeseen reasons (e.g., genetic mutation), and never gets the opportunity to develop and be viable. Sadly, the mother may not complete this loss biologically, and medical intervention is necessary to prevent the illness or death of the mother. This miserable requisite is in no way akin to an intentional termination of a baby's life.

The extent of abortion is terrible.[44] Statistics are kept regularly by the CDC[45] and the Guttmacher Institute[46] and, although they use different methods to get their numbers, here is a distillation of what the numbers show:

- *Since the Roe v. Wade Supreme Court decision on January 22, 1973, over 60 million abortions have been performed in the United States.*

---

[44] The federal prosecution case against Kermit Gosnell, operator of the Women's Medical Society of Philadelphia, PA profoundly illustrates the horrors of abortion and the notorious lack of regulation in this ghastly business. Also noteworthy is the infamous Live Action sting operation of a New Jersey Planned Parenthood clinic in 2011.

[45] For US statistics from the CDC, see: https://www.cdc.gov/reproductivehealth/data_stats/abortion.htm.

[46] For US statistics from the Guttmacher Institute, see: https://www.guttmacher.org/united-states/abortion. For global abortion statistics from the Guttmacher Institute, see: https://www.guttmacher.org/global/abortion.

- *Locations with the highest reported abortion rates include Washington, D.C., New Jersey, and New York. In New York City, approximately 1 in 3 pregnancies end in abortion.*
- *Locations with the lowest reported abortion rates include Idaho, South Dakota, and Wyoming.*
- *According to the statistics available from 2018, abortions disproportionately occur in unmarried women in their 20s.*
- *Among teenage pregnancies, approximately 1 in 5 ends in voluntary abortion.*
- *Voluntary abortion becomes a less likely option after one has initially chosen it; 60% of those who undergo abortion are first-timers, while those who have had three or more abortions make up a mere 6%.*
- *Reported abortions have decreased relatively consistently in the United States since 1990 (however, even a single voluntary abortion is a reprehensible tragedy!).[47]*

Methods of Abortion[48]

The "Abortion Pill" (i.e., the combination of Mifepristone and Misoprostol) is a non-surgical abortion that blocks progesterone, a natural hormone necessary for sustaining life in-utero, causing the baby to starve to death as the nutrient lining around the baby disintegrates. This option is advertised as non-invasive, safe, and simple, but the actuality could not be more different. The FDA regularly receives hundreds of cases of excessive bleeding, infections, and death. Two specific cases worth researching in order to understand this horrific reality include: Holly Patterson, who died as a result of being given this protocol by a Planned Parenthood in Hayward, CA, and another mother whose case is documented in chapter 2 of Abby Johnson's *The Walls Are Talking*.[49]

For pregnancies between 6 and 24 weeks, there are several methods for abortion that all incorporate similar methods and procedures. Suction Aspiration, also known as Vacuum Aspiration, is performed between 6 to 12 weeks after the woman's last menstrual period. The doctor inserts a long plastic tube

---

[47] Examination and interpretation of this data are helpfully made by the non-profit organization Abort 73. Their website is a valuable compendium of resources: https://abort73.com.

[48] This section is dependent on the work of Erhardt, Aaron. *Silenced Cries: A Study of Abortion*. Erhardt Publications, 2009.

[49] Johnson, Abby, and Kristin Detrow. *The Walls Are Talking: Former Abortion Clinic Workers Tell Their Stories*. Ignatius Press, 2018.

connected to a suction device into the womb, the baby is suctioned out, and then discarded. Dilation & Curettage (D&C) is performed between 12 to 15 weeks after the woman's last menstrual period. With this method, the baby may first be cut apart before it is suctioned out in pieces and discarded. Dilation & Evacuation (D&E) is performed between 12 to 24 weeks after the woman's last menstrual period. At most abortion clinics, it is standard to apply an off-label use of a medicine called Digoxin to stop the baby's heart and then extract the baby from the uterus. Abortion providers select this procedure when the baby is too large to be vacuumed through suction tubing. The doctor widens the cervix and dismembers the baby using forceps. The body is pulled out in pieces and discarded. In some cases, providers crush the skull to ease removal. Such practices, as well as the next category below, are described in graphic detail by the reformed abortion provider Dr. Anthony Levatino in his testimony before the Committee on the Judiciary at the House of Representatives on October 8, 2015.

Dilation & Extraction (D&X), also known as Partial-Birth Abortion, is performed after 21 weeks. The doctor grips the baby's leg using forceps and pulls him through the birth canal. The baby is delivered feet first, leaving the head in the birth canal. The physician then inserts a sharp instrument into the base of the skull, and suctions the brain out. The skull collapses, and the baby is discarded. This method burst onto the scene during President Bill Clinton's administration when, in 1996, he vetoed a bill banning this cruel and inhumane practice. Succeeding presidents have continuously volleyed similar bills, most notably George W. Bush, who said regarding Partial-Birth Abortion: *"For years, a terrible form of violence has been directed against children who are inches from birth, while the law looked the other way."* He continued, *"The best case against partial birth abortion is a simple description of what happens and to whom it happens. It involves the partial delivery of a live boy or girl, and a sudden, violent end of that life. Our nation owes its children a different and better welcome."*[50]

Saline Solution is another torturous abortion procedure involving injecting a potent salt solution into the baby's sac. The baby swallows the solution and is poisoned by it, while its skin is simultaneously severely burned by the same solution. The baby rarely dies immediately and is sometimes still alive when delivered the next day. For an informed explanation and defense against this grotesque form of abortion, refer to the testimony of Gianna Jessen, a survivor of Saline Solution Abortion, before the Constitution Subcommittee of the House Judiciary on April 22, 1996.

---

[50] "President Bush Signs Partial Birth Ban Act of 2003," https://www.whitehouse.gov/news/releases/2003.

Major Catalysts in Support for Abortion

Given the well-known realities behind abortion procedures and the advent of ultrasound technology where you can actually watch and listen to a baby in-utero as it struggles to survive such heinous acts, why would anyone voluntarily get an abortion?

Eugenics has played a foundational, formative role in the support of abortion. During the first half of the 20th century especially, eugenics dominated the philosophical landscape, searching for ways to eliminate all corrupted and mutated genes from the world's population. Key figures such as Margaret Sanger, Adolf Hitler, and Dr. Kevorkian illustrated the extreme lust for eliminating those arbitrarily deemed unworthy of life. The concept superficially seems to offer merit. After all, who wouldn't want to avoid the plagues of cancer, mental deficiency, and deformity? The ugly truth is much, much different. You see, all human life is corrupted on a genetic level. There is not a single person in the world today without some genetic imperfection and anomaly. Eugenics then is merely a systematized elimination of those deemed inferior by the egotistical managers of influential enterprises, groups such as Planned Parenthood today.

Perhaps the worst catalyst of abortion acceptance was the court decision that opened the floodgates for abortion—Roe v. Wade. In the original case, the plaintiff was Norma McGovey, pseudonym Jane Roe, a 21-year-old mother who had an unplanned pregnancy. Her testimony is that she was manipulated into the case and encouraged to lie about the circumstances of her pregnancy by her ultra-feminist lawyer Sarah Weddington. Though rarely mentioned, Norma McGovey never had an abortion after winning the case. In an interesting turn of events, the former "Jane Roe" became dedicated to reversing the decision![51] She called the entire abortion industry a sham and dedicated her life to undoing the law bearing her name.

Another reason for widespread support of abortion is because of abortion being philosophically and ethically portrayed as a praiseworthy victory in the progressive efforts of extremist women's rights advocates and ultra-feminism. Men, government, other institutions, and even children themselves are typecast as holding women back from their potential. Evolved societies, or so the

---

[51] *Ad hominem* attacks have been levied against Norma McGovey, calling her an opportunistic pathological liar because of her mixed emotions and opposing statements after the court case. Whether or not she was, in the end, is irrelevant. If she legitimately felt manipulated into the case, her testimony stands, and the resultant attacks of pro-abortion groups show validity to her statements. If she merely said these things to appease anti-abortion groups and gain a paycheck, it illustrates a fractured psyche, deeply affected by the case and testifying to the moral repugnance and callous of abortion.

story goes, would never inhibit women in such a way as to shackle them down as mothers. Such is undoubtedly the case in Hollywood propaganda pieces such as the film *If These Walls Could Talk,* where several scenarios are fallaciously presented by high-paid actresses in a way that elicits sympathy for women seeking an abortion. As one writer voiced:

> *"This issue gets presented as if it's a tug of war between the woman and the baby. We see them as mortal enemies, locked in a fight to the death. But that's a strange idea, isn't it? It must be the first time in history when mothers and their own children have been assumed to be at war. We're supposed to picture the child attacking her, trying to destroy her hopes and plans, and picture the woman grateful for the abortion, since it rescued her from the clutches of her child."*[52]

What Does the Bible Say About Abortion?

After discovering the true nature of abortion and the underlying philosophical foundations propping up support for this murderous practice, one should have a clear picture of its moral and ethical abhorrence. This knowledge comes without an appeal to the Scriptures but only serves to undergird what God has already revealed about such barbarism.

God's creation of life imbues it with sanctity. As He breathed His Spirit into the nostrils of mankind (Genesis 2:7) and fashioned him as a potter fashions clay (Isaiah 64:8), He imprinted in mankind His own image (Genesis 1:26-27). Human life is more important than the lives of any animal (Genesis 9:4-6); more than food or shelter (Matthew 6:25-34); more than any hobby or convenience (Matthew 19:26); more important than anything physical! Edgar Ramirez keenly observed this value by saying, *"For me, no ideological or political conviction would justify the sacrifice of a human life. For me, the value of life is absolute, with no concessions. It's not negotiable."* Given this God-imposed sanctity, any action against another human being is a grave matter. Murder, rape, theft, abuse, and any other comparable actions are an offense to God and should certainly offend the sensibilities of those created in His image.

There is perhaps no greater affront to the sanctity of life than when one commits a violent offense against someone whom God sees as especially worthy of compassion, specifically a child. Children in the womb are holy, living, and deserving of protection (cf. Jeremiah 1:5; Psalm 139; Luke 1:41). In fact,

[52] Matthewes-Green, Frederica. "When Abortion Suddenly Stopped Making Sense." *National Review,* 30 May 2019, https://www.nationalreview.com/2016/01/abortion-roe-v-wade-unborn-children-women-feminism-march-life/.

under the Law of Moses, the violent perpetrator of the death of a child in the womb would receive retributive justice, and his or her life would be forfeit. Exodus 21:22-25 states:

> "If men struggle with each other and strike a woman with child so that she gives birth prematurely, yet there is no injury, he shall surely be fined as the woman's husband may demand of him, and he shall pay as the judges decide. But if there is any further injury, then you shall appoint as a penalty life for life, eye for eye, tooth for tooth, hand for hand, foot for foot, burn for burn, wound for wound, bruise for bruise."

In the Scriptures, God consistently condemns child sacrifice. He condemned child sacrifice on altars of pagan idols (e.g., Deuteronomy 18:10; 2 Kings 16:3; 17:17; 21:6; 23:10; Jeremiah 32:35; Ezekiel 16:21; 20:26, 31; 23:37). God condemned the ripping open of pregnant women by foreign or domestic powers in efforts at self-magnification (e.g., Amos 1:13). He even connected the destruction brought on by sin to the tearing open of pregnant women and the destruction of their babies (e.g., Hosea 13:16).

The simple truth is that all lives are valuable to God whether we properly esteem them so or not. This includes people of any skin tone, the rich and the poor, the physical specimens and the physically deformed, the brilliant and those of low intelligence, children and adults, the old and those in the womb. He knits us together and breathes into our nostrils the breath of life. He loves us so much that despite our corruption by sin, He gave up the life of His only begotten Son to redeem us. God gave it all because He valued us, and that settles it. He is the highest court in any land. If any earthly government mandates that Christians oppose God's ordinance, we owe our allegiance to Him alone.

Answering False Defenses of Abortion

A large part of Christians' responsibility towards abortion lies in acknowledging and passionately defending what the Lord says (Proverbs 15:28; 1 Peter 3:15). This requires all of what we have discussed so far. However, even with these points, specific issues arise that require more fastidious attention and more thought-out reasoning. Let us now develop an apologetic that answers several key responses from the pro-abortion camp.

"It's Just a Fetus; It's Not Really a Person!"

This challenge may come from either ignorance or deception. The Scriptures candidly affirm that a fetus is a human being (e.g., Psalm 139:13-16;

Isaiah 44:24a). In addition to the Scriptures, let us examine the truth from a biological perspective.

Consider the concept of life itself. When does life begin? How can you tell whether something, such as a cell, is alive or not? Biologically speaking, growth and multiplication define life. Living cells grow, move, produce, and multiply. Proliferation is exactly what is happening after an egg and sperm join to form a zygote! Within one day of conception, the zygote is dividing rapidly into many cells, which separate to become different parts of the body. Non-living matter does not multiply. It does not replicate. It does not differentiate into different body parts. As such, life clearly begins at conception when the fertilized egg begins to grow.

The next question we must answer is when a living entity might be considered human. What determines whether a life form is a human? Biologically speaking, genetics objectively determine humanity. When an egg and sperm join, this is the beginning of a new human with its own unique DNA, different from its mother. This unique DNA will determine eye color, skin color, skin tone, fingerprints, and a million other individual characteristics (cf. Ecclesiastes 11:5; Job 10:8-11). Given this surefire consideration and what has been addressed above, abortion is the intentional ending of a human being's life based, biologically speaking, life and DNA both start at conception.

"Abortion Is Medically Required!"

Similar to the previous argument, this retort comes from either ignorance or deception. Listen to the testimony of the following medical professionals regarding abortion, particularly during the third trimester:[53]

> *"As an OB/GYN physician for 31 years there is no medical situation that requires aborting/killing the baby in the third trimester to 'save the mother's life.' Just deliver the baby by C/Section and the baby has a 95+% survival with readily available NICU care even at 28 weeks. C/Section is quicker and safer than partial birth abortion for the mother."* (Dr. Lawrence K. Koning)

> *"As a board-certified practicing OB/GYN physician for over 30 years, I need to say publicly and unequivocally, that there is never a medical reason to kill a baby at term. When complications of pregnancy endanger a mother's life, we sometimes must deliver the baby early, but it is always*

---

[53] Each of these testimonies was posted on the doctors' respective Facebook pages in response to the passing of the Reproductive Health Act.

with the intent of doing whatever we can to do it safely for the baby too. The decision to kill an unborn baby at term is purely for convenience. It is murder...God help us." (Dr. David McKnight)

"I want to clear something up so that there is absolutely no doubt. I'm a board-certified OB/GYN who has delivered over 2,500 babies. There's not a single fetal or maternal condition that requires third trimester abortion. Not one. Delivery, yes. Abortion, no. There is absolutely no medical reason to kill a near term or term infant, for any reason." (Dr. Omar L. Hamada)

"As an OBGYN I will not support this in my practice. The government may falsely lead women to think it's safe and easy to have an abortion in the late 2nd or 3rd trimester but the young mother could end up losing her life as well. I support and have dedicated my life to women's health and [the Reproductive Health Act] is NOT a win for women in any way. It will be the young and the vulnerable who will be the victims to this." (Dr. Rebecca Cisneros)

In addition to the medical perspective, the truth from the legal perspective is interesting to consider. Laws that allow abortion are fraught with inconsistencies and inaccuracies in the legal realm. Despite the Roe v. Wade decision by the Supreme Court, there is abundant disparity in the laws regarding abortion in our land. Counties, districts, and states have differing and contradictory laws; property rights are guaranteed to unborn children; the injury or murder of a pregnant woman is punishable twofold. Moreover, laws such as the Reproductive Health Act are conditioned upon "protecting the patient's life or health." This is marketed as medical necessity and portrayed as a mother-or-child scenario. Technically speaking, this is not an accurate representation. When the common person hears "necessary," they assume an either-or scenario. Legally this is not the case. Legally, "necessary" is at the discretion of the practitioner, as is "the patient's life or health." The bills, however, define "necessary" and "patient's life or health" in broad sweeping terms derived from the Doe vs. Bolton Supreme Court case, which states:

"Whether, in the words of the Georgia statute, 'an abortion is necessary' is a professional judgment that the Georgia physician will be called upon to make routinely. We agree with the District Court, 319 F. Supp., at 1058, that the medical judgment may be exercised in the light of all factors – physical, emotional, psychological, familial, and the woman's age – relevant to the well-being of the patient. All these factors may relate to health."

In other words, a physician could decide almost anything is a threat to the mother's health under these terms. That is why people correctly call such measures "abortion on demand;" even if that is not what the law is explicitly calling for, it is what the measures legally allow. Our government and society have truly become Judah of old (cf. Micah 3:1-4, 8-12).

Even if the allegation that abortion is medically "required" were true, it still does not justify any and all abortions. By the same logic, if you say sometimes shooting a person can save another's life (e.g., in the case of self-defense), should you conclude it is morally acceptable to shoot people anytime, for any reason? Consider the profound impact and dedication shown by a mother who willingly sacrifices herself for a child! If a mother jumped in front of a bus to save her toddler, she would be esteemed as a hero. How inconsistent then to praise a woman for choosing self over her child in abortion! As demanding as it would be, it would be honorable, courageous, and praiseworthy for a mother to show the same love and sacrifice as Jesus.

"Abortion Need to Be Available for Victims of Rape!"

This is a classic example of argument solely based in emotion and not from emotions in partnership with statistical evidence (cf. Proverbs 18:17). In 2004, the Guttmacher Institute anonymously surveyed 1,209 post-abortive women from nine different abortion clinics across the country. Of the women surveyed, 957 provided a primary reason for having an abortion. Less than 0.5% said they were the victims of rape! In other words, 4 out of over 1,200 women said rape was the reason they had an abortion. This survey was anonymous, so any shame factor for rape victims was methodologically minimized. Regardless, rape is an extremely tiny percentage of what leads mothers to abort their babies. So, is abortion necessary or even beneficial in such terrible circumstances?

Rape and molestation are indeed tragic, yet many have endured such trials by choosing not to abort their babies. Many children born as a result of rape have gone on to be influential people in the world. One 17-year-old woman who was raped became mother to Layne Beachley, a seven-time World Champion Surfer. Another woman was raped at 16 years old and gave birth to Kelly Wright, former *Fox & Friends* weekend co-anchor. Kelly's mother always told him that despite the circumstance of his conception, God had a purpose for his life. Still another woman was raped at 17 years old and conceived Faith Daniels, a well-known television personality. Faith has said, *"It really doesn't matter how you were conceived, only what you've become."* Valerie Gatto, Miss Pennsylvania 2014, is the daughter of a woman raped at knifepoint at 19. Valerie travels the country now, teaching women how to protect themselves from assault. She has said, *"I believe God put me here for a reason: to inspire people, to encourage them, to give them hope that everything is possible and you can't let your circumstances define your life."*

The reality is that abortion magnifies the trauma of rape. The mother and baby are both helped by preserving life, not by perpetuating violence! Many incorrectly assume that survivors of rape always desire abortions. In the only major study of pregnant rape victims ever done, 80% chose against abortion![54] Similarly, victims of incest rarely ever voluntarily choose abortion![55] Many women who have had abortions report that their abortions felt like a degrading and brutal form of medical rape.[56] Sexual rape robs a woman of her purity; medical rape robs a woman of her maternity. Going through with the child's birth may be therapeutic for rape victims because they choose a totally selfless act of generosity that displays courage, strength, and honor. Why then are people pushing for abortion in this scenario when it is precisely the opposite of what is most advantageous and beneficial for the victim?

What do survivors of rape actually say and believe? (cf. Proverbs 18:13; Amos 1:13-15)[57]

"I soon discovered that the aftermath of my abortion continued a long time after the memory of my rape had faded. I felt empty & horrible. Nobody told me about the pain I would feel deep within causing nightmares & deep depressions. They had all told me that after the abortion I could continue my life as if nothing had happened." (Jackie Bakker)

"I, having lived through rape, and also having raised a child 'conceived in rape,' feel personally assaulted and insulted every time I hear that abortion should be legal because of rape and incest. I feel that we're being used by pro-abortionists to further the abortion issue, even though we've not been

---

[54] Sandra Mahkorn, "Pregnancy and Sexual Assault," *The Psychological Aspects of Abortion*, eds. Mall & Watts, (Wash., D.C., University Publications of America, 1979) 55-69.

[55] Maloof, "The Consequences of Incest: Giving and Taking Life" *The Psychological Aspects of Abortion* (eds. Mall & Watts, Wash., D.C., University Publications of America, 1979) 84-85.

[56] Francke, *The Ambivalence of Abortion* (New York: Random House, 1978) 84-95, 167.; Reardon, *Aborted Women – Silent No More* (Chicago: Loyola University Press, 1987), 51, 126.

[57] These testimonies are common to many sources, but these are taken from: "Rape, Incest, and Abortion." *Iowans For Life*, 14 Mar. 2017, www.iowansforlife.org/2017/03/rape-incest-abortion/.

asked to tell our side." (Kathleen DeZeeuw)

"Throughout the years I have been depressed, suicidal, furious, outraged, lonely, and have felt a sense of loss... The abortion which was to 'be in my best interest' just has not been. As far as I can tell, it only 'saved their reputations,' 'solved their problems,' and 'allowed their lives to go merrily on.'... My daughter, how I miss her so. I miss her regardless of the reason for her conception." (Edith Young, a victim of incest at 12 years old who was forced to commit an abortion)

Are we interested in hearing what these women have to say, or are we only interested in misrepresenting and victimizing them further? The baby is never to blame for the sins of a father or a mother, no matter how violent, and should never be penalized.

"You Can't Tell a Woman What to Do with Her Own Body!"

This argument is a classic red herring (cf. Proverbs 17:15). A woman has every right to control and be responsible for her own body. She has the right to use numerous methods to prevent conception if she does not want to become pregnant. She has the right to refrain from activity known to lead to pregnancy by practicing sexual abstinence. She has the right to be married and have a family if she so desires, just as she has the right to be single.

Once pregnancy occurs, it is no longer the woman's body that is in question; the baby, while dependent on the woman, is not itself the woman's body. The placenta and umbilical cord connect a mother and child, but, more importantly, they separate two distinct bodies. This organ and pathway exist precisely because the baby has a different circulatory system than the mother, and their blood must not intermingle. If the fetus were not a separate human being, the placenta and umbilical cord would not be required to separate them!

What about the related objection: *"You have no right to judge someone for their personal decision"*? If I truly believe that abortion is wrong, that it kills an innocent person, and if I understand the facts of science that prove it is murder, then how can I say that it is agreeable for anyone to have the right to make that decision? That is like saying that I think it is wrong to murder a person, and I would not do it, but I cannot impose those beliefs on anyone else! It is no different from arguing that though I think it would be wrong to hold a pillow over the face of someone, I should not impose my beliefs!

The Scriptures command God's people to judge un-hypocritically (Matthew 7:1-5), with righteous judgment (John 7:24), and to call evil what it is (Ephesians 5:6-17). Engaging in such God-approved behaviors will cause some to hate you, but it is necessary and vital to the Christian walk (cf. Proverbs 24:11-12). When we know the right thing to do, we must do it, or it is a sin (James 4:17). Taking a stand against abortion may even require resisting governmental authorities who forego their God-given responsibility to reward what is good and punish what is evil (Romans 13:1-7).

How Can Christians Effectively Address Abortion?

What seems so obviously cruel and brutal has become common, even encouraged. How shameful and repulsive, sickening and heartbreaking (Proverbs 6:17). Christians must further stem the tide of this descent into depravity. Christians must learn how to answer arguments in favor of abortion calmly and collectively, logically and in an informed fashion (Proverbs 15:28). If we can give these responses, we will help educate, inform, and convict others regarding this wicked act. We will shed light in an increasingly dark world if we can do this. But words alone are not enough.

In addition to knowing the truth about abortion and persuading others to avoid it, Christians have other responsibilities toward this awful act. Ultimately, Christians have a duty to make abortion an unreasonable option in the face of well-supported and well-funded alternatives. If Christians encourage those considering abortion to consider adoption instead, it begs the question, who will adopt these children? Who will foster these children? Or will they end up being further traumatized by those leveraging the system for ungodly pursuits? Furthermore, will the refusal to accommodate abortion be followed with financial obligation and support to those who choose otherwise? Who will support these moms? Or will complaints of taxation or avoidance of charitable organizations due to materialistic greed be the reality? What programs will you support that benefit such persons? Or, at its root, what will you individually and specifically do when you look a person in the eye who is in need?

Indeed, there are options available, but only if you are genuinely concerned about upholding the sanctity of life and not a political ideology. You could get involved in organizations such as Save the Storks, which offers support, resources, and education to men and women to make life-affirming decisions for themselves and their children.[58] You could fund organizations such as Sa-

---

[58] Learn more about this organization at: https://www.savethestorks.com.

[59] Learn more about this organization at: https://www.sacredselections.org.

cred Selections, which facilitates adoption.[59] You can partner with organizations such as And Then There Were None, which helps abortion workers to leave the business, finding healing, forgiveness, and a purpose in Christ.[60] You could foster in your local foster care system. You could volunteer at pro-life and post-trauma clinics, or pray outside of an abortion clinic. Studies have shown that when anti-abortion advocates congregate around these facilities, these clinics experience a 75% no-show rate from their patients.[61] In addition to these courses of action, you can play an active role in drafting legislation that prohibits abortion and provides an actionable framework to support pro-life decisions. You can participate in the Right to Life march.[62] You could buy groceries for women in need. You can teach your sons and daughters about consensual sex and its beauty within the holy arrangement of marriage. You can train your children not to objectify or disrespect the opposite sex and to value the sanctity of life. Better yet, show them your respect for your mate! Show the world that your children are a blessing and are arrows in your quiver! (Psalm 127) Show them that babies in-utero can sometimes survive complex illnesses, and parents can grow exponentially by choosing life even in the event of their child's death, thereby showing consistency in viewing life as sacred at all points of existence.[63] Christians can show consistency by having hard discussions about spiritual and medical ethics questions regarding the use of

---

[60] Abby Johnson's work through this organization is unrivaled. The organization's website is: https://www.abortionworker.com. Also consult her books *The Walls Are Talking* and *Unplanned* (also a motion picture). In the former work, one repentant abortion worker describes the horrors of the experiences of abortion workers by saying: *"Abortion clinic workers have experienced evil in a very tangible way. We have seen it in the glass dishes that hold the parts of the aborted babies. And we have even smelled evil. Abortion has a very distinct smell— one that you will never be able to forget, no matter how long you have been away. That evil becomes a part of you. It's what numbs you to the brutality. It's what keeps you there every day, until the evil all around you is just all in a day's work."* (pages 120-121)

[61] Johnson and Detrow, *The Walls Are Talking,* 150.

[62] For excellent resources regarding this rally, as well as voting and legislative matters regarding abortion, see: https://www.nrlc.org.

[63] Two inspiring stories might be researched in this regard. One is detailed in: Smith, Angie. *I Will Carry You: The Sacred Dance of Grief and Joy.* B&H, 2010. Another is the case of Justin and Amanda Mock and their baby Abigail whose journey with Osteogenesis Imperfecta is detailed on their Facebook blog, "Perfectly Imperfecta: The Adventures of Abigail."

[64] The organization Children of God for Life has a host of resources, charts, and graphics that aid in these discussions. All will benefit from looking at their resources on their website: https://www.cogforlife.org.

fetal cell lines in vaccination production and the suspension of residual human zygotes in the case of in-vitro fertilization.[64] You can choose your words wisely regarding rape, survivors of rape, those who have had abortions, and those who have participated in an abortion. There are a plethora of opportunities to display the sincerity of your relationship to Christ! The question is: will you give more than just inflamed narratives? As Joni Tada says, *"If you truly believe in the value of life, you care about all of the weakest and most vulnerable members of society."*

Closing Thoughts

God loves you and values you. You may know someone who has had an abortion; you may be the result of a failed abortion; you may have had an abortion. God loves you and paid the ultimate sacrifice to save you from your sins. Unlike the vacillation of imperfect and immoral societies and courts, that will never change. Won't you take Him up on His free offer of salvation to you, His child and the bearer of His glorious image?

"Can a woman forget her nursing child and have no compassion on the son of her womb? Even these may forget, but I will not forget you. Behold, I have inscribed you on the palms of My hands" (Isaiah 49:15-16). God knows every one of the millions of innocent babies slain in the place where they should be most protected. He mourns their earthly rejection, but comforts them in His arms.

Do not be silent in regards to abortion. God commands that we speak up. So, let's get educated, and inform others of the evils of abortion. If you have supported abortion, do support it, or maybe even have had an abortion, as terrible as that is, forgiveness is available for you. Jesus died on the cross to deliver you from all guilt. Only in Him can you find peace and deliverance. Draw near to Him and He will draw near to you (James 4:4).

Thought Questions

1) What emotions arose as you read this chapter and how did this information affect you?

_____

_____

2) In what ways are voluntary and spontaneous abortion different? How can a lack of differentiation between these two matters lead to confusion?

_____

_____

3) If you are able, watch the testimony of former abortion provider Dr. Anthony Levatino before Congress. Why are voices such as his so impactful in the pro-life movement?

_____

_____

4) What defenses for abortion have you most often dealt with or heard? What have you learned in this chapter that would aid your response to such arguments?

_____

_____

5) How can showing compassion and mercy toward needful expectant mothers help make abortion an unthinkable option?

_____

_____

6) Biblically speaking, what does it mean to be "pro-life"?

_____

_____

7) What will you do this week to help expecting mothers and the unborn who are in need?

_____

_____

CHAPTER 7

Adoption & Fostering

As is the case with cancer, ignoring psychosocial problems rarely makes matters better; overlooked, these issues tend to worsen, with disastrous spiritual implications. Sadly, Christians often ensnare themselves in this precise folly by labeling worldly problems as solely "social" or "political," though issues rarely fall so neatly into single categories like this. With oversimplistic labels, Christians can become callous to the spiritual realities behind psychosocial issues, perpetuating and increasing negligence. This failure to acknowledge such a connection inhibits Christians from offering viable and realistic alternatives to immoral, unethical, and ungodly decisions that otherwise plague our world. Not only that, but neglect also gives a reasonable pretext for atheists to attack Christianity. This should not be!

This disastrous cycle is perhaps nowhere better illustrated than with respect to adoption and foster care. Accusations of negligence and lack of sympathy against Christians abound in this area and, judging from the comments heard even within the walls of worship assemblies, there is much merit to these accusations. Many people, Christians included, are hesitant or even hostile to the idea that there are spiritual responsibilities involved toward adoption and fostering. As a preacher, I have had several Christians express concern over using the pulpit to even broach such a topic—some well-meaning, some woefully ignorant, and some simply heartless. I have also had many Christians so enthusiastic about hearing this addressed from the pulpit that I was empowered to make the subject a pulpit mainstay. I hope that the discussion in this chapter will help all to see that adoption and fostering are not only psychosocial matters but also spiritual matters that the Bible addresses and that God's people have responsibilities to fulfill. May we grow to realize that greater activism in these areas would provide reasonable alternatives to abortion and serve as a preventative for human trafficking, let alone illustrate concrete acts of compassion on behalf of the church.

A Theological Foundation

God's well-attested love for humanity transcends words. Nevertheless, in His infinite wisdom, God has appropriated human language to convey His blessings and will for His creation within the Scriptures. In the Bible, we find such words—forgiveness, atonement, propitiation, calling, and election. These words are illustrative enough to give us a glimmer of God's love for us. He loved the world so much that He sent His one and only Son to die for us (John 3:16; 1 John 3:16).

While words like these tend to be the focus of theologians and technical Bible students, there is one term that conveys God's love in an especially emotive and unique way – adoption. The word (Greek: *huiothesia*) is used several times in the New Testament, always in Paul's letters, to show us unequivocally that God is gracious, loving, and tenderhearted to those made in His image. This divine choice to adopt is usually expressed openly in the light of our desperate situation brought on by sin.[65] God reveals this helplessness by stating through His apostle Paul,

> *"For while we were still helpless, at the right time Christ died for the ungodly. For one will hardly die for a righteous man; though perhaps for the good man someone would dare even to die. But God demonstrates His own love toward us, in that while we were yet sinners, Christ died for us"* (Romans 5:6-8).

Before we consider the passages specifying this theological idea, let us consider some preliminary matters to aid our understanding. The following examinations will serve to root all of God's people together in the truth that God's adoption of Christians serves as a theological foundation for Christians to be involved in adoption, fostering, and other related support activities.

Understanding Backgrounds in the Bible

The New Testament is written against the backdrop of the Greco-Roman

---

[65] There is a beautiful, and horrific, image used in Ezekiel 16:1-14 that illustrates this well. In this passage, God has compassion on an abandoned child and then later marries her as a metaphor for His relationship with His wayward people. Her ingratitude is shown in her continued rebellion after such compassion.

civilization. Adoption was an impressively profound action used even by the Roman emperors to endow their successor with their identity.[66] Such is well-attested in ancient times, as modern commentators explain:

> *"...in the Roman world of the first century AD an adopted son was a son deliberately chosen by his adoptive father to perpetuate his name and inherit his estate; he was no whit inferior in status to a son born in the ordinary course of nature, and might well enjoy the father's affection more fully and reproduce the father's character more worthily."*[67]

> *"Adoption was a powerful figure to the ancient Mediterranean people and it is to us...The son, in turn, totally surrendered himself to the new father in order to receive his name and inheritance. The father gave great gifts to the son. The son responded with respect for the father. Love was given and love was returned. The relationship could be wonderfully fulfilling to both, particularly if the adopted son were poor and in need prior to the adoption. This analogy from Roman sociology fits well the picture of the sinner adopted into the family of God."*[68]

Far removed from this culture, studying Greco-Roman conceptions of family and adoption augments one's appreciation for the biblical doctrine of adoption. The greatest of these is *patria potestas*, in which the father possessed autocratic authority over the son for his entire life (for a daughter, a father maintained the same authority until she was married). This dominance included the right to imprison, scourge, sell, or even kill his child. Even when the son became an adult, this dynamic did not change. One concept specific to the adoption procedure is *mancipatio*—the emblematic sale of a child involving copper and scales. The father symbolically sold and bought back the child two times and then sold them a third time, but did not purchase them back. Another component to this ancient adoption process was *vindicatio*, in which the person seeking to adopt would approach a Roman magistrate with a case for their *adoptio*. If approved, the child would officially be theirs for all time. After completing this process, the biological parents had no claim to the child; adoption was the transference of total power over that child. For this reason, it was a solemn exchange that required seven witnesses.

---

[66] Examples include, but are not limited to Augustus' adoption of Tiberius and Claudius' adoption of Nero.

[67] Bruce, F.F. *Tyndale New Testament Commentaries: Romans.* Eerdmans, 1984, 157.

[68] Caldwell, Charles Grover. *Ephesians.* Guardian of Truth, 1994, 22.

Interesting as they are, Greco-Roman standards were not the exclusive background for adoption in the Bible. The New Testament also draws on a long history of Jewish conceptions of adoption. Unfortunately, the Jewish system was not as clear as the Greco-Roman one. Various mandates in the Law of Moses seem to have had a comparable function to adoption. Adoption in the Old Testament seems well displayed in Jacob's adoption of Ephraim and Manasseh (Genesis 48:5), Pharaoh's daughter's adoption of Moses (Exodus 2:10), and Mordecai's adoption of Esther (Esther 2:7, 15). Adoption is also culturally reflected by the Jews in Joseph's adoption of Jesus, a son biologically not his own. Paul even mixes Jewish and Greco-Roman conceptions in his metaphorical treatment of Israel as a collective body (Romans 9:4).

Understanding these backgrounds for adoption in the Bible empowers us to appreciate God's concern for orphans, which can find expression through adoption and fostering. Studying adoption in the Bible with such knowledge illuminates our theological understanding of Who God is and provokes us to heed His call to pay-it-forward. Again, New Testament commentators have respected this connection and often discuss it in their commentaries:

"Men and women were created for life in fellowship with God, as children with the Father (Gn. 1:26; Acts 17:28). By sin that privilege was forfeited, but by grace, in and through Christ, restoration to sonship is made possible (John 1:12). Adoption is the best way to describe this (cf. Rom. 8:15, 23; Gal. 4:5), because adopted children have their position by grace and not by right, and yet are brought into the family on the same footing as children by birth."[69]

"The adoptee is taken out of his previous state and is placed in a new relationship with his new paterfamilias. All his old debts are canceled, and in effect he starts a new life...The idea of having a new state in a new family and in effect starting a new life finds obvious parallels within the writings of the New Testament...God is willing to adopt us as his sons, if we are willing to be adopted by him."[70]

---

[69] Foulkes, Francis. *Tyndale New Testament Commentaries: Ephesians.* Eerdmans, 1989, 56-57.

[70] Longstreth, Jason. "Our Adoption As Sons" in *Blessed Be God: Studies in Ephesians.* Florida College Press, 2010, 63-65. Let the reader note that Jason Longstreth has been an ardent advocate for adoption and has adopted four children of his own.

Usage in the New Testament

The key to understanding the Christian's responsibilities with respect to adoption and fostering is contingent upon understanding God's personal investment in His people through this process. This is our goal as we direct our attention to the specific New Testament verses that establish the theological underpinnings of adoption and fostering.

Ephesians 1:5-6

While sitting in chains, the Holy Spirit moved Paul to write of adoption in his letter to the Ephesians. Amid a dense assortment of blessings from the heavens (1:3-14), Paul writes: *"God predestined us to adoption as sons through Jesus Christ to Himself, according to the kind intention of His will, to the praise of the glory of His grace, which He freely bestowed on us in the Beloved."* Paul specifies that God planned to adopt believers into sonship before the creation of the world! As one writer voiced:

> *"God intentionally purposed to adopt us as sons. He longingly desired to do so as a man or woman might want more than anything else in the world to be able to adopt a child. God wants us! Further, the adopted child needs to know that he is wanted by his parents. In spiritual adoption the will (thelēmatos) of God has never been at issue. He has freely exposed his innermost emotions which shout his desires for children upon whom he can bestow his love. Our willingness to receive the adoption and accept him as our Father is the issue!"*[71]

Another emotionally observed, *"When the Father chose a people for himself, deciding to adopt them as his own children, he was motivated by love alone. Hence, what he did was a result not of sheer determination but of supreme delight."*[72] To His glorious praise, God's will is definitively manifested in the death, burial, and resurrection of Jesus. Through the cross of Christ, God implements His grace in the hopeless narrative of our lives! For this reason, God is exceedingly worthy of all praise, honor, and glory. F.F. Bruce explains:

> *"The grace of God in redeeming sinful children of Adam and adopting them as His own sons will be throughout eternity the most glorious theme*

---

[71] Caldwell, *Ephesians*, 24

[72] Hendriksen, William. *Exposition of Galatians, Exposition of Ephesians*. Baker, 1979, 79.

of praise to His name...Be it noted again that all the blessings which are
ours by God's grace are ours in Christ; there is no way apart from Him in
which God either decrees or effects the bestowal of His grace on men."[73]

Romans 8:15, 23

Writing to the Romans, whose knowledge of and appreciation for adoption
was culturally embedded on every level, Paul uses adoption as a metaphor for
God's relationship to the Christian. He states, *"for you have not received a spirit*
of slavery leading to fear again, but you have received a spirit of adoption as
sons by which we cry out, 'Abba! Father!'" (8:15) Such a blessing is highlighted
against the dismal reality of all mankind falling prey to sin. We were all condemned in unrighteousness by the law of God as we walked according to the
flesh; yet, through Jesus Christ, we are delivered from condemnation as we
walk in the Spirit (Romans 7:24-8:14). The Holy Spirit testifies with our spir-
its that as many as have received Jesus and walk in Him are children of God.
These two witnesses imitate the aforementioned Roman requirement of witnesses at an adoption. Adopted by God, Christians confidently approach Him
with the most intimate of relationships, signified by 'Abba' (cf. Mark 14:36).
What a marvelous gift! William Barclay memorably describes this by stating:

> *"It was Paul's picture that when a man became a Christian he entered into*
> *the very family of God. He did nothing to deserve it; God, the great Father,*
> *in his amazing love and mercy, has taken the lost, helpless, poverty-strick-*
> *en, debt-laden sinner and adopted him into his own family, so that the*
> *debts are cancelled and the glory inherited."*[74]

Paul builds on the theme of adoption several verses later: *"And not only*
this, but also we ourselves, having the first fruits of the Spirit, even we ourselves
groan within ourselves, waiting eagerly for our adoption as sons, the redemption
of our body" (8:23). This inaugurated eschatology shows a "now, but not yet"
graduation of the blessing of God's adoption of the believer. As a result of sin,
our flesh and the entirety of the world became subjected to futility. At Jesus'
return, this will dramatically change:

> *"The fullness of the adoption, their complete admission to the privileges*

---

[73] Bruce, *Ephesians*, 30.

[74] Barclay, William. *Ephesians*. Daily Study Bible Commentaries. Saint Andrew Press, 1975, 107.

of the sons of God, shall be in the day of judgment, in the presence of the universe, and amidst the glories of the final consummation of all things... he looks forward to that complete deliverance, and to that elevated state, when, in the presence of an assembled universe, he shall be acknowledged as a child of God."[75]

Galatians 4:4-7

Writing to the Galatian churches, Paul again uses the imagery of adoption to illustrate God's love for His people. He states,

"But when the fullness of the time came, God sent forth His Son, born of a woman, born under the Law, so that He might redeem those who were under the Law, that we might receive the adoption as sons. Because you are sons, God has sent forth the Spirit of His Son into our hearts, crying, 'Abba! Father!' Therefore, you are no longer a slave, but a son; and if a son, then an heir through God."

Much akin to the usage in Romans, the Holy Spirit is contrasting the believer's pre-adoption standing to his post-adoption standing. All were condemned in sin by the law of God, particularly under the Law of Moses, as they walked according to the flesh. Through the Law's education, in partnership with the atonement of Jesus, people have come of age and been adopted as sons, no longer serving in inferiority but living as heirs of God. Several commentators well-highlight this change:

"The main idea of adoption seems to be this: we were children of the Devil (John 8:44), in slavery to sin and doomed to eternal damnation. In the abundance of his marvelous grace, God adopted us as his children. The blessedness of the relationship as a child of God is seen in contrast with the relationship of a servant (v. 7)."[76]

"Under the Jewish law they had felt that they were slaves or servants. Now through faith they can feel that they are sons—children. A son obeys from love, a servant from fear. Now they are no longer servants, but sons, and

---

[75] Barnes, Albert. *Romans*. Baker, 1956, 193-194.

[76] Willis, Mike. *The Book of Galatians*. Guardian of Truth Foundation, 1994, 185-186.

the son is the heir of the heritage of the father."[77]

"The idea is, that as the Lord Jesus was enabled to approach God with the language of endearment and love, so they would be. He, being the true and exalted Son of God, had the same spirit...it was not permitted slaves to use the title of Abba in addressing the master of the family to which they belonged. If so, then the language which Christians are here represented as using is the language of freemen, and denotes that they are not under the servitude of sin."[78]

What Christians Gain by God's Choice

The believer's blessings and advantages through God's adoption are manifold and include:

- A new nature from God (John 1:12-13; James 1:18; 2 Peter 1:3; 1 John 5:18). This new nature is in contrast to formerly being children of wrath (Ephesians 2:3).
- A revitalized image bearing a new similitude of God's likeness (Romans 8:29; 2 Corinthians 3:18; Colossians 3:10; 2 Peter 1:4). This revitalized image is in contrast to our former fallen identity as children of Adam (Romans 5) and of Satan (cf. John 8:44).
- A new spirit, the spirit of Jesus, which frees us from guilt, bondage, and fear of death (Romans 8:15, 21; 2 Corinthians 3:17; Galatians 5:1; Hebrews 2:15; 1 John 5:14). This spirit results in holy boldness and royal dignity (Hebrews 10:19, 22; 1 Peter 2:9; 4:14).
- A new name (1 John 3:1-2; Revelation 2:17; 3:12) and a new family (Romans 8:15-16).
- A reassurance of God's love (John 17:23; Romans 5:5-8; Titus 3:4; 1 John 4:7-11).
- A new hope – eternal inheritance (Romans 8:17, 23; James 2:5; 1 Peter 1:3-4; 3:7; Philippians 3:21).
- Protection, consolation, and provision (Psalm 125:2; Isaiah 46:13; Luke 12:27-32; John 14:18; 1 Corinthians 3:21-23; 2 Corinthians 1:4).
- Discipline (Psalm 51:11-12; Hebrews 12:5-11).

There is simply no reason to reject God's adoption or to be indifferent

---

[77] Lipscomb, David. *Second Corinthians and Galatians*. Gospel Advocate, 1958, 243.

[78] Barnes, Albert. *2 Corinthians and Galatians*. Baker, 1955, 361-362.

to this kindhearted act in light of these overwhelming benefits. Colly Caldwell portrayed the magnitude of God's grace well:

"Imagine yourself an orphan child, cold and hungry, walking the streets in search of food and shelter. A dedicated Christian, loving and kind, takes notice of your plight. This Christian is wealthy and successful, but he and his wife have no children. He stops beside you and stoops to look you in the eye. As he smiles through tears of compassion, he says, 'Please come home with me and let me adopt you into my family.' That, of course, means that you will be cared for, loved, protected and nurtured in spiritual and physical things. It means that you will inherit his estate as if you had been naturally born to him. Will you turn and walk away? Can you imagine the lonely, hungry, fatherless child rejecting such an offer? So many turn away from God. He is offering much more than any man could offer. How foolish we are when we reject the Lord!"[79]

God acted first, adopting His people by the good pleasure of His will and as an expression of the sincerest love in the universe (John 14:18). God's nature is to be a *"Father to the fatherless,"* Who *"makes a home for the lonely"* (Psalm 68:5-6). He executes justice, defends, and gives them food and clothing (cf. Deuteronomy 10:18; Psalm 10:14; 27:10; Jeremiah 49:11; Hosea 14:3). If God's nature is to care in this fashion, what does that say of His people? (Genesis 1:26-27; 2 Peter 1:1-4).

Adoption, Fostering, and Divine Expectations

Under the Old Testament, God repeatedly commanded His people to defend, uphold, nurture, clothe, and feed the fatherless and other needful people (e.g., Deuteronomy 24:17, 21). In fact, a feast was held every three years in order to uphold the fatherless and other persons worthy of special compassion (Deuteronomy 14:28-29). At this feast, those who were lacking were to eat and be satisfied so that God would bless His people. This, and other stipulations in the Law of Moses, were to ensure that God's people exhibited His character of compassion. However, abject failures to meet the needs of the fatherless compounded over time. On numerous occasions, God called His people to amend their ways specifying their failures in this area (e.g., Psalm 82:3-4; Isaiah 1:16-17; Jeremiah 7:5-7). In short, caring for the fatherless and widows were essential; anything less brought condemnation (e.g., Deuteronomy 27:19; Exodus 22:22-23). Indeed, the patriarch Job serves as an example *par excellence* of a

---

[79] Caldwell, *Ephesians*, 25-26.

righteous person whose actions involved visiting orphans (Job 29:12-17). Note also that God specifies this type of behavior as foundational to pure religion (Micah 6:6-8; cf. Matthew 9:13; 23:23).

The New Testament reiterates this condition, transcending the division of the covenants. The obvious New Testament Scripture renewing God's emphasis on adoption and fostering is James 1:26-27:

> *"If anyone thinks himself to be religious, and yet does not bridle his tongue but deceives his own heart, this man's religion is worthless. Pure and undefiled religion in the sight of our God and Father is this: to visit orphans and widows in their distress, and to keep oneself unstained by the world."*

These verses serve a twofold purpose. James 1:26 serves as a negative example. If you claim to be a Christian, but your speech does not match up, then your religion is vain. James 1:27 serves as a positive example. If you claim to be a Christian, then the claim is substantiated by your words and actions, namely in caring for orphans and widows and keeping yourself unstained by the world. Two commentators explain:

> *"If these things are found, they show that there is true piety. If they are not, there is none...If a man, from proper motives, is the real friend of the widow and the fatherless, he will be the friend of every good word and work, and we may rely on him in any and every way in doing good...If a man is truly benevolent, he bears the image of that God who is the fountain of benevolence...If he has not these things, he cannot have any well-founded evidence that he is a Christian; for it is always the nature and tendency of religion to produce these things. It is, therefore, an easy matter for a man to determine whether he has any religion; and equally easy to see that religion is eminently desirable. Who can doubt that that is good which leads to compassion for the poor and the helpless, and which makes the heart and the life pure?"*[80]

> *"The kind of 'religion that God our Father accepts' is the kind that exerts a positive influence on one's life. This verse...presents a concrete way of insisting that genuine religion is a life-changing force. One's religion should be more than external; it must spring from an inner spiritual reality that*

---

[80] Barnes, Albert. *James*. Baker, 1951, 33-34.

expresses itself in love to others and holiness before God."[81]

James 1:27 makes a point of denoting the role of the believer to *"visit orphans and widows in their distress."* *"Visit"* is *episkeptesthai* and means "to see or inspect with a view of assisting." This word is used this way in Judges 15:1 (in the Septuagint); Matthew 25:36, 43; Luke 1:68, 78; 7:16; Acts 7:23; 15:14, 36; and Hebrews 2:6. Reviewing this usage,

> *"It is plain to see that this word involves personal contact, visiting a person, going to see him. It is not about building institutions or merely sending money. Nor is it about 'churches' acting collectively, but rather deals with individual responsibility, as the following clause proves beyond any question. James strikes a downright blow here at ministry by proxy, or by mere gifts of money. Pure and undefiled religion demands personal contact with the world's sorrow: to visit the afflicted, and to visit them in their affliction."*[82]

Furthermore, it is significant to note that the verb "visit" is present infinitive, suggesting continuous, habitual action (cf. Mark 14:7). This indicates that the obligation remains so long as the need continues. Since the need always exists, the responsibility always exists! In continuously obeying God's command, the believer pays forward the gift of his or her own adoption in the gospel (James 3:13). In so doing, one may actively *"keep oneself unstained by the world."* The use of "oneself" along with the previous verse ("anyone who thinks himself...") places these commands in the spiritual context of the individual, rather than the collective. This is a matter of personal sanctification. As Daniel King puts it:

> *"A close scrutiny of the passage before us will find quite readily that there is nothing here that remotely resembles an institution of human ingenuity... Creation and maintenance of such organizations is a matter of individual preference and conscience, personal choice, and private enterprise. They have absolutely nothing to do with the work of the New Testament church and should not therefore be viewed as worthy objects of congregational support from local church treasuries...It is not a forty-second cousin to*

---

[81] Barker, Kenneth L., and John R. Kohlenberger. *Zondervan NIV Bible Commentary.* Zondervan Pub. House, 1994, 1024.

[82] Mott, L.A. *Thinking Through James.* Sunesis Publications, 2015, 32.

what James was describing when he wrote as he did."[83]

How Can Christians Effectively
Address Adoption & Fostering Needs?

Christians need to transcend lifeless, cold, stifling preparation for a ritualistic debate on authority and the role of the individual versus the role of the collective. Lest I be misunderstood, I fully acknowledge that knowledge in these areas is necessary and vital to the livelihood of the church, and I commonly preach it from the pulpit. However, debate without action is hollow and godless; being able to distinguish between the proper function of the collective church and those things which are the role of the individual believer (e.g., 1 Timothy 5:16) is only meaningful if we measure up to those collective and personal responsibilities. Asserting this truth is meant to both reinforce the stalwart efforts of those who historically stood against institutionalizing the church and also to respond to the pro-institutional charge that "anti's" rarely, if ever, perform such individual actions effectively (1 Peter 2:12). We need good debate to defend sound doctrine as well as practical action in the realm of the individual and the collective if we are to move forward with the approval of the Head of the church. The real question is, how can individual Christians actively play a vital role in paying forward God's adoption? How can Christians be zealous for good deeds (Galatians 6:9-10; 1 Timothy 6:17-18; Titus 2:14; 3:8, 14; Hebrews 10:24) in a way that does not violate the proper role and function of the church collective?

Undoubtedly, one of the most outstanding actions or answers we can give to this calling would be to personally adopt a child or even children! According to the Dave Thomas Foundation, there is an average of 250,000 children adopted per year, with 9,000 adopted internationally.[84] This seems a great work, and it is, but also consider that there are 150 million orphans worldwide and that adoptions are trending downward. To offer a visual, if each child in need of adoption lined up shoulder to shoulder, the line would be 30,000 miles long! Of these cases, 14 million age out of foster care systems per year. In the face of this enormous need, it is instructive to note that 81.5 million Americans have considered adoption. If even 1 in 500 of these individuals did adopt, all kids in the United States currently in need would be in homes! It has been repeatedly, and correctly, said by adoptive parents, *"I always wondered if I was able to adopt, but then I realized that no child was ready to be an orphan."* To further

---

[83] King, Daniel. *James.* Guardian of Truth Foundation, 2015, 220-222.

[84] https://www.davethomasfoundation.org/

illustrate and personalize this, one man asked his adopted daughter what she would say to those considering adoption. She said:

> *"They need to think less about themselves and more about kids who need help. Kids need someone to call 'Mom' and 'Dad,' give them love, help them when they are sick, and hug them goodnight. They also need someone to be goofy with. Families need to ask, 'Is there room at my table for one more?' You can change someone's life and maybe they will change yours."*[85]

If you want to pursue adoption, you can do this through the public or private system.[86] If done publicly, there are typically more resources readily available, and they are all free assets! This includes tuition assistance, health insurance, counseling, etc. Public adoption is the adoption of children who are in the foster care system due to the termination of parental rights. Those interested may view these children in need via the state database system where you live. Take the time to look at your state's website and see these children.[87] Private adoption agencies are another route.[88] Whichever method is chosen,

---

[85] Wilson Adams records this account in at least two places. The first is in the online discussion board for Let Children Smile, an organization dedicated to raising awareness and providing information, support, and positive direction for post-adoption families. Their website is: http://www.letchildrensmile.org. The second place is in Wilson Adams's book accounting their adoption of Lea entitled, *I Am Lea November*.

[86] If you are interested in learning more about adoption and like to read, here are some books that would be helpful: *Parenting with Connection* by Karyn Purvis, *The Connected Child* by Karyn Purvis, *The Body Keeps The Score* by Bessel van der Kolk, *Adopting Older Children* by Stephain Bosco-Ruggiero, Gloria Russo Wassell, and Victor Groza, *In Defense of the Fatherless* by Sara Brinton and Amanda Bennett, *Fields of the Fatherless* by Tom Davis, *Parenting Adopted Adolescents* by Gregory C. Keck, *Parenting the Hurt Child* by Gregory C. Keck, *Daring to Hope* by Katie Davis Majors, *Adopted for Life* by D. Russell Moore, *The Collapse of Parenting* by Leonard Sax, and *Too Small to Ignore* by Wes Stafford.

[87] For example, if you live in Kentucky, the websites you need to visit are: Cabinet for Health and Family Services (CHFS) Kentucky Foster Adoptive Caregiver Exchange System (KY FACES) at https://prdweb.chfs.ky.gov/kyfaces/Home and also Kentucky Adoption Profile Exchange (KAPE) at https://prdweb.chfs.ky.gov/kape/index.aspx.

[88] We cannot overstate how important one particular group has been in the adoption of hundreds of children in need by families of Christians. Sacred Selections is an organization run by Dana and David Carrozza that facilitates adoptions, both in the United States and abroad. They hold fundraising events at their branch chapters throughout the year. Their website is http://www.sacredselections.org. The apologetic value and influence of the Carrozza's is incalculable.

desirous families have to jump through many hoops, and it is an arduous process, potentially more so for Christians. One preacher and his wife tried to be approved to adopt and were denied twice. Due to the nefarious actions of their caseworker, they were rebuffed because of their faith!

Another great work that Christians can be involved in is the foster care system. There are 400,000 children in the foster care system in the United States. Like adoption, this process is also somewhat complex. To be approved, a family or individual has to meet a host of criteria, pass background checks, have home studies, and wait…and wait…and wait again. Once approved, the foster parent(s) care for the child/children until parents meet specific guidelines for reconciliation. If the parents do not meet those guidelines in the time allowed (typically a year or more), parental rights are terminated, and the child is then qualified to be adopted. The truth is that fostering can be emotionally exhausting. You may not feel the parents or child/children are ready to be reunited; you may become very attached; you may feel shortchanged; etc. However, foster parents provide a home for those children in distress and a positive influence that may profoundly affect them. As a dear sister in Christ candidly shared:

> "These children certainly do have afflictions. There is satisfaction knowing that you are pleasing to God as you show these children His love. Even if they are only in your home for a few months they maybe are going to church for the first time, they hear our prayers, they see a good marriage with love and respect, they feel warmth and nurturing. We are surprised that more members of the church are not at least involved in some way with helping these children. They need people to take them under their wings and help to heal them. I encourage others to get involved. These are children who've been abused, neglected, lived in multiple homes, may have bad behaviors and lack of boundaries. Most children that we have had have enjoyed going to church with us. And their eyes light up when we've told some about heaven. A place where no one cries and no one hurts."

This may all seem intimidating and justifiably so. However, intimidation should not stop a servant of God from aiding the afflicted. One Christian foster parent in Virginia voiced frustration in this regard: "It is super hard trying to sway people into becoming foster parents because they say 'I couldn't do it' and seem to be more concerned about how they would feel instead of how the child feels in that situation." She also said, "People like to say you never know what you are going to get with foster kids, but the truth is you never know what you will get with your own kids! A person's history or family history does not necessarily define them and what they will become."

Maybe you are not ready to commit fully to adoption or foster care. Is there some other way in which you can serve? Yes! You can sign up for Emergency Care (cf. Luke 10:25-37). This means that you would be the first contact for children pulled from homes prior to being entered into the foster care system. You would give the child a place to stay until a permanent foster family is found, typically around two weeks. You have to keep your phone on 24/7, and a child can be dropped off within 1-3 hours after being taken from the family. Generally, you sign up for this on a monthly basis, and you have the benefit of the "honeymoon period" of a month before trauma exhibition.[89] Another option is to sign up for Respite Care. Everyone needs a break, especially foster parents. Foster children cannot just be watched by anybody and everybody. Many states require specific licensing to babysit foster children, which requires a background check, classes, fingerprints, First Aid/CPR training, and a copy of your driver's license. Respite Care helps support parents with life obligations and can provide the opportunity for time away. A third avenue for supporting children in foster care is to become a Court Appointed Special Advocate (CASA).[90] These individuals are authorized volunteers who can spend time with children, get to know them, and speak with everyone in their life to determine how a child's life can be improved in collaboration with the judge overseeing the child's case (cf. Proverbs 31:8-9). There are currently more than 85,000 CASA volunteers serving over 260,000 children each year. Certainly, more volunteers would prove helpful!

Maybe you do not feel ready to commit to these areas in such a formal way. You can still serve in other beneficial ways. Listening, offering meals, celebrating victories, using kind speech[91], purchasing gift cards, doing laundry, delivering care packages, playdates, purchasing memberships and day passes, tutoring, volunteering, etc. are all examples of ways we can serve, help, and actively respond to God's calling regarding adopted and/or foster children and their parents and guardians. As Kelly Meldrum says, *"As a foster parent who is*

---

[89] Two organizations deserve mention here with respect to providing resources and counseling for parents of children who are adopted or are in the foster care system: the Association for Training on Trauma and Attachment in Children (https://www.attach.org/) and Leaving the Pit Behind (http://www.LeavingThePitBehind.org.).

[90] The National CASA Association website has a host of helpful information (http://www.casaforchildren.org).

[91] Some further guidance here on statements to avoid is necessary. Do not ever say: "How much did he cost?" "What happened to the real parents?" "Which of your children are yours?" "Is it hard to love a child that isn't blood related?" "Why did you adopt from there?" "Well, what did you expect when you took someone else's kid?" "If you had to do it again, would you adopt?"

overwhelmed on my best days and hiding in my closet on the worst, I generally accept offers of help in any capacity. You don't even have to be creative!" Above all else, pray (James 5:16). Wilson Adams provides wise direction here:

> *"Pray for the children who will lie down in an unfamiliar bed in a stranger's home tonight. Pray for the parents who had their kids removed today. Pray for the restoration and reunification of families. Pray for healing for the kids who have lost faith in everyone and everything that was supposed to keep them safe. Pray for the judges, attorneys, social workers, advocates, and counselors who are tasked with making potentially life-altering decisions and recommendations for children in care. Pray for the families who have voluntarily opened their homes to brokenness and heartache. Pray for the hearts of God's people to be broken and enflamed by the children in crisis in our country."*

A Closing Thought

One Christian expresses the current state of affairs this way: *"We [Christians] are seriously lacking in caring for our orphans, and it is such a huge opportunity to bring them to Christ. Not only the children, but their families too. It is a huge opportunity to minister to those that need Him most."* Let's turn this tide by becoming actively involved in practical help to those who are troubled. Our involvement is needed not merely because it will curtail a psychosocial issue but also because it will pay God's love forward to the lost children of the world. Being active in this way provides a strong apologetic for Christianity and decisively answers the challenge of antagonists that Christians are negligent in helping others, particularly children, in need. We close with this final impassioned statement from a New Testament commentator:

> *"The Church exists that its members may be inspired to become a fountain of spiritual sympathy to the widow, and a ministry of moral help to the orphan. A congregation can offer no comelier praise than the music of constant acts of loving-kindness and tenderness and self-sacrifice. Where this worship is not rendered, the grandest sanctuary, so called, will be rather only a sepulcher of souls, and the most aesthetic church-service a 'vain oblation.' The true gospel cultus lies in personal acts of sympathy and kindness, done to the poor out of love to Jesus, and because the poor are his 'brethren' (Matt. xxv. 34—40). Every professing Christian should therefore try the reality and strength of his piety by this test: Does he give himself to*

the celebration of the true full ritual of Christ's house—that which lies in a life of purity and charity?"[92]

---

[92] Jerdan, C. *The General Epistle of James.* Pulpit Commentary, Eerdmans, 1962, 19.

Thought Questions

1) What emotions arose as you read this chapter and how did this information affect you?

_____

_____

2) In what ways can activism and participation in adoption and fostering help limit abortion and human trafficking?

_____

_____

3) How can God's adoption of Christians serve as an inspiration to get involved in adoption and fostering?

_____

_____

4) What is pure and undefiled religion in the sight of God?

_____

_____

5) What necessary considerations should be made when choosing to adopt or foster?

_____

_____

6) Explain why an institutional view of the church is not in line with God's approved methods of attending to orphans and children in need.

_____

_____

7) What will you do this week to aid the adoption and fostering community?

_____

_____

CHAPTER 8

Human Trafficking

Many subjects in the Scriptures are comfortable to discuss. Conversing about grace, love, faith, joy, and hope delights our souls as we meditate on marvelous blessings from God and extensions of His character in our own lives. However, other subjects are challenging to discuss: the graphic nature of sin, the eternal torment of Hell, sexual immorality, marriage, divorce and remarriage, etc.

One especially difficult, but necessary, subject to address rarely gets treatment from the pulpit. In fact, discussing it brings all to a solemn level of discomfort and grief. In this chapter, we consider what the Bible says about the human trafficking epidemic and what responsibilities the people of God have in addressing this spiritually-rooted evil plaguing our world. Please keep in mind this subject is incredibly relevant to the age we live in and that it is a spiritual issue as much as it is a psychosocial one. May we never ignore or label this as anything otherwise!

What Is Human Trafficking?

Human trafficking has gained widespread attention in recent years outside of the church but does not seem to be discussed as much within the church. Primarily, light has been shed on this epidemic through news reports, national criminal cases, popular movies (e.g., *Taken*), and various activist celebrities (e.g., Ashton Kutcher[93], Emma Thompson). The reader may even be familiar with the "red x" used in advertisements, campaigns, and drawn on individ-

---

[93] Ashton Kutcher's famous impassioned plea before Congress can be watched in full at: www.youtube.com/watch?v=V0e-y2qrneA%2F.

uals' hands to symbolize opposition to human trafficking. Initiatives on the part of society at large have been bittersweet as they help to curb the effects of traffickers and save victims, but they also show us that sin is alive and well in the world.

So, what exactly is human trafficking? The United Nations defines human trafficking in its famous Palermo Protocol (Article III, Paragraph a) as:

"The recruitment, transportation, transfer, harbouring or receipt of persons, by means of the threat or use of force or other forms of coercion, of abduction, of fraud, of deception, of the abuse of power or of a position of vulnerability or of the giving or receiving of payments or benefits to achieve the consent of a person having control over another person, for the purpose of exploitation. Exploitation shall include, at a minimum, the exploitation of the prostitution of others or other forms of sexual exploitation, forced labour or services, slavery or practices similar to slavery, servitude or the removal of organs."[94]

The US Department of Homeland Security similarly describes human trafficking:

"Human trafficking involves the use of force, fraud, or coercion to obtain some type of labor or commercial sex act. Every year, millions of men, women, and children are trafficked worldwide – including right here in the United States. It can happen in any community and victims can be any age, race, gender, or nationality. Traffickers might use violence, manipulation, or false promises of well-paying jobs or romantic relationships to lure victims into trafficking situations."[95]

These two organizations, internationally and nationally, attest to the two-pronged approach of human traffickers: the labor trade and the sex trade. The data suggests that human trafficking is the fastest growing business in organized crime and the second most lucrative commodity traded illegally after drugs and guns. Let's take a look at some of that data.

---

[94] UN General Assembly, *Protocol to Prevent, Suppress and Punish Trafficking in Persons, Especially Women and Children, Supplementing the United Nations Convention against Transnational Organized Crime*, 15 November 2000.

[95] "What Is Human Trafficking?" *Department of Homeland Security*, 6 May 2020, www.dhs.gov/blue-campaign/what-human-trafficking.

The Extent of the Problem

Globally, the statistics are alarming. According to the International Labour Organization (ILO), 4.5 million people worldwide are coerced into the sex trafficking trade every year as part of a $32 billion annual industry.[96] The ILO data also shows that 22% of human trafficking victims go into the sex trade and that 22% make up 66% of the profits of human trafficking, itself a $150 billion industry. This high demand is all the more shocking when one considers that 25% of trafficking victims is a child. Current estimates suggest that there are 25 million slaves worldwide at any given time. That number is three times the population of New York City! The average cost of a slave is $90, and the average life expectancy in the trade is seven years.

Nationally, the statistics are disturbing. According to the US State Department's *Trafficking in Persons Report,* between 600,000 and 800,000 people are trafficked across international borders every year, of which 80% are female, and 50% are children.[97] The average age of a child entering the sex trade in the US is 13 years old. The CNN Freedom Project Ending Modern Day Slavery estimates 14,500-17,500 people are trafficked into the US each year.[98] In the US alone, sex trafficking amounts to a $9.5 billion/year industry. These statistics primarily reflect what is known or well-evidenced. Consider also that tens of thousands of people go missing every year—how many of these are trafficking victims?

Locally, the statistics and evidence are distressing. Officials are concerned about human trafficking in hundreds of cases each year. Every year, major cities throughout the US prepare for the risk of human traffickers leveraging large events to supply the ungodly demand. Living in Louisville, it is now commonplace each year to have human trafficking arrests during the Kentucky Derby and other city events.[99] We are all seeing and hearing more accounts of human trafficking in our neighborhoods and near our homes, in store parking

---

[96] *Forced Labour, Modern Slavery and Human Trafficking,* www.ilo.org/global/topics/forced-labour/lang--en/index.htm.

[97] See the full 2019 report on human trafficking statistics and preventative measures at: https://www.state.gov/reports/2019-trafficking-in-persons-report/.

[98] "The CNN Freedom Project." CNN, Cable News Network, www.cnn.com/interactive/2018/specials/freedom-project/.

[99] One example: Aulbach, Lucas. "In Kentucky Derby Sex Trafficking Case, Police Tout Emphasis on Recovery for Women." *Courier-Journal,* 6 May 2019, www.courier-journal.com/story/news/crime/2019/05/06/louisville-police-work-with-women-victims-kentucky-derby-human-trafficking-arrests/1119816001/.

lots, parks, and malls. This is happening in all of our communities; however, trafficking is a more significant threat for those in major cities because of their location and population statistics. Proximity to interstates, major waterways, airports, and other transportation mediums are all major catalysts for this ungodly and cruel activity.

Consider one Christian's inspiring journey to advocacy against human trafficking:

> "Human trafficking is a huge problem that is hidden in our society. From the clothing industry and hospitality industry to the pornography industry, it is all impacted (and sometimes inseparable) from human trafficking. Human trafficking is one of the fastest rising crimes worldwide, yet our media does little to cover it. As for my beginnings, I had a friend who was an advocate for a non-profit that raised funds and awareness regarding the extent and problem of human trafficking. After learning the facts about it, I couldn't in good conscience not do something about it. I am now an advocate for the same company and it brings me satisfaction to bring this issue to people's attention. I sincerely believe that Christians have a responsibility to be involved in the abolishment of human trafficking. We are to look out for the interest of others, especially for the innocent (children are at the most risk of being sexually trafficked). We can't turn a blind eye to such horrendous events. Since I don't think it is possible to abolish human trafficking completely while there is evil in this world, I suppose I hope that human trafficking becomes a topic like abortion that all Christians advocate for the ending of. I believe that if more people are aware of it and how prevalent it is, we can prevent it or better help those who are in it to escape and learn to live fruitful lives for the Lord."

Contributing Factors to This Psychosocial Problem

Human trafficking has a litany of contributing factors. In order to understand the issue well, it must not be isolated from these causes. Human trafficking does not just "happen." Other factors play a part in increasing this demand and the acceptability of human trafficking. One author explains,

> "Sex trafficking is part of a larger continuum in America that runs the gamut from homelessness, poverty, and self-esteem issues to sexualized television, the glorification of a pimp/ho culture—what is often referred to as the pornification of America—and a billion-dollar sex industry built on

the back of pornography, music, entertainment, etc."[100]

Perhaps the most foundational cause for human trafficking is the surge in sexual perversion, specifically catalyzed by pornography. The objectification of men, women, and even children in general within today's societal norms, let alone through porn mediums, is grossly toxic. Sexual perversions are humdrum or even celebrated. The non-profit organization Fight the New Drug aptly describes the situation:

"The porn industry is tied inescapably to sex trafficking. No, not every video and image on every porn site is trafficking-related, but exploitative images and videos are often indistinguishable from regularly consensual content. Porn is a risk factor that has been connected to heavy involvement in sex trafficking, it normalizes the actions trafficking victims are forced into, it desensitizes victims of sex trafficking to those actions, and it's used as 'advertising' by both pimps and traffickers. Clicking, downloading, or consuming videos and images sends the message that we accept sexual entertainment at the cost of sexual exploitation, and earns advertising dollars that fund increased trafficking and exploitation."[101]

Another major contributing factor of human trafficking has to do with fractures in the home. Note these statistics regarding human trafficking survivors:[102]

- *49% were physically assaulted as children*
- *57% were sexually abused as children*
- *85% were victims of incest as children*
- *61.5% were frequently hit, slapped, pushed, or had objects thrown at them by a member of their household*
- *40% of the above were kicked, beaten, raped, threatened, and/or attacked with a weapon by a member of their household.*

---

[100] Whitehead, John W. "The Essence of Evil: Sex with Children Has Become Big Business in America." *The Rutherford Institute*, 23 Apr. 2019, www.rutherford.org/publications_resources/john_whiteheads_commentary/the_essence_of_evil_sex_with_children_has_become_big_business_in_america.

[101] "Home." *Fight the New Drug*, https://www.fightthenewdrug.org/.

[102] "YOUR Neighborhood Needs Help #HelpERASE." *ERASE Child Trafficking*, www.erasechildtrafficking.org/.

Other common and alarming risk factors include youth, poverty, unemployment, desperation, homelessness (see Chapter 12), mental disorders (see Chapters 2-3), a desire to be loved, immigration status, homes in countries torn by armed conflict, civil unrest, political upheaval, corruption, or even natural disasters.

Many of these catalysts are directly connected to a lack of adoption and fostering by God-fearing families (see Chapter 7), and words-only anti-abortion politicking (see Chapter 6). How significant a decline this industry might have with a more outstanding commitment to providing godly homes for these children! How significant a reduction if fractures in the family were limited and a path of healing was actively pursued when they did occur? Turning a spiritual blind eye to psychosocial issues plays a definite role here. The desensitization of society compounds neglect, which certainly impacts the church. Christians must face the reality that the television programs we have watched, the organizations we have supported, the websites we have visited, etc. have all played a part in this toxic and ungodly business. Our choices coupled with our lack of action have contributed to the acquiring and sale of human beings created in God's image. Sins of omission hold the same cost as sins of commission (James 4:17). It's not just "the world" who has done this; it is sinners, including you and me, who have driven this business by our own lusts.

Does the Bible Address This Problem?

Starting at the very beginning of Scripture, we learn and understand that mankind is created in the image of God. Genesis 1:26-27 reads,

> *"Then God said, 'Let Us make man in Our image, according to Our likeness; and let them rule over the fish of the sea and over the birds of the sky and over the cattle and over all the earth, and over every creeping thing that creeps on the earth. God created man in His own image, in the image of God He created him; male and female He created them."*

James 3:8-12 builds on this God-imprinted identity of mankind by rebuking inflammatory speech toward one's fellow person:

> *"But no one can tame the tongue; it is a restless evil and full of deadly poison. With it we bless our Lord and Father, and with it we curse men, who have been made in the likeness of God; from the same mouth come both blessing and cursing. My brethren, these things ought not to be this way. Does a fountain send out from the same opening both fresh and bitter water? Can a fig tree, my brethren, produce olives, or a vine produce figs?*

Nor can salt water produce fresh."

In Matthew 5:20-30, Jesus likewise rebukes careless speech towards one's fellow person and further expounds upon this matter by condemning evil thoughts toward one's fellow person, including even sexual fantasies:

"'For I say to you that unless your righteousness surpasses that of the scribes and Pharisees, you will not enter the kingdom of heaven.

You have heard that the ancients were told, 'You shall not commit murder' and 'Whoever commits murder shall be liable to the court.' But I say to you that everyone who is angry with his brother shall be guilty before the court; and whoever says to his brother, 'You good-for-nothing,' shall be guilty before the supreme court; and whoever says, 'You fool,' shall be guilty enough to go into the fiery hell. Therefore, if you are presenting your offering at the altar, and there remember that your brother has something against you, leave your offering there before the altar and go; first be reconciled to your brother, and then come and present your offering. Make friends quickly with your opponent at law while you are with him on the way, so that your opponent may not hand you over to the judge, and the judge to the officer, and you be thrown into prison. Truly I say to you, you will not come out of there until you have paid up the last cent.

You have heard that it was said, 'You shall not commit adultery'; but I say to you that everyone who looks at a woman with lust for her has already committed adultery with her in his heart. If your right eye makes you stumble, tear it out and throw it from you; for it is better for you to lose one of the parts of your body, than for your whole body to be thrown into hell. If your right hand makes you stumble, cut it off and throw it from you; for it is better for you to lose one of the parts of your body, than for your whole body to go into hell."

Such stern condemnation of evil words and thoughts toward one's fellow person would render an action like human trafficking unthinkable to the spirit of Christ's instruction. No doubt, the fiery Hell reserved for evil words and thoughts is the same fiery Hell to which an unregenerate human trafficker is destined. This clear principle is well-established in the Scriptures. Even so, the Bible does offer specific illustrations of and condemnations for human trafficking.

Jacob's son Joseph was a clear survivor of human trafficking. Sadly, this transpired at the hands of his own brothers, the patriarchs of Israel, due to their slight at Jacob's favoritism of Joseph. Many chapters of Genesis are devoted to this narrative and the resulting consequences from this betrayal, which typifies Christ's betrayal by His own. Note the following passages which identify this as an act of human trafficking:

> "Then [Joseph's brothers] sat down to eat a meal. And as they raised their eyes and looked, behold, a caravan of Ishmaelites was coming from Gilead, with their camels bearing aromatic gum and balm and myrrh, on their way to bring them down to Egypt. Judah said to his brothers, 'What profit is it for us to kill our brother and cover up his blood? Come and let us sell him to the Ishmaelites and not lay our hands on him, for he is our brother, our own flesh.' And his brothers listened to him. Then some Midianite traders passed by, so they pulled him up and lifted Joseph out of the pit, and sold him to the Ishmaelites for twenty shekels of silver. Thus, they brought Joseph into Egypt" (Genesis 37:25-28)

> "Meanwhile, the Midianites sold him in Egypt to Potiphar, Pharaoh's officer, the captain of the bodyguard..." (Genesis 37:36)

> "Now Joseph had been taken down to Egypt; and Potiphar, an Egyptian officer of Pharaoh, the captain of the bodyguard, bought him from the Ishmaelites, who had taken him down there." (Genesis 39:1)

Joseph's case is a powerful attestation to God's own people historically playing a role in human trafficking. The patriarchs' decision was condemnable, but the longsuffering spirit of Joseph saw God navigating his life through these horrors to establish a foothold for His people in a time of calamity. Had Joseph not been sold into slavery and been trafficked, Israel would have perished during the famine discussed in the last several chapters of Genesis. Joseph became a victor and a provider of life; his hopelessness had created hope for Israel.

Joseph's case was not unique. God condemns several nations for human trafficking in the Bible, especially in the prophets. Listen to God's rebuke of the Philistines and Tyre through the prophet Amos (1:6-9):

> "Thus says the Lord,
> 'For three transgressions of Gaza and for four
> I will not revoke its punishment,
> Because they deported an entire population
> To deliver it up to Edom.
> So I will send fire upon the wall of Gaza

And it will consume her citadels.
I will also cut off the inhabitant from Ashdod,
And him who holds the scepter, from Ashkelon;
I will even unleash My power upon Ekron,
And the remnant of the Philistines will perish,'
Says the Lord God.

Thus says the Lord,
'For three transgressions of Tyre and for four
I will not revoke its punishment,
Because they delivered up an entire population to Edom.'"

In addition to individual and collective examples of human trafficking, the Bible also explicitly condemns kidnapping, a necessary feature of human trafficking. Kidnapping is forbidden in both the Old Testament and New Testament:

"He who kidnaps a man, whether he sells him or he is found in his posses-
sion, shall surely be put to death." (Exodus 21:16)

"If a man is caught kidnapping any of his countrymen of the sons of Israel,
and he deals with him violently or sells him, then that thief shall die; so
you shall purge the evil from among you." (Deuteronomy 24:7)

"But we know that the Law is good, if one uses it lawfully, realizing the fact
that law is not made for a righteous person, but for those who are lawless
and rebellious, for the ungodly and sinners, for the unholy and profane,
for...kidnappers and liars and perjurers, and whatever else is contrary to
sound teaching, according to the glorious gospel of the blessed God, with
which I have been entrusted." (1 Timothy 1:8-10)

The Scriptures outright condemn human trafficking. Not only that, but the facilitating sins of kidnapping, sensuality, sexual immorality, etc., are likewise wholly abhorred by the Lord, as indeed they should be by all His people.

How Can Christians Effectively Address Human Trafficking?

Having played a part in the industry, even indirectly, Christians should be highly motivated to dismantle that same industry. This is an indispensable responsibility of discipleship to Jesus. One foundational area that merits fastidious attention is for believers to develop a greater moral sensitivity (Psalm 82:3;

Proverbs 31:8-9; Hebrews 10:34). Perpetrators tend to act in ways that can be preventable if believers are observant, while those trapped in the industry tend to exhibit signs of trafficking. Let's research and be aware of the red flags.

Another foundational area where Christians can hamstring the human trafficking industry is to cultivate and encourage sexual fulfillment through God's intended mediums, laying aside sexual perversions (1 Thessalonians 4:3-8; 1 Corinthians 6:9-11; Hebrews 13:4). One Christian offers some counsel related to this and also includes another area worthy of attention:

> *"The two main industries that are responsible for the majority of human trafficking worldwide are the pornography and fashion industries. For the first, and just obviously, don't consume porn. It just creates more demand. The same goes for the fashion industry, however it is more difficult to determine which have played a part in human trafficking. Try to shop ethical brands or thrift your clothes!"*

Practical helps are also important to consider. Advocacy, counseling, and offering encouragement to survivors can be a lifesaving ministry that a Christian can fulfill (Psalm 35:10; 82:4; Isaiah 58:6-7; 61:1-3). All Christians should use their particular skills and experiences to fight human trafficking. This may include taking advantage of citizenship rights that enable one to give a voice to the voiceless (cf. Acts 16:37-38; 22:25-28; 25:11). In so doing, one may support the development of and enforcement of laws through God's ministerial governmental medium (Romans 13:1-7; 1 Peter 2:13-18). Christians can also serve by acknowledging and aligning with parental concerns for their children in order to build a greater community of protection for all families. Story after story comes out about people's children and family members being taken. This constant anxiety weighs on the hearts of many and can cripple social interaction that has enormous impacts even on things like evangelism or coming to church. Another equally powerful means of thwarting the spread of human trafficking is to consider how you might help children in need through adoption and fostering, or by supporting adoptive and foster families. Most importantly, share the gospel broadly. You never know if you might pull a sufferer out, or change a perpetrator of human trafficking into a disciple. Let all believers grow to see people through God's compassionate eyes (Matthew 25:31-46; Jeremiah 22:16).

Whatever course of action you decide to pursue, pray! Pray for the survivors. Pray for the perpetrators. Pray for the officers trying to enforce laws. Pray for the legislators crafting laws. Pray for counselors and the reform of former perpetrators and supporters. The US State Department's *2019 Trafficking on Human Report* gives us a sense of direction for what we can pray for in the governmental realm. Included in the report is a listing of fourteen recommendations for improvement, which serve well to pray for and aid in developing, depending on our skills and influence. The listing includes:

- *Increase investigation and prosecution of labor trafficking cases.*
- *Increase the number of requests by federal law enforcement officials for Continued Presence and conduct targeted training to ensure such officials apply for Continued Presence in a timely manner and in all appropriate circumstances.*
- *Shorten processing times and improve training for adjudicators to reduce obstacles for victims to appropriately obtain trafficking-related immigration benefits.*
- *Proactively identify potential trafficking victims among populations vulnerable to human trafficking.*
- *Increase the number of trafficking investigations and prosecutions.*
- *Seek to ensure immigration enforcement does not hinder human trafficking criminal law enforcement or victim protections.*
- *Increase equitable access to comprehensive victim services across the country and improve access to short-term and/or transitional housing for all victims.*
- *Encourage state, local, and tribal authorities to implement policies not to prosecute victims for the unlawful acts their traffickers compelled them to commit.*
- *Remove the restriction on victim assistance funding for legal representation of victims in vacatur and expungement cases for the unlawful acts their traffickers compelled them to commit.*
- *Mitigate vulnerabilities in employment-based or other nonimmigrant visa programs in the United States, including by increasing oversight of labor recruiters to ensure compliance with federal, state, and local regulations.*
- *Increase training of prosecutors and judges on mandatory forfeiture and restitution for trafficking victims.*
- *Increase survivor engagement, including by more systematically incorporating survivor input when forming policies, programs, and trainings.*
- *Increase prevention efforts, including through outreach to and intervention services for marginalized communities.*
- *Strengthen efforts to reduce the demand for commercial sex and labor trafficking.*

Education must replace ignorance, and passion must replace apathy. There are a host of resources that Christians should become familiar with in their efforts to fight human trafficking. Here is a brief listing of informative resources:

- **Erase Child Trafficking**— https://www.erasechildtrafficking.org/
- **Fight the New Drug**— https://fightthenewdrug.org/
- **Hope for Justice**— https://hopeforjustice.org/
- **International Labour Organization**— https://www.ilo.org/global/lang--en/index.htm
- **IOM Counter-Trafficking Data Collaborative (CTDC)**—This is the first global data hub on trafficking. As of January 25th, 2019, they had 91,416 survivor cases from 172 countries. https://www.ctdatacollaborative.org/
- **Polaris Project**—Operates the **National Human Trafficking Hotline** (888) 373-7888 as well as a textline called **BeFree** (233733). https://polarisproject.org/
- **Stop the Traffik**— https://www.stopthetraffik.org/
- **The Dressember Foundation**—This organization has advocates who wear a dress or tie every day of December in an effort to raise funds to support rescue missions and provide for victims who have been rescued. https://www.dressember.org/
- **The National Center for Missing & Exploited Children**— https://www.missingkids.org/
- **TraffickCam**—This app allows you to take pictures of your hotel room and upload them onto a database that can help agencies identify and match locations to those shown in abuse videos in order to capture perpetrators. https://www.traffickcam.com/
- **US Department of Health & Human Services (HHS), Administration for Children & Families (ACF), Office on Trafficking In Persons (OTIP)**— https://www.acf.hhs.gov/otip
- **US Justice Department, Civil Rights Division, Human Trafficking Prosecution Unit (HTPU)**— https://www.justice.gov/crt/human-trafficking-prosecution-unit-htpu
- **US State Department**—The Department of State leads the US global engagement to combat human trafficking and supports the coordination of anti-trafficking efforts across the US government. https://www.state.gov/policy-issues/human-trafficking/
- To report suspected human trafficking to federal law enforcement, call **1-866-347-2423.**
- **SESTA** and **FOSTA** bills signed into effect by President Donald J. Trump
- **Trafficking Victims Protection Act of 2000 (TVPA)**

- The Palermo Protocol to Prevent, Suppress and Punish Trafficking in Persons, Especially Women and Children, supplementing the United Nations Convention against Transnational Organized Crime

A Closing Thought

God has charged His people to be zealous for good deeds (Ephesians 2:10; Titus 2:11-14). One of the worst psychosocial situations that exist in the world today is human trafficking. People are being taken, stolen from their homes and families, and objectified as labor or sex slaves. This is a real problem that we can and should be taking the proper steps to address. As Christians, we must engage this psychosocial issue in whatever capacity our sphere of influence, skillset, and resources allow.

Let us boldly shed light on the horrors of evil in this world (Ephesians 5:11-16). Let us advocate for the distressed and afflicted as Jesus would, because if we do not, we will be held liable by the judgment of God's wrath. We will also give grounds for the world to justifiably attack Christianity as a system filled with hypocrites apathetic to the plight of the stricken. Let us provide love, forgiveness, reconciliation, grace, and compassion to both the victims of human trafficking as well as the perpetrators who will turn from their evils.

Thought Questions

1) What emotions arose as you read this chapter and how did this information affect you?

_____

_____

2) How significant of a problem is human trafficking?

_____

_____

3) What are some of the biggest risk factors for human trafficking and how can Christians lessen these factors?

_____

_____

4) What does the Bible say regarding human trafficking?

_____

_____

5) What are some of the signs of human trafficking and what can individual Christians and congregations do to watch out for these signs?

_____

_____

6) Choose one of the resources listed in this chapter to further research concerning the issue of human trafficking. What did you learn and how can you apply this as a conscientious Christian?

_____

_____

7) What resource(s) can you use this week to help combat human trafficking?

_____

_____

CHAPTER 9

Homosexuality

Do you know someone who has fallen away from Christ and pursued a homosexual lifestyle? Do you know someone who was never a Christian and actively lives a homosexual lifestyle? Chances are that you do, and sadly, you will likely experience this more as homosexuality becomes not only normalized, but celebrated. No doubt, the late-twentieth and early twenty-first century have seen exponential growth in the acceptance and popularity of homosexuality. Too many factors have contributed to this for us to discuss in detail, but we will overview some of the same considerations we have already undertaken regarding other psychosocial issues. With this discussion, keep in mind that the goal of the Christian is to understand the will of God, to convey the will of God to others, and to snatch the fallen soul out of the snares and fires of the evil one (James 5:19-20; Jude 1:17-23). In this journey and with this dedication, Christians can demonstrate sincere love.

Homosexuality as a Psychosocial Issue

With the widespread acceptance of homosexuality, many ask whether homosexuality should even be identified as a psychosocial issue. However, it is imperative for Christians to see that homosexuality is not merely a matter of what inconsequentially goes on between consensual adults. Quite the contrary actually; in reality, LGBTQ+ activists target every basic element of society. There are issues here that defy neutrality. To achieve these goals, activists cunningly craft the image of homosexuality in a way that undermines elemental socio-spiritual successes. To that end, they have been highly effective not only in society at large but even in influencing the church. Listen to these two appraisals of this insidious influence:

"One of the most pervasive issues of our time is the movement to embrace homosexual behavior, same-sex 'marriage,' and the marred versions of masculinity and femininity that accompany this lifestyle. References sympathetic to the homosexual lifestyle appear now in books, on television, in films, and in video games and graphic novels. Even the popular social networking platform Facebook announced the addition of 'gay marriage timeline icons' for users. And of course, the crowning moment for the LGBT movement was the decision to legalize gay 'marriage' by the Supreme Court in Obergefell v. Hodges. Our children and teens are inundated with a message of 'tolerance' and 'acceptance' of homosexual behavior, and sadly even some professing Christians are preaching this message."[103]

"Due to the emotional and highly personal nature of the homosexuality discussion, many in the church are choosing to focus on sobering statistics...and bend biblical truth to fit with the cultural narrative as an attempt to fix these problems. And what is the cultural narrative? That so-called discrimination causes nearly irreparable harm and that the only answer is full inclusion and acceptance. But we should not be taking our cues from the culture! We need to look to God's Word for an unchanging standard of truth. Otherwise, we are simply blown here and there by every wind of doctrine (Ephesians 4:14) that comes and goes as we make man, not God, the authority for morality."[104]

As these quotes make clear, embracing sin and emboldening others in their rejection of God's commands is not biblically-based compassion or love; it is a self-serving guise of sympathy and irreverence that distances others from their Creator and His plan for human sexuality and marriage. Efforts on the part of mainstream churches such as the United Methodist Church, the Episcopalian Church, the Catholic Church, and others to normalize, celebrate, and fellowship active participants in homosexual unions are not reflective of a prioritization of the objective standard of God's Word, but rather of the influence of the world upon these organizations. Mankind's redefinition of sin does not change God's definition, for God is the only One qualified to define something as a sin, and He has clearly done so in the Scriptures.

---

[103] Golden, Steve. "Pro-Gay Theology: Does the Bible Approve of Homosexuality?" *Answers in Genesis,* 29 Jan. 2013, answersingenesis.org/family/homosexuality/pro-gay-theology-does-the-bible-approve-of-homosexuality/.

[104] Foley, Avery. "Can the Church Embrace Homosexual Behavior in the Name of Love?" *Answers in Genesis,* 29 Mar. 2017, answersingenesis.org/sin/can-church-embrace-homosexual-behavior-in-name-of-love/.

How have such efforts on the part of activists been so influential even in churches? What has been their methodology? In addition to the tactics addressed above, part of the success of activists is due to the perpetuation of several instrumental myths. One popular myth is that homosexuals make up as much as 10% of the population; however, it is obviously advantageous for the LGTBQ+ community to inflate this statistic. Support for this notion is found in the infamous *Kinsey Reports* (1948, 1953); yet, modern studies show that the *Kinsey Reports* are altogether flawed. There is counterevidence from more recent studies showing this percentage to be 1-3%.[105] Despite these lower numbers, Americans in particular grossly overestimate the number of people who engage in homosexual relationships and activities at nearly tenfold rates.[106]

Another well-circulated falsehood is that homosexual relationships are wholesome and fulfilling. However, the reality is that homosexual couples are statistically far less likely to be monogamous, a truth deeply affecting both individual psyches and society at large.[107] Many think homosexuality is an ordinary, healthy lifestyle. However, the activities and issues occurring within the homosexual community would repulse Jesus' followers, as attested by reformed homosexuals.[108] So, are homosexuals as healthy as everyone else? Up until 1973, homosexuality was considered a mental disorder in the *Diagnostic and Statistical Manual of Mental Disorders* because homosexuals exhibited generalized impairment and distress in social effectiveness and functioning.[109] Because of pressure from the homosexual community, the APA eliminated homosexuality from the *DSM*! Let's take a quick look at some data regarding

---

[105] Gates, Gary J. "How Many People Are Lesbian, Gay, Bisexual, and Transgender?" *Williams Institute*, 14 July 2020, williamsinstitute.law.ucla.edu/publications/how-many-people-lgbt/. "Topic: Homosexuality." *Statista*, Statista Research Department, 9 June 2017, www.statista.com/topics/1249/homosexuality/.

[106] Robison, Jennifer. "What Percentage of the Population Is Gay?" *Gallup.com*, Gallup, 30 June 2020, news.gallup.com/poll/6961/what-percentage-population-gay.aspx.

[107] See: Hanna Rosin, "The Dirty Little Secret: Most Gay Couples Aren't Monogamous," *Slate*, June 26, 2013, http://www.slate.com/blogs/xx_factor/2013/06/26/most_gay_couples_aren't_monogamous_will_straight_couples_go_monogamish.html; and Meredith May, "Many Gay Couples Negotiate Open Relationships," *SFGate*, July 16, 2010, http://www.sfgate.com/news/article/Many-gay-couples-negotiate-open-relationships-3241624.php.

[108] Ligon, Amy, and Bree Stevens. "#OnceGay Stories - *Changed* - #ONCEGAY STORIES." Changed, 9 Dec. 2020, https://www.changedmovement.com/stories.

[109] For a helpful resource on this subject, see: Stoller, Robert J., et al. "A Symposium: Should Homosexuality Be in the APA Nomenclature?" *American Journal of Psychiatry*, vol. 130, no. 11, 1973, pp. 1207–1216., doi:10.1176/ajp.130.11.1207.

the common effects of homosexuality:

- The median age of death of those with AIDS is 39; for those homosexuals without AIDS, the median age of death is 42. In all, homosexuals exhibit a 20-30-year decrease in life expectancy.[110]
- According to the Herrell, et al. Twin study, twins reporting a same-gender sexual orientation are 6.5x more likely to report having attempted suicide than their heterosexual twin.[111]
- According to the Sandfort, et al. Netherlands Study, homosexual men are: 3x more likely to be diagnosed with mood disorders, 7x more likely to be diagnosed with bipolar disorder, 2.5x more likely to be diagnosed with anxiety disorder, and 6x more likely to be diagnosed with OCD. According to the same study, homosexual women are 3.5x more likely to be diagnosed with substance abuse disorders and 8x more likely to be diagnosed with drug dependence.[112]
- According to the Siever Body Dissatisfaction Study, homosexual males are far more likely to develop eating disorders than heterosexual females.[113]
- According to a CDC press release: homosexual males are 44x more likely to have HIV than heterosexual males, primary and secondary syphilis incidence was >46x greater among homosexual males than heterosexual males, primary and secondary syphilis incidence was >71x greater among homosexual females than heterosexual females.[114]

---

[110] Satinover, Jeffrey. *Homosexuality and the Politics of Truth.* Baker Books, 1998.

[111] Herrell, Richard, et al. "Sexual Orientation and Suicidality." *Archives of General Psychiatry,* vol. 56, no. 10, 1999, p. 867., doi:10.1001/archpsyc.56.10.867.

[112] Sandfort, Theo G. M., et al. "Same-Sex Sexual Behavior and Psychiatric Disorders." *Archives of General Psychiatry,* vol. 58, no. 1, 2001, p. 85., doi:10.1001/archpsyc.58.1.85.

[113] Siever, Michael D. "Sexual Orientation and Gender as Factors in Socioculturally Acquired Vulnerability to Body Dissatisfaction and Eating Disorders." *Journal of Consulting and Clinical Psychology,* vol. 62, no. 2, 1994, pp. 252–260., doi:10.1037/0022-006x.62.2.252.

[114] Center for Disease Control, National Center for HIV/AIDS, Viral Hepatitis, STD, and TB Prevention. (2010). HIV among gay, bisexual and other men who have sex with men (MSM). Retrieved from website: http://www.cdc.gov/hiv/topics/msm/pdf/msm.pdf. See also, Center for Disease Control, National Center for HIV/AIDS, Viral Hepatitis, STD, and TB Prevention. (2010). CDC analysis provides new look at disproportionate impact of HIV and syphilis among US gay and bisexual men. Retrieved from website: http://www.cdc.gov/nchhstp/Newsroom/msmpressrelease.html.

- According to the Daling, et al. STD study, homosexual males are 33x more likely to develop anal cancer.[115]
- According to a report from the Oasis Foundation titled "In the Name of Love: The Church, Exclusion and LGB Mental Health Issues," 24% of gay men admitted to trying to kill themselves, while 54% admitted to having suicidal thoughts, 1 in 14 gay and bisexual men deliberately harmed themselves in the year 2011–2012 compared to just 1 in 33 men in general who have ever harmed themselves, 42% of young LGBT people have sought medical help for anxiety or depression, and 52% of young LGBT people report self-harm either now or in the past.[116]

Sadly, these statistics are often falsely reinterpreted by LGBTQ+ advocates as representations of faults within the church—such as hypercriticism, ostracization, and hatred—and not with the lifestyle itself.[117] Considering all factors, particularly the wide acceptance and celebration of homosexual lifestyles, the response of the church seems to play a minimal role in any of these markers. Even so, it is accurate that the church has not always excelled at effectively addressing homosexuality.

Another propagated lie is that homosexuals cannot change and have no reason to change. This is perhaps the most destructive deception, for it can lead to the abandonment of all hope for deliverance as well as spiritual apathy and death. Militants do not want society to know that homosexuals can, and indeed should, change their lifestyle and actions.[118] In reality, numerous professionals, friends, family members, and religious organizations have successfully helped homosexuals change their lives, but it is certainly not easy! Temptations will still abound, and opportunities to sin will always arise, but Christians can and should resist! So, rather than dismiss these illicit activities,

---

[115] Daling, J.R., et al. "Sexual Practices, Sexually Transmitted Diseases, and the Incidence of Anal Cancer." *New England Journal of Medicine*, vol. 318, no. 15, 1988, pp. 990–992., doi:10.1056/nejm198804143181511.

[116] Foley, Avery. "Can the Church Embrace Homosexual Behavior in the Name of Love?" *Answers in Genesis*, 29 Mar. 2017, answersingenesis.org/sin/can-church-embrace-homosexual-behavior-in-name-of-love/.

[117] For one example, see: Knapton, Sarah. "Church Is Driving Gay People to Suicide, Warns Christian Charity." *The Telegraph*, Telegraph Media Group, 10 Feb. 2017, www.telegraph.co.uk/science/2017/02/10/church-driving-gay-people-suicide-warns-christian-charity/.

[118] "Former LGBTQers Testify: If You No Longer Want to Be Gay or Transgender, You Don't Have to Be." *CBN News*, 10 Jan. 2020, www1.cbn.com/cbnnews/us/2020/january/former-lgbtqers-testify-if-you-no-longer-want-to-be-gay-or-transgender-you-dont-have-to-be.

or be indifferent to a consensual evil, let us be passionate to help those who struggle with temptation!

What Does the Bible Say About Homosexuality?

The Bible establishes God's will for people and relationships throughout the ages (cf. Isaiah 45:19; Ephesians 3:3-5; 5:17). In some ways, variations did occur among the three different dispensations – the Patriarchal age, the Mosaic age, and the Age of the Church – but we typically see the same fundamental requirements in respect to moral areas, including homosexuality.

The Patriarchal Age

In the age of the patriarchs, God held same-sex relations in contempt. The case of Sodom, Gomorrah, and the cities of the plains (Genesis 18-19) openly displays this intolerance. God was disgusted with the vile activities of the city: *"And the Lord said, 'The outcry of Sodom and Gomorrah is indeed great, and their sin is exceedingly grave.'"* (18:20). Their cities had become so corrupted by evil that God decreed these metropolises were to be obliterated by fire and brimstone from the heavens. God announced this planned destruction to Abraham since his nephew Lot lived in the city of Sodom. In response, Abraham interceded on behalf of Lot and asked that God spare the city. Abraham negotiated with God to preserve the city for fifty righteous souls (18:22-26). Holding out little hope for righteousness in these cities, Abraham continued to implore God for an ever-decreasing number until he reached only ten righteous souls (18:27-33). God agreed to spare the city for a measly ten righteous souls.

Two angelic agents of God entered Sodom to inspect the city and to communicate God's will to Lot, but the deep depravity of the city ultimately led to a horrific situation. Lot offered to host the messengers in his house in order to protect them from staying the night in the exposed part of the city. After serving them a quick meal, the agents of Satan descended on the home with violence in their hearts and evil on their minds. The text relates,

> *"Before they lay down, the men of the city, the men of Sodom, surrounded the house, both young and old, all the people from every quarter; and they called to Lot and said to him, 'Where are the men who came to you tonight? Bring them out to us that we may have relations with them.' But Lot went out to them at the doorway, and shut the door behind him, and said, 'Please, my brothers, do not act wickedly. Now behold, I have two daughters who have not had relations with man; please let me bring them*

out to you, and do to them whatever you like; only do nothing to these men, inasmuch as they have come under the shelter of my roof.' But they said, 'Stand aside.' Furthermore, they said, 'This one came in as an alien, and already he is acting like a judge; now we will treat you worse than them.' So they pressed hard against Lot and came near to break the door" (19:4-9).

Note the all-encompassing description of the evildoers: they came from every part of the city, were young and old, small and great. They all violently desired to sodomize the men.[119]

Few should struggle to see why God decreed judgment against such people. The simple truth is that not even ten righteous souls could be found in Sodom, yet God dragged Lot and his family out of the city to safety (19:12-16). The narrative ends in exceeding sadness with the destruction of Sodom (19:23-25, 27-29), the death of Lot's wife because of her adoration for the city of Sodom (19:17, 26), and the incestuous relations of Lot and his daughters which result in the Moabite and Ammonite peoples (19:30-38). All of this destruction resulting from these populations' lust for homosexual mistreatment of the body. While man saw fit to pursue his own desires, God resoundingly demonstrated that such activity brought condemnation and judgment.

Sodom, therefore, serves as a negative example for Christians to learn from if they are to abide in the lovingkindness of God:

"For if God did not spare angels when they sinned, but cast them into hell and committed them to pits of darkness, reserved for judgment; and did not spare the ancient world, but preserved Noah, a preacher of righteousness, with seven others, when He brought a flood upon the world of the ungodly; and if He condemned the cities of Sodom and Gomorrah to destruction by reducing them to ashes, having made them an example to those who would live ungodly lives thereafter; and if He rescued righteous Lot, oppressed by the sensual conduct of unprincipled men (for by what he saw and heard that righteous man, while living among them, felt his righteous soul tormented day after day by their lawless deeds), then the Lord knows how to rescue the godly from temptation, and to keep the unrighteous under punishment for the day of judgment, and especially those who indulge

---

[119] Advocates for homosexuality, particularly those of the infamous Queen James Version of the Bible, suggest that the issue in Genesis 19 is not homosexuality but gang rape or lack of hospitality. This argument runs aground on the Hebrew of the text and defies Jude 6-8, which specifies Sodom's issue as sexual immorality in which the people of the city pursued strange flesh, a clear reference to homosexuality.

the flesh in its corrupt desires and despise authority" (2 Peter 2:4-10). *"Now I desire to remind you, though you know all things once for all, that the Lord, after saving a people out of the land of Egypt, subsequently destroyed those who did not believe. And angels who did not keep their own domain, but abandoned their proper abode, He has kept in eternal bonds under darkness for the judgment of the great day, just as Sodom and Gomorrah and the cities around them, since they in the same way as these indulged in gross immorality and went after strange flesh, are exhibited as an example in undergoing the punishment of eternal fire"* (Jude 1:5-7).

The Mosaic Age

When God gave a law to His new nation Israel, He gave legislation regarding religious, civil, social, and personal matters. His precepts set Israel apart from other nations (Exodus 19:5-6). Some of these matters included relationships between individuals and even went to great lengths to cover nearly every conceivable perversion of God's intent for one man to be married to one woman for life (e.g., Leviticus 18; Deuteronomy 27). Many of these perversions carried the death penalty so as not to create a social epidemic of sin. Homosexuality is specifically listed among these sins. Listen to just a few of these laws and consider God's opinion of such activities and lifestyles: *"You shall not lie with a male as one lies with a female; it is an abomination"* (Leviticus 18:22) and, *"If there is a man who lies with a male as those who lie with a woman, both of them have committed a detestable act; they shall surely be put to death. Their bloodguiltiness is upon them"* (Leviticus 20:13).[120]

Though God was clear regarding His desire for mankind to abstain from the fleshly lusts of homosexuality, violations of this decree frequently occur during the Mosaic Age, so much so that Israel and Judah are both likened unto Sodom and Gomorrah (e.g., Isaiah 1:9-10; 3:9; Jeremiah 23:14; Lamentations 4:6; Ezekiel 16:46, 48, 49, 53, 55, 56; Amos 4:11). Notably, this rebellion among God's peculiar people continues in the New Testament, as does the comparison to Sodom (e.g., Matthew 10:15; 11:23-24; Luke 17:29). On other occasions in the Old Testament, the byword is used of other nations who were not subject to the Law of Moses but were subject to basic, inherent moral expectations

---

[120] Here is another place where advocates of homosexuality have made grotesque changes in the Queen James Version of the Bible. To these passages is added the wholly unwarranted phrase, *"in the temple of Molech,"* to minimize the restrictions here to only contexts of ritual impurity. Not only are these phrases totally absent from all manuscripts of these passages, but the addition of this phrase is inconsistently applied, for if the phrase were added throughout Lev 18 and 20, slaughtering of children, incest, bestiality, and other behaviors would only be wrong in religious ceremonies.

(e.g., Babylon in Isaiah 13:19 and Jeremiah 50:40; Edom in Jeremiah 49:18; Moab and Ammon in Zephaniah 2:9). On still other occasions, the specific issue of sodomy and homosexuality are condemned, and the accusers are removed from the people (e.g., 1 Kings 22:46).

The Church Age

In law and example, homosexuality was denounced under the age of the patriarchs and under the Law of Moses. What about under the new covenant of Christ? Jesus Himself speaks against same-sex relationships in His response to another perversion of marriage—divorce without cause—in Mark 10:2-9 and its parallels. He forthrightly establishes God's intent for marriage is between one man and one woman, for life; all exceptions to this necessarily involve sin and jeopardize the soul, whether heterosexual or homosexual in nature. In the beginning God created one male and one female who were given the charge to procreate, populate, and rule the Earth (Genesis 2:18-24). Adam and Eve supply the compositional archetype for all other sexual relationships.

Christ further spoke through His authoritative apostles (cf. Matthew 10:14; John 14-16; 1 Corinthians 2:10-13; 13:8-10; 2 Timothy 3:16-17) on marriage and homosexual relations. The Holy Spirit instructs Christians to keep the marriage bed undefiled (Hebrews 13:4), to abstain from sexual immorality (e.g., 1 Corinthians 6:18-20; 1 Thessalonians 4:3-8), and particularly to not engage in homosexual acts under penalty of spiritual death. Regarding the latter instruction, two passages are worthy of citation:[121]

"Or do you not know that the unrighteous will not inherit the kingdom of God? Do not be deceived; neither fornicators, nor idolaters, nor adulterers, nor effeminate, nor homosexuals, nor thieves, nor the covetous, nor drunkards, nor revilers, nor swindlers, will inherit the kingdom of God. Such were some of you; but you were washed, but you were sanctified, but you were justified in the name of the Lord Jesus Christ and in the Spirit of our God" (1 Corinthians 6:9-11).

"But we know that the Law is good, if one uses it lawfully, realizing the fact that law is not made for a righteous person, but for those who are lawless and rebellious, for the ungodly and sinners, for the unholy and profane, for those who kill their fathers or mothers, for murderers and immoral men and homosexuals and kidnappers and liars and perjurers, and whatever

---

[121] 1 Corinthians 6:9-11 and 1 Timothy 1:8-11 specifically condemn both the passive (Greek: *malakos*) and active (Greek: *arsenokoites*) members of a homosexual relationship.

else is contrary to sound teaching, according to the glorious gospel of the blessed God, with which I have been entrusted" (1 Timothy 1:8-11).

The apostle Paul even explains why homosexual relations are wrong else-where—they are unnatural, fleshly, and carnal (Romans 1:18-32). Paul specifies that God's judgment abides on those who even support or advocate for such sinful lusts and activities (1:32).

Why Does the Bible Speak So Strongly Against Homosexuality?

Homosexuality is fundamentally wrong because it violates God's plan for the home (Matthew 19:2-9). Jesus makes clear the origin of marriage goes back to the beginning. God created and specifically designed two complementary people – Adam and Eve. Jesus affirms human sexuality is under divine authority; the very fact that man is the result of God's creative power is the basis of this authority in directing what activities are wholesome and what activities are damaging (cf. Romans 9:20). God is the One Who determines who shall lawfully be joined together; Jesus exercises this authority under the new covenant (Hebrews 1:2; Matthew 19:9). Jesus forcefully restricts the expression of human sexuality to scriptural marriage. Therefore, people, including the Supreme Court of the United States, have not been granted the prerogative of setting the terms of the marriage covenant (Matthew 19:6). The order of creation is lifetime, monogamous, heterosexual marriage (Matthew 19:5, 8; Romans 7:2-3).

Homosexuality is also sinful because it involves fornication for the unmarried (1 Corinthians 7:2-5). God does not demand that anyone and everyone get married, but He does restrict sexual intercourse to scriptural marriage (7:2-3). He simply does not offer same-gender or opposite-gender sexual relationships to the unmarried (7:2); as such, all sexual relationships outside scriptural marriage are sinful (1 Corinthians 6:9). Moreover, when a man leaves his wife to have sexual relations with a man, or a woman leaves her husband to have sexual relations with a woman, adultery occurs. The marriage bed is defiled thereby (Hebrews 13:4).

Furthermore, homosexuality is sinful because it is explicitly reproached in the New Testament (Romans 1:26-27; cf. 1 Timothy 1:9-10). The context of these verses describes the causes and consequences of pagan lifestyles. The overall problem for a person living a pagan lifestyle is his or her foundational rejection of God's authority (see Romans 1:28). Each person then has a significant choice to make: they can expel God and His authority from their lives or bring their conduct into harmony with His will. The type of individuals described in Romans 1 chose the former and their course became one of cumulative evil. In this particular context, Paul explained that homosexuality is self-abusive (1:24), disgraceful/vile (1:26), and unnatural (1:26-27). It is contrary to God's created order! It is an unseemly and vulgar error (1:27). It is forbidden by God and thus condemned (1:18, 28). Homosexuals receive the recompense of their error in themselves (1:27). Therefore, sexual deviation is not only a rebellion, but the activity itself is a punishment!

Finally, homosexuality is sinful because it has always been sinful! There was never a time when people were without law from God (Romans 5:13). Since sin is present in the world and since sin is lawlessness, the conclusion is that law has always existed for people. This is especially true for homosexuality because the marriage law was universal from the beginning. The sinfulness of homosexuality is exemplified in every single age. In the Patriarchal Age, we have the destruction of Sodom. It is clearly abhorrent and condemned under the Law of Moses. As we have already seen, it is likewise condemned in the New Testament.

How Can Christians Effectively Address Homosexuality?

Though it may seem different for diverse reasons of background and bias, Christians have the same responsibility regarding homosexuality as they do with other sins. The Christian must diligently shed light on the ugliness of sin and preach repentance to a lost and dying world. With compassion and love, firmness and caution (1 Timothy 5:22b; Jude 17-23), Christians can have an effective experience in addressing homosexuality. Such an opportunity would be different from the prevailing norm, according to one Christian who candidly shares:

> *"In my experience, Christians are not afraid to address homosexuality, at least not by way of condemnation. I have heard many sermons and engaged in several discussions with Christians who readily agree homosexuality is a sin and can lead to condemnation in hell. But I have not observed many Christians—including myself—actually addressing homosexuality with someone who is tempted by, or actively engaged in, homosexual sin. This failure stems less from fear, in my view, as uncertainty on how to address the topic with someone who struggles with a temptation that is not easy for every Christian to understand. This difficulty is compounded by the fact that, as a general rule, Christians have often heard homosexuality condemned, but rarely thought about how best to approach someone struggling with it."*

Another Christian, who himself struggles with homosexuality, concurs, citing several impediments to discussions on homosexuality:

> *"Honestly, I think there is a spectrum of stigma when it comes to sin and the church. Sexual sins are definitely looked at more critically. However, adultery, fornication, divorce, and lust all seem to elicit at least a degree of universal empathy. But sins of perversion, of which homosexuality and transgenderism are the most relevant right now, are lacking in empathic response. These sexual sins are definitely treated with a range of stigmatism and judgment. Responses range from, 'Well, they just choose to be that way, and they just need to stop,' (which betrays a deep ignorance of the situation) to evangelical churches picketing with hateful signs conveying the most heinous blasphemy and disregard for the command to love our neighbor. With such ignorance and vitriol, it can be hard for a person struggling to understand their temptations or to bring their desires under submission to the Spirit. It can also make it hard to see the church as a safe place to have that conversation. Many righteous and faithful people in the church would not and do not respond with such prejudice, but those who do respond in such a way do so with such a loud voice that their discrimination is perceived as the common voice of the church."*

He further explains,

> *"Some members of the church are totally unafraid to address homosexuality, and they do so with a lack of wisdom, understanding, or love. Another group, who possesses the wisdom to know that they don't fully understand homosexuality and the love to not want to be hurtful, are afraid to address it. It comes down to a sad irony that the ones who are afraid to address it out of sympathy are the ones who ought to speak up, and the brazen ones who speak without wisdom are the ones who should be humbled and be silent."*

For Those Who Do Not Themselves Struggle with Homosexuality

For those who do not struggle with homosexual ideation or temptation, you face an uphill battle. First of all, you must keep in mind that apathy due to discomfort or other reasons is unwarranted and will bring condemnation on the Day of Judgment. A lack of response is as condemnatory as an inappropriate response. No Christian can afford to be afraid to address a matter of sin in his fellow human (2 Timothy 1:7), so reach out! (cf. Galatians 6:1) Often, Christians are either paralyzed by cowardice or are patently overaggressive in this area, and those trapped by Satan go on living under his power. Related to this, if you know a brother or sister in Christ who is entangled in this sin and refuses to repent, you must not save face by acting as if nothing is wrong. If he or she is an unrepentant Christian actively engaging in a homosexual lifestyle, you must withdraw fellowship, and he or she must be marked as fallen until they seek and pursue repentance and are then restored (cf. 1 Corinthians 5:9-13; 2 Thessalonians 3:14-15). A response is undoubtedly necessary and vital to discipleship, but there will be obstacles. Avery Foley offers direction:

> *"The attitude here is important. We do not rebuke or discipline others with a 'holier-than-thou' attitude or in a mean-spirited or disgusted fashion. But rather, in love and humility (2 Thessalonians 3:13–15), we use God's Word (2 Timothy 3:16) and biblical principles to expose sin and stir people toward repentance.*
>
> *Of course, they may not listen or may even get angry or offended. Discipline, church or otherwise, is unpleasant (Hebrews 12:11). Being told your actions, thoughts, or attitudes are sinful hurts, regardless of the sin. No one wants to be told they are wrong, but wise is the man or woman who heeds instruction and correction (Proverbs 1:7, 28:26), repents, and asks the Lord for forgiveness. But if someone gets offended, let it be over the truth, not over our attitude or tone."*[122]

One self-inflicted struggle is due to deeply ingrained biases towards homosexuality. Christians have often been guilty of condemning homosexuality while simultaneously being idle in preaching against illicit heterosexual relationships such as fornication or pornography use. Here is one Christian's evaluation of this disparity:

> *"Homosexuality is treated differently than other sins in the church. Most sexual sins and temptations are taboo subjects, but homosexuality is even more so. Christians are more inclined to react negatively toward a brother or sister struggling with homosexual temptation or sin than with a non-married, heterosexual couple struggling with sexual temptation or sin. I believe this disparity stems from the likelihood that most, if not all, Christians have struggled with heterosexual temptation at some point in life. This temptation, and the accompanying sin, is thus more relatable to the average believer. It is therefore easier to make excuses for the sin.*

---

[122] Foley, Avery. "Can the Church Embrace Homosexual Behavior in the Name of Love?" *Answers in Genesis,* 29 Mar. 2017, answersingenesis.org/sin/can-church-embrace-homosexual-behavior-in-name-of-love/.

Homosexual temptation and sin, by contrast, is less common, or at least less openly common. Since we are often most blind to the sins and temptations we ourselves experience, and often harshest with the ones we do not, Christians tend to have a much harsher view of homosexual sins and temptations than other sins."

As this brother highlights, all sexual activities outside of the proper marital relationship are against the law of God and should be unequivocally and equally condemned. Imbalance in this area can bring, and often has brought, reproach upon Christianity for hypocrisy. Christians must be vigilant not to put sin into manmade categories by which we become the judge, for there is only one Judge and Lawgiver (James 4:12). Sin is sin, and it all drives a wedge between man and God (Romans 6:23). Granted, many sins seem to be isolated, and the difference with respect to homosexuality tends to be that homosexuality seems more multi-faceted since it becomes a dominating lifestyle. Perhaps this is a reason for lack of ministry among those who struggle with homosexuality? Yet, is that complexity not found in other areas where we are more diligent in responding? Do not lies, fornication, stealing, slander, outbursts of anger, and other sins become patterns as well? Christians would do well here to apply the oft-memorized verse, *"For all have sinned and fallen short of the glory of God"* (Romans 3:23).

Another struggle for Christians is not as self-inflicted. LGBTQ+ advocates often accuse believers of infringing on the rights of homosexual couples to express themselves freely, claiming the infringement is a testimony to a Christian's lack of love. To this accusation, the Christian should not be silent, at least until first meeting an important responsibility. The Christian should agree that all people have the free will to do as they please; however, the Christian must also reinforce that if a person chooses to do something which the Lord expressly condemns, that person is no longer living according to God's law, but by his or her own direction (cf. Proverbs 14:12; Jeremiah 17:9). This decision puts a person into opposition to God, and all those in opposition to God will not be welcomed into the heavenly kingdom (cf. Proverbs 3:5-6; Matthew 7:21-23). If the individual is antagonistic or belligerent after sharing these truths, then one should dust their feet off and walk away. This response is in full-accord with Christ's vision for preaching and evangelism (Matthew 10:14; Acts 18:6). Recognize that in this process, enemies of the Lord will use hateful speech against you (Proverbs 13:19; Luke 16:15). You will be accused of hypocrisy. You will be charged with being unloving to your friend, family member, coworker, or acquaintance. Yet, the reality is that love can only act in truth (1 Corinthians 13:6). Christians are to consider themselves blessed when people revile them falsely in the name of Christ (Matthew 5:11; 1 Peter 3:13-

17; 4:14). Again, Avery Foley offers valuable advice:

"Will everyone respond positively to the gospel? Of course not. The gospel is a stumbling block and foolishness to those without the Spirit (1 Corinthians 1:23). Some will get angry, some will mock and jeer, others will be offended and maybe call you a homophobe or bigot. But others will want to hear more now or maybe down the road. Let them be offended by the gospel, not by our attitudes, tone of voice, or body language (John 6:60-69)."[123]

For Those Who Do Struggle with Homosexuality

For those Christians who struggle with homosexual temptation, you will have an added burden in resisting the flesh in this area. This may be your "cross to bear," but know that you need not bear it alone! As with all other areas of temptation, fellowship with believers, prayer, and accountability will help you practice self-control and self-denial (Matthew 16:24-27). By definition, followers of Christ submit themselves to all of Christ's teachings (Luke 6:46). If He taught that homosexuality violates God's will, then a believer must follow suit (1 John 2:3-6). While you may possess certain feelings and desires, you can, and you must, master them! (Romans 13:13-14) Victory is available in Christ; He will provide ways of escape for you in areas of temptation and has not—and will not—give you more than you can overcome through Him! (1 Corinthians 10:13; Philippians 4:13)

For encouragement in this battle, keep in mind the victories of those who resisted as you do, as well as those who struggle today alongside you! Among other places, 1 Corinthians 6:9-11 speaks of some Christians who had previously engaged in homosexual relations, but they had effectively turned the tide! Please also remember that your struggle does not make you inferior to or less forgivable than anyone else. Others' lack of temptation in this area does not make them superior or more forgivable. Instead, acknowledge that each person struggles and stumbles in many ways (James 3:2a). One Christian offers enabling and powerful advice for you in this regard:

"Temptation is not the same as sin. Even Jesus was tempted by Satan, and yet he was at all points pure and holy. The fact that you are tempted by homosexuality does not make you dirty, unclean, unworthy, or sinful. It is succumbing to the temptation, not the temptation itself, that is sinful. The fact that you struggle with homosexual temptation does not make you a

---

[123] Ibid.

sinner. Know this too, I will fight with you. All sin separates from God, and that includes mine. When I lie, I stand just as condemned as an individual who succumbs to homosexual temptation. The sin—whatever it may be—that we give in to condemns us. The blood of Christ equally cleanses both of us. So, while I may not suffer from the same temptation, I struggle against sin too. And that means we can both be there for each other and lift each other up in our joint struggle against sin, whatever form it takes."

Another Christian, who struggles with homosexual temptation, shares:

"There's not a silver bullet here. By the grace of God, I have a point of common ground here. I've never proclaimed it from the pulpit, but I have often in private conversations, with people struggling with sexual sin, confessed my own history of struggling with homosexuality. As with any other sin, the people struggling with homosexuality are actual human beings created in the image of God and listening is pivotal for those who want to help. For the one who struggles with homosexual temptation, it ultimately comes down to two things: 1) Do we find our primary identity in our sexual desires or in our relationship with Jesus Christ? and 2) Are we able to deny ourselves and sacrifice our sexual desires on Jesus' cross in order to follow Him into holiness?"

A Closing Thought

While our society may debate the so-called rights of individuals to engage in perverse and homosexual relations in marriage or otherwise for as long as God sees fit to suffer it, Christians can know beyond the shadow of a doubt what our Creator's stance is regarding homosexuality. God is indisputably opposed to homosexual relationships, whether they are called marriage or not. Such activities and behaviors transgress the ordinances He established and maintained from the beginning. Marriage is between one man and one woman, for life.

Our responsibility as Christians is like unto what we have toward other areas of sin. We need to know what the Bible teaches. We must not be indifferent to homosexuality but must instead expose it as the sin that it is and offer help to those who wrestle with it. Avoiding it or writing it off as merely a personal preference without lasting significance is harmful to souls and society. We need to passionately persuade others to accept God's truth.

You may suffer from temptations regarding same-sex desires. You may agonize with the question of rights and liberties for same-sex relationships. But you must master yourself and prove that which is the good and perfect and acceptable will of God (Romans 12:1-2). Whatever your struggle, I ask that you face it head-on and that you share your burden with other Christians so they may pray and strengthen you. You can, by God's grace, cease your sin.

Thought Questions

1) What emotions arose as you read this chapter and how did this information affect you?

_____

_____

2) Is homosexuality more shameful than other sexual sins like fornication? Why or why not?

_____

_____

3) Is there room for approving of governmental sanctions of homosexual unions and marriages, but spiritually disapproving of them?

_____

_____

4) Has God ever approved of homosexual relationships?

_____

_____

5) How is homosexuality abusive to the body?

_____

_____

6) Is homosexual temptation the same as homosexual sin?

_____

_____

7) What will you do this week to biblically respond to homosexuality?

_____

_____

_____

CHAPTER 10

Transgenderism

O ne of the most bewildering situations for a conscientious Christian is how to interact with a person who is transgender or is an advocate of transgenderism. The matter was rarely, if ever, encountered in the younger years of most people alive today. However, in the past couple of decades, the movement has certainly gained traction, to the point where we currently have 1.4 million individuals identifying as transgender in the United States, with 0.7% of adults ages 18-24 and 0.5% of adults 65 and older identifying as transgender.[124] Though these numbers are proportionately small, transgenderism exerts a profound voice in the world. We regularly hear terms like cisgender, transgender, transsexual, intersex, gender-fluid, non-conforming, preferred-gender-pronouns, etc. With this recent and widespread support for transgenderism, Christians need to equip themselves to the end that we may better understand this issue and better communicate with those who are themselves transgender, as well as those who advocate for transgenderism.

What Is Transgenderism?

Defining terms is often the best place to begin when dealing with an area that is unknown or uncomfortable. Unfortunately, defining terms with respect to transgenderism is complicated by various factors, including but not limited to: ever-shifting terminology, fluid definitions between organizations and individuals, and conflicting criteria put forth by the psychological community.

---

[124] Flores, Andrew R., et al. "How Many Adults Identify as Transgender in the United States?" *Williams Institute*, 27 Apr. 2020, https://www.williamsinstitute.law.ucla.edu/publications/trans-adults-united-states/.

The best way Christians can gain a working knowledge of transgenderism is by delineating three basic types of transgenderism. In doing so, this provides some direction in how to approach a transgender or pro-transgender person.

Biological Transgenderism

Biological transgenderism is a medical reality that Christians must not overlook. Due to chromosomal aberrations, physiological mutations, and biological deficiencies, a person's gender may not be as easy to establish when compared to non-affected others. Examples of these medical issues include:

- 5-alpha-reductase-deficiency
- 17-beta-hydroxysteroid dehydrogenase deficiency
- Congenital adrenal hyperplasia
- Androgen insensitivity syndrome
- Reifenstein syndrome

These sorts of disorders can result in three primary complications:

- Hermaphroditism, where both genitalia are fully occurring in a single person
- Female Pseudohermaphrodites with ovaries and some male genitalia, but no testes
- Male Pseudohermaphrodites with testes and some female genitalia, but no ovaries

Biological transgenderism presents an assortment of difficulties for the Christian. The fallout from sin has perverted something as singularly fundamental as sex determined by genetics. Yes, God created male and female (Genesis 1:27-28; 2:7, 8; 18-24; Matthew 19:4); sin however, has eroded that very fabric and introduced something that does not obviously conform to that dualistic nature. Can and should Christians condemn someone for something they have no control over? To what degree do accountability and responsibility get involved here? Such questions are indeed challenging, yet there is hope in this area for some direction and answers. Genetic research has advanced incredibly, allowing study and testing to deduce the nature of biological transgender issues. This effectively provides a framework by which a biologically transgender individual can move forward. This same framework can provide Christians with objective data to encourage proper gender conformity to that intended gender preceding the aberration. Of course, this entails immense financial cost and psychological strain. Are Christians prepared to offer assistance in these areas? They should be!

At the same time, it is important to note that these corruptions of gender are incredibly uncommon, weighing heavily on the use of previously-mentioned complications being used as a reliable pretext for any and all pro-transgender arguments. Research has consistently shown these sorts of issues only occur in 0.02% of people, and even less have full-fledged abnormalities.[125] This begs the question: should Christians develop a systematized spiritual understanding of something that so infrequently occurs and that is an obvious corruption to the human genome? Indeed, most examples of transgenderism do not result from biological phenomena. Dr. Paul McHugh, University Distinguished Professor of Psychiatry at Johns Hopkins Medical School, notes this by confidently asserting:

> "Although much is made of a rare 'intersex' individual, no evidence supports the claim that people such as Bruce Jenner have a biological source for their transgender assumptions. Plenty of evidence demonstrates that with him and most others, transgendering is a psychological rather than a biological matter."[126]

Psychological Transgenderism

According to Dr. McHugh's professional assessment, understanding psychological transgenderism may be the key to being adequately informed of others' struggles, being sufficiently equipped to share the gospel with transgender individuals, and caring for those who wrestle in this manner within the church of Jesus Christ.

A variety of psychological conditions and traumas result in complications regarding one's perception of his or her gender. Gender Identity Disorder (GID), now referred to as Gender Dysphoria (GD), is a mental disorder where cognitive dissonance is particularly attached to gender and a person's thoughts constantly provoke agitation and anxiety over his or her gender. Body Dysmorphic Disorder (BDD) is a mental disorder which causes a person to reject a part of their body so strongly that they inflict bodily harm on themselves, typically trying to sever the body part from their body altogether. Lesser or more acute degrees of this disorder, especially genitalia dysmorphia, can result

---

[125] "16 FACTS about Gender Dysphoria/Gender Identity Disorder." *Real Impact Help Center,* 26 Aug. 2019, https://www.intercom.help/real-impact/en/articles/3499539-16-facts-about-gender-dysphoria-gender-identity-disorder.

[126] McHugh, Paul. *Transgenderism: A Pathogenic Meme.* Public Discourse: The Journal of the Witherspoon Institute, 21 July 2020, https://www.thepublicdiscourse.com/2015/06/15145/.

in maladaptive psychological projections related to transgenderism. To these diagnostic conditions may be added the fallout of diverse physical and psychological traumas. These traumas, particularly sexual traumas, may produce a mental disorder that causes one to reject or hate the gender they were born with, or the gender the perpetrator does or does not have.

Psychological transgenderism accounts for far more cases than biological transgenderism. This becomes apparent when considering the specific demographic of teenagers, which has been the source of considerable study by psychologists. Among teens who claim to be transgender, 63% have previously been diagnosed with at least one mental health disorder or neurodevelopmental disability, and 96% engage in self-harm![127]

This abundance of cases, particularly with complications among teenagers, produces manifold difficulties for the Christian who seeks to be kind, provide adequate direction, and perhaps even overcome personal psychological challenges. The diagnostic criteria for these disorders are ever-changing due to social pressures towards acceptance.[128] This is seen in simple comparisons between the various *DSM* versions released by the APA and changes with the *ICD* versions released by the WHO. These difficulties and changing standards may cause us to provide exemptions and allowances where they should not be made, or conversely, not to extend compassion where compassion is desperately needed. The APA and WHO have introduced further confusion by creating an arbitrary distinction between "sex" (biologically-determined) and "gender" (what sex a person *feels* closer to). This sociological restructuring has caused much confusion, consternation, and even suicide or death due to lack of clarity regarding gender. Students of behavioral science, medical professionals tending to their patients, and blossoming young people are among the most seriously affected.

Social Transgenderism

With the two aforementioned categories, responsibility and accountability are not as easy to determine. A third category—social transgenderism—can be more objectively determined, but first, we must understand whence social transgenderism has arisen.

For generations, moral relativism has run amuck in every level of society.

---

[127] Sochor, Andy. *Transgenderism (Season 13, Episode 4).* 28 May 2019. https://www.plainbibleteaching.com/podcast/transgenderism-season-13-episode-4/. Refer also to the DSM-5.

[128] Belluck, Pam. "W.H.O. Weighs Dropping Transgender Identity from List of Mental Disorders." *The New York Times,* The New York Times, 26 July 2016, https://www.nytimes.com/2016/07/27/health/who-transgender-medical-disorder.html.

Truth is seen as relative and in the eye of the beholder. Not even the field of genetics has eluded being detrimentally affected by this widespread, nonsensical, and self-defeating philosophical commitment. Flagrant misunderstandings of gender roles have further amplified this crucial error. For example, the simple ability to perform a traditionally gender-specific task has caused entire societies to throw out gender conceptions altogether, refusing to consider quality of performance, biological and psychological make-up, after-effects of performing such tasks, etc. Beware the conflation of ability with responsibility!

Related to gender role understanding and acceptance, all should be careful to recognize that adolescents may, and often do, go through a stage where they wonder about their gender. Instructively, the *DSM-5* even admits that 98% of gender-confused boys and 88% of gender-confused girls accept their biological sex after puberty without any counseling! Sadly though, we are seeing massive spikes in transgender identification and gender-reassignment surgery among young people especially, and many are accelerating this downward spiral. Research out of Brown University suggests that this uptick may represent the development of a maladaptive coping mechanism similar to an eating disorder.[129] Journalist Abigail Shrier writes,

> *"Between 2016 and 2017, the number of females seeking gender surgery quadrupled in the United States. Thousands of teen girls across the Western world are not only self-diagnosing with a real dysphoric condition they likely do not have; in many cases, they are obtaining hormones and surgeries following the most cursory diagnostic processes. Schoolteachers, therapists, doctors, surgeons, and medical-accreditation organizations are all rubber-stamping these transitions, often out of fear that doing otherwise will be reported as a sign of 'transphobia'—despite growing evidence that most young people who present as trans will eventually desist, and so these interventions will do more harm than good.*
>
> *The notion that this sudden wave of transitioning among teens is a worrying, ideologically driven phenomenon is hardly a fringe view. Indeed, outside of Twitter, Reddit, Tumblr, and college campuses, it is a view held by a majority of Americans. There is nothing hateful in suggesting that most teenagers are not in a good position to approve irreversible alterations to their bodies, particularly if they are suffering from trauma, OCD, depres-*

---

[129] Littman L (2018) Parent reports of adolescents and young adults perceived to show signs of a rapid onset of gender dysphoria. PLoS ONE 13(8): e0202330. https://doi.org/10.1371/journal.pone.0202330.

sion, or any of the other mental-health problems that are comorbid with expressions of dysphoria. And yet, here we are.

While gender dysphoria has always been vanishingly rare among females, social contagion has not. These are the same high-anxiety, depressive (mostly white) girls who, in previous decades, fell prey to anorexia and bulimia or multiple personality disorder. Now it's gender dysphoria, sometimes along with some or all of those other conditions. Parents are being presented with the seductive idea of transition as a utopian cure-all."[130]

Societal pressures regarding guilt and entitlement also play a role here. Self-labeling victimization is wildly in-vogue. What greater attention-getter could one have than to identify as something different than their biology? Such interdependent factors result in two sides of the same coin: conformism to progressive conceptions of gender fluidity or non-conformism to traditional, biological, and spiritual conceptions of gender.

With social transgenderism, there are also difficulties facing the Christian. The discomfort with this category comes primarily with the accountability factor being higher here than with psychological or biological issues. This is a deliberate, significant choice that amounts to intentional and consistent self-deception and self-misrepresentation. Another side of this is social pressures potentially leading to psychological malfunction, so how and where do we draw a line? Transgender advocates ignite political and governmental change, stigmatizing those who dissent. They become a spiritually evil and totalitarian source of tyranny against conscientious Christians and the church.[131] Can we draw a line? Again, Dr. Paul McHugh offers impassioned insight:

"The idea that one's sex is fluid and a matter open to choice runs unquestioned through our culture and is reflected everywhere in the media, the

---

[130] Shrier, Abigail. "Gender Activists Are Trying to Cancel My Book. Why Is Silicon Valley Helping Them?" *Quillette*, 19 Nov. 2020, https://www.quillette.com/2020/11/07/gender-activists-are-trying-to-cancel-my-book-why-is-silicon-valley-helping-them/. Abigail Shrier's book, *Irreversible Damage: The Transgender Craze Seducing Our Daughters*, is worth reading as well.

[131] For further discussion see: Roberts, Rebekah. "Transgenderism Is Leading Us towards Totalitarianism: The Van Maren Show Episode 9." *LifeSiteNews*, 20 Mar. 2019, www.lifesitenews.com/news/transgenderism-is-leading-us-towards-totalitarianism-the-van-maren-show-episode-9. Also, Prager, Dennis. "Meanwhile, This Is What LGBTQ Organizations Are Doing to Society." *Townhall*, 13 Aug. 2019, http://www.townhall.com/columnists/dennisprager/2019/08/13/meanwhile-this-is-what-lgbtq-organizations-are-doing-to-society-n2551561.

theater, the classroom, and in many medical clinics. It has taken on cult-like features: its own special lingo, internet chat rooms providing slick-answers to new recruits, and clubs for easy access to dresses and styles supporting the sex change. It is doing much damage to families, adolescents, and children and should be confronted as an opinion without biological foundation wherever it emerges. But gird up your loins if you would confront this matter. Hell hath no fury like a vested interest masquerading as a moral principle."[132]

The Moral, Societal, and Spiritual Fallout of Transgenderism

Already we have seen glimpses of the fallout of transgenderism. To this may be added clear-cut measures of the sinfulness of sin (cf. Romans 7:11-13) and the ugliness that sin's corruption of gender has incited.

Transgenderism and advocacy for transgenderism often come from and result in physical, psychological, and emotional abuse. As seen in the sources cited above, social and psychological transgenderism have a high correlation with initial trauma and with perpetuating trauma for others. This is particularly true of children and adolescents. The American College of Pediatricians released a statement that the movement to indoctrinate children with the idea that they can pick their gender is a substantial form of child abuse.[133] Truthfully, medically-enabled and socially-pressured transition surgeries are causing the mutilation of children, adolescents, and adults. Walt Heyer has an entire website dedicated to the details and accounts of numerous issues resulting from transgenderism, especially how most survivors feel overlooked, neglected, and betrayed by society over their traumas.[134] One compelling point from this compendium of resources is the 40% suicide rate post-transition surgery.[135] He gives one specific account of a teenager named Nathaniel who regretted the sex change he was pressured into by family, friends, and medical professionals. Nathaniel sadly describes his experience post-surgery:

---

[132] McHugh, Paul. *Transgenderism: A Pathogenic Meme*. Public Discourse: The Journal of the Witherspoon Institute, 21 July 2020, www.thepublicdiscourse.com/2015/06/15145/.

[133] An online PDF of this statement may be read at: https://acpeds.org/assets/imported/9.14.17-Gender-Ideology-Harms-Children_updated-MC.pdf.

[134] https://sexchangeregret.com/

[135] One of many studies on this significant increase in suicide rates among post-transition surgery patients was done at the Department of Clinical Neuroscience in Stockholm, Sweden. Researchers found a drastically higher general morbidity rate after surgery and a rate of suicide 20x higher than patient's peers.

"Now that I'm all healed from the surgeries, I regret them. The result of the bottom surgery looks like a Frankenstein hack job at best, and that got me thinking critically about myself. I had turned myself into a plastic-surgery facsimile of a woman, but I knew I still wasn't one. I became (and to an extent, still feel) deeply depressed."

Heyer also has a book entitled *Trans Life Survivors*, where he shares the stories of thirty people who regret their sex changes. Another noteworthy case was the first "legally non-binary person" in the United States named Jamie Shupe, who now has de-transitioned. He acknowledges pressures put on him, a history of sexual and physical abuse, and PTSD as a soldier. He says, *"My psyche is eternally scarred, and I've got a host of health issues from the grand medical experiment."* Introducing more debate about a trait as fundamentally determined as gender clearly causes more strain on human beings' mental faculties. Two biologists wrote a sharp critique regarding this effect of social pressure, stating:

"Biologists and medical professionals need to stand up for the empirical reality of biological sex. When authoritative institutions ignore or deny empirical fact in the name of social accommodation, it is an egregious betrayal to the scientific community they represent, and it is dangerously harmful to those most vulnerable."[136]

Add to these clearly abusive and psychological traumas the marked increase in human trafficking, divorce, homosexuality, marital strain, polygamy, and other issues, and transgenderism cannot simply be labeled a matter of individual choice devoid of negative consequence. Furthermore, consider the implications and debates that have arisen in the medical field regarding treatment protocols, bathrooms, economic issues, politicking, controversies in sports with transgender athletes[137], Drag Queen Story Hour, and dilemmas in the church, and we can obviously see the deleterious effects of transgenderism.

---

[136] Wright, Collin M., and Emma N. Hilton. "The Dangerous Denial of Sex." *The Wall Street Journal*, Dow Jones & Company, 13 Feb. 2020, www.wsj.com/articles/the-dangerous-denial-of-sex-11581638089.

[137] E.g., Stanescu, Bianca. "Transgender Athletes Don't Belong in Girls' Sports. Let My Daughter Compete Fairly." *USA Today*, 19 June 2020, https://usatoday.com/story/opinion/2020/06/19/transgender-athletes-robbing-girls-chance-win-sports-column/4856486002/.

What Does the Bible Have to Say About Transgenderism?

Does the Bible address transgenderism? Few passages speak on transgenderism explicitly, yet this dearth is supplemented with passages offering implicit principles.

At a foundational level, the Bible explicitly affirms divinely designed and respected binary gender:

> "*Then God said, 'Let Us make man in Our image, according to Our likeness; and let them rule over the fish of the sea and over the birds of the sky and over the cattle and over all the earth, and over every creeping thing that creeps on the earth.' God created man in His own image, in the image of God He created him; male and female He created them.*" (Genesis 1:26-27)

> "*Then the Lord God formed man of dust from the ground, and breathed into his nostrils the breath of life; and man became a living being...Then the Lord God said, 'It is not good for the man to be alone; I will make him a helper suitable for him.' Out of the ground the Lord God formed every beast of the field and every bird of the sky, and brought them to the man to see what he would call them; and whatever the man called a living creature, that was its name. The man gave names to all the cattle, and to the birds of the sky, and to every beast of the field, but for Adam there was not found a helper suitable for him. So the Lord God caused a deep sleep to fall upon the man, and he slept; then He took one of his ribs and closed up the flesh at that place. The Lord God fashioned into a woman the rib which He had taken from the man, and brought her to the man. The man said,*

> '*This is now bone of my bones,*
> *And flesh of my flesh;*
> *She shall be called Woman,*
> *Because she was taken out of Man.'*

> *For this reason a man shall leave his father and his mother, and be joined to his wife; and they shall become one flesh. And the man and his wife were both naked and were not ashamed.*" (Genesis 2:7, 18-25)

> "*And He answered and said, 'Have you not read that He who created them from the beginning made them male and female?'*" (Matthew 19:4)

This dualism is not inconsequential as it carries unique design and gender role differences that God commands to be respected and observed:

"In the same way, you wives, be submissive to your own husbands so that even if any of them are disobedient to the word, they may be won without a word by the behavior of their wives, as they observe your chaste and respectful behavior. Your adornment must not be merely external—braiding the hair, and wearing gold jewelry, or putting on dresses; but let it be the hidden person of the heart, with the imperishable quality of a gentle and quiet spirit, which is precious in the sight of God. For in this way in former times the holy women also, who hoped in God, used to adorn themselves, being submissive to their own husbands; just as Sarah obeyed Abraham, calling him lord, and you have become her children if you do what is right without being frightened by any fear. You husbands in the same way, live with your wives in an understanding way, as with someone weaker, since she is a woman; and show her honor as a fellow heir of the grace of life, so that your prayers will not be hindered." (1 Peter 3:1-7; cf. Ephesians 5:22-33; Titus 2:3-8)

"Likewise, I want women to adorn themselves with proper clothing, modestly and discreetly, not with braided hair and gold or pearls or costly garments, but rather by means of good works, as is proper for women making a claim to godliness. A woman must quietly receive instruction with entire submissiveness. But I do not allow a woman to teach or exercise authority over a man, but to remain quiet. For it was Adam who was first created, and then Eve. And it was not Adam who was deceived, but the woman being deceived, fell into transgression. But women will be preserved through the bearing of children if they continue in faith and love and sanctity with self-restraint." (1 Timothy 2:9-15; cf. 1 Corinthians 11:1-16; 14:34-35)

These differences do not make one gender more superior than the other concerning merit or salvation (Galatians 3:28). Indeed, males and females are complementary to one another and equal in the sight of God. However, the Bible lays out binary gender, and scientific and genetic research confirms there are thousands of gender differences.[138] As such, the Bible makes clear that all should make an effort to distinguish and display their gender in a clear, mod-

---

[138] Bergman, Jerry. "Male-Female Differences Supported by Scripture and Science." *The Institute for Creation Research*, 2018, www.icr.org/article/male-female-differences-supported.

est manner (cf. 1 Corinthians 11:1-16; Deuteronomy 22:5; Romans 1:24-27). The Bible altogether condemns deception and misrepresentation, including in the area of gender (Romans 1:28-32; Ephesians 4:25; Revelation 21:8). Likewise, the Bible affirms the value of a male and female relationship in marriage (Genesis 2:24) and unequivocally condemns perversions of this relationship, including those pursuing transgenderism (Hebrews 13:4; 1 Thessalonians 4:3-8; 1 Corinthians 6:9-11; Romans 1:24-27).

These considerations granted, the Bible also reveals that the Fall has brought catastrophic effects (Genesis 3:16-19, 23-24; Job 14:1-2; Romans 8:19-23). The unavoidable reality is that these effects are often expressed in a variety of genetic, biological, behavioral, and mental disorders. Of course, a time will come when internal forms of dissonance will all pass away (cf. Revelation 21:4), but people do face coping and warring with these issues now. So, how can Christians then respectfully and effectively address the matter of transgenderism?

How Can Christians Effectively Address Transgenderism?

The diligent Christian will actively work to be prepared to address the various challenges of transgenderism inside and outside the church. This will serve as a hallmark of the Christian apologetic during the present worldview climate. To that end, I offer a handful of recommendations and encouragements.

First, it is okay to be uncomfortable around transgender persons and advocates of transgenderism. The perversion of binary gender, whether intentionally or as a byproduct of sin, is unnatural. As such, discomfort is a testament to abhorring what is evil and clinging to what is good (Amos 5:15; Romans 12:9). Transgenderism is not the biological rule. It is atypical from what would, under normal considerations, be expected. Moreover, misrepresentation and deception are both sins. If these two factors are at play, then sin is directly at play. Any and all sin should cause revulsion.

Despite appropriate discomfort, do not be afraid or intimidated to start a conversation. We can seriously doubt that Jesus felt no qualms in the presence of any sinner; yet, He saw fit to engage in discussions that challenged their sins and the tragic effects of evil in the world. There is no room for timidity or fear of reprisal in the life of a devoted servant of Christ (Matthew 10:32-33; 2 Timothy 1:7). Love and compassion reach outward; fear and apathy retreat inward. These individuals can talk; they are not alien, though they may be alien sinners! They have the God-given ability to communicate, and we have a responsibility to reach all who are in the world. Jesus came to seek and to save sinners (Matthew 20:28; Luke 19:10). Jesus came to heal infirmities (Luke 5:31). If those goals are not our goals, we are not being transformed by the renewing of our minds; we are being conformed to the world (Romans 12:1-2).

In order to effectively gain ground in a conversation, it is imperative that the Christian gain as much information as possible about the type of transgenderism with which one is dealing. Different types of transgenderism will require different tactics. In the matter of biological and psychological transgenderism, what accountability can you attribute? Sin has caused a genetically and psychologically toxic result. What degree of accountability will God give? Until you can answer these and similar questions at least somewhat definitively, be careful about imposing a standard, lest it be self-created. These individuals need compassion and sympathy first and foremost. Regarding social transgenderism, a firmer obligation must be met. Willful repudiation of God's holy and righteous intent for males and females requires a robust, more overt response.

With any divinely-approved effort at apologetics, conversation must be in season and gracious, respectful, kind, and loving (Romans 12:16; Colossians 3:12-14; 4:5-6; 2 Timothy 2:14-26). Do not unnecessarily cause offense, as this will give a ground of accusation against Christianity and also hurt people who are in need of love. You represent your Lord; act as He would act. Be kind and respectful. This person is created in the image of God, and the Spirit produces kindness in His people (Galatians 5:22-23). If you are unkind, whose fruit are you bearing? Certainly not His! You can love without supporting someone's actions. Make sure to be clear that your love for them is seen in your willingness to have a conversation and getting to know and understand them. If you did not care, you would not bother! If you can keep these factors in mind, you have done your duty, regardless of the response it elicits.

Throughout your efforts, be firm in your convictions. Relativity and spinelessness have vastly contributed to what we face today. The use of names or preferred pronouns you know to be clear perversions of truth will put you under condemnation. Words have meaning, and the improper use of words will be held against you in God's court (Matthew 12:33-37). This is especially true in the workplace, where LGBTQ+ entities have successfully created a hostile work environment for employees. Regardless of what a company states, you have the legal right to request a reasonable accommodation, notably one for your religion. The same legislation and civil rights regulations that transgender advocates appeal to are the same guidelines supporting your religious freedom. Even so, you will have to use impeccable wisdom in how you ask questions and interact with transgender individuals (cf. Matthew 10:16; James 1:5). You will have to respect your conscience in a way that may end up getting you fired. In that case, the question will be: Do you love your job more than you love the command of the Lord?

A Closing Thought

There is a large degree to which this chapter will not have addressed all of your questions. However, the Christian's goal is to see with the eyes of Jesus, to take a stand where a stand needs to be taken, and to love our fellow brothers and sisters in mankind. Christians have responsibilities vis-à-vis transgenderism. Do not stick your head in the sand. Do not say what should not be said. Do not do what should not be done. Do not approve where approval is not warranted. Do all things with love and respect. Do be sympathetic and compassionate. Do desire salvation for everyone. May God grant us all wisdom and love, and may we be vessels of His love and thoughtfulness.

Thought Questions

1) What emotions arose as you read this chapter and how did this information affect you?

_____

_____

2) Why do you think transgenderism seems stranger than other perversions?

_____

_____

3) What are the different types of transgenderism and why is it important for Christians especially to understand their differences?

_____

_____

4) What is complementarianism and what does it have to do with gender?

_____

_____

5) What are some gender differences that the Bible speaks about? How can these be better recognized and celebrated?

_____

_____

6) How important is positive teaching regarding godly gender roles in young people?

_____

_____

7) Armed with a biblical worldview, what will you do this week to positively influence society's notions of gender?

_____

_____

CHAPTER 11

Racism

Consider your experiences with racism, its history in our country, and its presence and impact today. Do you feel like racism is more prevalent than ever, or at least that the cultural discussion regarding racism is as fiery as ever? Perhaps you strongly feel that more discussion is needed. You may even believe that racism is nowhere near the issue that it was in previous generations. Many opinions circulate, and one's views come out of diverse experiences. In humbly pooling our thoughts with others of different understandings, we can get a more accurate appreciation for what areas have developed and what areas still need development. In cooperation, we can move forward arm-in-arm and have productive discussions regarding the sins of racism and prejudice.

Racism as a Psychosocial Issue

Racism is currently at the forefront of societal discussion, as it should be! Part of this is genuine and authentic in motivation, as people strive for equal treatment, an end to hostilities, and reasonable reparations for past abuses. Another side of this is not so altruistic. For this corrupt side, racism is a political pawn by those with little to no interest in injustices. The former motivations are praiseworthy, and the latter are condemnable. Both of these desires have been displayed at different times and in different ways in media coverage. News outlets, in particular, have done this while spotlighting a selection of recent cases involving police brutality, injustices, and riots that have broken out in response to these incidents. The list of these cases includes, but is not limited to: Trayvon Martin, Eric Garner, Michael Brown, Akai Gurley, Tamir Rice, Freddie Gray, Philando Castile, Stephon Clark, Botham Jean, Atatiana Jefferson, Breonna Taylor, Ahmaud Arbery, George Floyd, and others. In some of these cases, claims of racial injustice were either validated immediately or over time, and partial or full justice was administered. In other instances, racial motivations have not been validated, and cries of injustice have continued, whether examination of each case's factors has, or has not, occurred.

The recently enhanced interest in race issues should not cause one to believe that these troubles are new. Since the Fall of Eden, racism has been a perpetual issue within every nation under heaven. Look to the annals of history, and nearly all people groups have committed atrocities against others. The majority of the discussion today is devoted to two tragic areas of sin: barbaric racism at the foundations of American history and systemic racism today, both dealing with racism primarily based on skin color. These two aspects of the discussion are helpful to differentiate and not to equivocate anachronistically. In addition to conversations regarding these two issues, we should be careful not to overlook other historical examples of racism and prejudice. Genocide and racism have existed for Jews, Native Americans, Latinx, Italians, the Irish, the Japanese, and a host of other peoples, and that is just in the last century! Consider also the historical and present tribal wars of Africa and South America, racism against Ashkenazi Jews, Romani, gypsies, and other people groups. It quickly becomes apparent that prejudicial problems occur on many levels and in many places. This acknowledgment is not to diminish any single example, but rather illustrate the magnitude of the problem of racism.

Again, this is not merely a problem outside in the world; racism is a problem facing the church as well. Here is one story of racism experienced in the life of a Christian from Manila, who now lives with his family in the United States:

"My experience with racism might be different from others. I had not given much thought on the prevalence of racism in America until I came face to face with it at the graduation ceremony of my oldest daughter in 2018. I sat there with my wife, children, son-in-law, and grandchildren looking forward to celebrating my daughter's graduation from phlebotomy school. In front of us, there was a group of Caucasian women, some middle-aged and others older. As I sat there with my family, joyfully talking with them, as many around us were also doing, one of the women in front of us turned her head, angrily looking just at me and said 'Shut your mouth!' I was surprised and in shock! What did I do to them that made them so angry? I looked at my son-in-law, a Caucasian police officer, and I saw his face was also completely in shock. I did not know what to do or say. After graduation, while we were taking pictures outside the building, my son-in-law came to me and said 'What happened back there?' I said, 'I have no idea! I didn't know what I did, I was just talking to you and all of the

sudden they look just at me and tell me to shut up!' My son-in-law shared with me that their motivations were possibly prejudicial because of my appearance and accent. It was like the scales fell from my eyes. I began to recognize that I had experienced similar forms of aggression and bias in my previous workplaces! Every day from that moment I always thought of this experience. I have since researched and wondered about the biological response that may be connected to racial thoughts. Spiritually, I believe that racism is rooted in anger and pride. These are a disease upon the world that often gets expressed in racist thoughts, behaviors, and actions. We must all be careful about pride and anger and refuse to give them a place in our hearts. If we can do that and pay attention to the warnings that the Word of God gives about them, we can fight racism in this world."

Another brother in Christ shares his experience:

"Racism is one of those cultures/practices that push you around or into a corner at times, forcing you to choose to cope with some aspect of it. You may not like certain people because of their skin color or based on hearsay. Some also choose a diluted version of racism by expressing it through a form of justification, meaning that one tries to justify racist thoughts and behaviors by labeling others as already being racially hostile toward them. Racism has a way of hiding or justifying itself in the mind of the racist.

When I was an ironworker, I often experienced racism in the form of sarcasm, jokes, plain writings on the porta-potty walls, lack of opportunities, etc. I talked with a Caucasian payroll manager for a company I contracted with once who, in short, told me that she feared being in the presence of black people up until adulthood because she had been shown all her childhood by the news, parents, and other media that blacks were a dangerous people. I asked her, 'Since I've known you in three years working around here, have I ever threatened or disrespected you? Have I not always been kind to you? Are we not having an intelligent and peaceful discussion?'

I've even experienced racism in the church by both black and white members. When I attended an institutional church in the past, I was denied the opportunity of being funded for preaching school because the black preacher didn't like the idea of me attending a predominantly white school. I was also denied preaching spots at a predominantly Caucasian congregation, even when they needed someone to preach and had no one on schedule to do so. At one point, racism caused me to feel the need to identify as so many others identified me.

In order to change these behaviors in the church, I think that it would be beneficial to have an in-depth study on human origin from a biblical perspective, on understanding how the idea/practice of racism originated, and on understanding preconceptions and stereotypes about different races. As we teach on the subject, we could make handouts with intimate questions to see how people really feel about racism and their perspective or experiences. The responses could be read anonymously with opportunity for discussion. I think this would be a way for people's emotions and true feelings to be revealed and possibly developed, corrected, or nurtured. A great starter question would be to ask, 'Do we think it's important to seriously discuss racism?' Oftentimes, we don't want to engage in the more challenging battles, but as Christians, we have to fight every battle, not just the ones we feel that we can easily win and move past. But it first has to be a study that is deemed important enough to cover. I also think we could challenge ourselves to talk with a couple of individuals one-on-one outside of the class regarding the subject."

Understanding Terminology in Racism Discussions

In any emotionally-charged discussion, there is danger stemming from two common problems. The first problem is using terminology in different ways than someone with an alternative viewpoint. Unaddressed, this inevitably leads to speaking past one another. How important it is to agree on the definitions of terminology before a conversation becomes heated! The second problem is ignorance, or total denial, of philosophical commitments and presuppositions. When these assumptions continue unrecognized and unchallenged, narrow-mindedness can cause one to withdraw into an echo chamber. As one shouts grievances and disagreements, their lack of openness to other viewpoints closes them off from engaging others constructively. Complementarity of thought is foregone, lines are drawn, and alliances form without adequate consideration of alternative views. In an effort to rise above both of these issues, let's define several key terms in the discussion of race and offer brief thoughts on the pros and cons of each idea.[139] Necessarily, this will be cursory and is merely one resource to facilitate understanding. Additionally, please keep in mind that there is variability in terminology that depends on a

---

[139] Definitions of these terms are taken from Project Change's "The Power of Words." Originally produced for Project Change Lessons Learned II, also included in *A Community Builder's Toolkit* – both produced by Project Change and the Center for Assessment and Policy Development with some modification by RacialEquityTools.org.

variety of conditions, including the intended audience's geographic location, age, generation, and political orientation.

Various terms describe varying types of racism. *Individual racism* refers to beliefs, attitudes, and actions of individuals that support or perpetuate discrimination, whether deliberate or in ignorance. Examples might include telling racist jokes or avoiding interaction with others who differ in culture or skin tone. In the case of unknowing expressions of this form of racism, the actions are often connected to *implicit bias*, which refers to negative associations that people unknowingly hold. These may be measured by an assessment known as the Implicit Association Test (IAT). Openly expressed individual racism is known as *interpersonal racism,* in which public expressions of prejudice, hate, bias, or bigotry between individuals occur. *Cultural racism* is a phrase used to convey what a culture racially deems appropriate, beautiful, and praiseworthy in advertisement, education, policies, laws, and entertainment. *Systemic racism,* or *Structural racism,* refers to the cumulative reinforcing norms and institutions in a population that adversely impact certain people groups. Cited examples typically include lower life expectancy for those who face higher exposure rates to environmental toxins, dangerous jobs, higher stress, worse healthcare coverage, or low-quality housing stock. *Institutional racism* refers to policies that disproportionately affect *emerging majorities* (formerly known as minorities). Examples might include red-lining (formally outlawed over 50 years ago) and the concentration of sanitation facilities in certain neighborhoods instead of others. *Internalized racism* refers to the acceptance of racial ideas by a victim of discrimination in a way that perpetuates racism toward their own people group. Examples might include participation in rewards systems for those of color who support initiatives against people of color, or refusing resources allocated toward one group based on a commitment to allocate those funds to everyone altogether. Generally speaking, the advantages these terms offer is that they highlight the multiple levels where racism can, and often does, occur, and they also provide specific instances that can be objectively measured by those who might deny racism as a reality in the present day. The downside of such terminology is that it often overgeneralizes matters, oversimplifying all of the factors that go into levels of decision-making, focusing on racism as an exclusive, or near-exclusive, motivation when this may not always be the case. Moreover, rather than employing gestalt unity to overcome these issues, identity politics are brought in, widening the chasms already carved out by racism.

As a result of these cited examples of racism, several important conversations tend to arise. In recent years, repeated volleys have debated such topics as equity versus equality, reparations, privilege, and microaggressions. *Equity* refers to when two or more people groups are standing on proportionately equal footing. This is illustrated in devoting lesser or greater resources to different communities based on availabilities or shortages. In contrast, *equality* refers to treating everyone the same by giving everyone access to the same opportunities. Equity would mean the distribution of 150 books across a group of 30 students, taking into consideration the current availability of books in the homes of those students. Equality would be simply giving five books to each student, whether they already have books or not. *Reparations* refers to making immediate and/or long-term restitution for racially motivated grievances. The chief positive to this idea is that it seeks, at least in claim, to give an equal voice and position to all in the form of redress to victims. The primary downside of this term's usage is that appropriate reparation can be hard to measure and can lead to faulty conceptions of entitlement, perpetuating issues across generations. The use of the term *privilege* tends to refer to those advantages of one people group over another based on systemic racism. The upside to this is that it attempts to acknowledge inequities. The downside of this is the subjectivity with which it is applied, often making gross overgeneralizations or projecting the guilt of past grievances upon those who had little, if any, part in those actual grievances. In other words, the sins of the father are projected onto the sons and daughters, bypassing individual responsibility and accountability to make reparations, thus failing to address the actual case of racism itself and instead creating new issues and aggressions (cf. Deuteronomy 24:16; Ezekiel 18:20). *Microaggressions* tend to refer to the everyday, nonverbal slights, snubs, and insults, whether intentional or unintentional, that communicate hostile, derogatory, or negative messages to target persons. The upside of this terminology is that it attempts to address individual racism that resides in the heart of the racist. The downside is that it often stereotypes and superficially judges according to appearance (cf. John 7:24).

Due to differing philosophies on causative issues in racism, differing theories, viewpoints, and responses have arisen. A few key points in this area are beneficial to define. *Critical Race Theory* claims to set many of the issues of racism within a broader framework of understanding, including economics, history, feelings and the unconscious, equality theory, legal reasoning, Enlightenment rationalism, and principles of constitutional law. The alleged benefit of this theory is that a broad network of thought tends to provide a surer foundation. Where this theory falls short is that it makes dangerous and divisive assumptions by marginalizing and isolating people groups further. *Racial Identity Development Theory* claims to discuss how people of different racial groups form their particular self-concept. *Cancel culture* is a cultural movement in which a person is ostracized for doing or saying something considered offensive or objectionable. Cancel culture has primarily taken on notoriety in discussions regarding free speech and censorship, particularly in the realms of entertainment and social media. One final term, *antiracism*, refers to not only avoiding racial behaviors but actively trying to altogether dismantle it.

Even with consensus on definitions, several additional roadblocks can inhibit meaningful discussion. These obstacles include confirmation bias and overgeneralization, media misrepresentation and sensationalism, projectionism, defeatism, and equivocation, amongst other issues. As always, self-control, patience, sincerity, honesty, humility, and balance will win the day. One writer eloquently conveys this effectiveness by saying:

> *"Neither the warmonger nor the pious bystander is a peacemaker. Those too heavenly or high-minded to soil their ceremonial garb by touching common ground and advocating for their neighbors aren't peacemakers. Moreover, those who exploit prayer as a copout to neglect the issues God has placed in their sphere of influence aren't peacemakers either. Their silence condones a conflicted state of affairs and makes them keepers of a riotous status quo.*
>
> *Peacemakers will engage the conflicts necessary to achieve racial justice, but they won't be carried away by the moment. In the tensest times, they'll watch their words, acknowledge their opponent's human dignity, and guard their hearts from tribalism. They'll address today's bleak situation with tenacity and moral imagination, rather than cynicism. This means peacemakers will seek out approaches that transcend the inadequate options offered by ideological conservatives and progressives. They won't run from reality, but they'll attempt to reach higher ground rather than settling for the base terrain immediately available."*[140]

Biblical Solutions for Racism

Spiritual Commonality in the Image of God

The Bible describes the creation of all people in the image of God. Genesis 1:26-27 reads,

> *"Then God said, 'Let Us make man in Our image, according to Our likeness; and let them rule over the fish of the sea and over the birds of the sky*

---

[140] Giboney, Justin. "Only Biblical Peacemaking Resolves Racial and Political Injustice." *ChristianityToday.com*, Christianity Today, 15 Jan. 2021, www.christianitytoday.com/ct/2021/january-web-only/only-biblical-peacemaking-resolves-racial-and-political-inj.html.

*and over the cattle and over all the earth, and over every creeping thing
that creeps on the earth.' God created man in His own image, in the image
of God He created him; male and female He created them."*

This fingerprint of God upon the soul of humanity establishes an equal
spiritual value among all people for all time. This special creation rules out any
rational basis for racism. In contrast, naturalistic evolution denies the equality of all people and has been the staging ground for discrimination through
the ages. Charles Darwin's two most notable works—*The Origin of Species by
Means of Natural Selection or the Preservation of Favored Races in the Struggle
for Life* and *The Descent of Man and Selection in Relation to Sex*—reflect evolution's racist division into superior and inferior races. Adolf Hitler, Margaret
Sanger, and others cited these works and this theory as justification for the
extermination of minorities, ethnic groups, and those with disabilities.[141][142] As
the late Harvard professor Stephen Jay Gould famously concluded, *"Biological
arguments for racism may have been common before 1859 [the year Darwin's On
the Origin of Species was published, EP], but they increased by orders of magnitude following the acceptance of evolutionary theory."*[143]

Consider two key examples that beautifully reflect humanity's spiritual
equivalence in the scriptural account of creation. One illustration is in the
Godhead—the Father, the Son, and the Holy Spirit—Who each equally share
the fullness of deity. God's very nature poignantly exemplifies cooperation and
equality. Another way this equality of spiritual essence is illustrated is in the
fact that the New Testament makes clear that all people have one heavenly
Father (Matthew 23:9; Ephesians 4:6) and one beloved Brother, Jesus Christ

---

[141] For the advantages of creationism over naturalistic evolution and the racist ideologies related to the latter, see: Lyons, Eric, and Kyle Butt. *Darwin, Evolution, and Racism.* www.apologeticspress.org/APContent.aspx?category+9&article=2724. Also, Parker, Eric. *Behold the Builder: Scientific Evidences for the Biblical God.* One Stone, 2019.

[142] Margaret Sanger, the progenitrix of Planned Parenthood, candidly said of her efforts that, *"We do not want word to go out that we want to exterminate the Negro population"* (Margaret Sanger, Letter to Dr. C.J. Gamble in 1939). One former abortion worker recently confirms this is an ongoing goal by stating: *"As many abortion clinics are, the one I worked at was strategically placed in a very poor and ethnically diverse section of the city. In fact, more than 70 percent of Planned Parenthood facilities are located in minority neighborhoods. The majority of our patients were Hispanic or African Americans, and many of them spoke very little English."* (Johnson, Abby, and Kristin Detrow. *The Walls Are Talking: Former Abortion Clinic Workers Tell Their Stories.* Ignatius Press, 2018, 129).

[143] Mitchell, Tommy. "How Many Races Did God Create?" *Answers in Genesis,* 1 Apr. 2014, answersingenesis.org/tower-of-babel/how-many-races-did-god-create/.

(Hebrews 2:11; Romans 8:29), Who laid down His life to establish harmony within our family. May we always honor, cherish, and celebrate that! (Matthew 22:37-40)

The Common Descent of Humans

Reinforcing equal spiritual footing is the common descent of all humans. The opening pages of Genesis establish that all people descend through Adam and Eve, the biological father and mother of all people. Later in Genesis, all people are identified as descendants of Noah, post-Flood. This aspect of our descent is detailed in Genesis 6-10, most notably in the "Table of Nations" in Genesis 10, where Shem, Ham, and Japheth were to fulfill the original creation mandate to go forth, multiply, fill, and subdue the Earth (cf. Genesis 1:28; 8:15-19; 9:1, 7, 18-19).[144] Sadly though, there were issues along the way (i.e., the Tower of Babel in Genesis 11), and God forced people to fulfill His commission by dividing languages.

Note in the aforementioned passages that God's desire was not to create a race of automatons with aesthetic, emotional, and cultural uniformity, but rather to express His own depth through variation by means of aesthetic, emotional, and cultural diversity. Any of these differences (e.g., differing eumelanin and pheomelanin levels, hair consistency, body shape, facial structure, height, weight, etc.) do nothing to change our common descent. Common origin is incontestable fact; however, cultural differences must also be acknowledged, embraced, and celebrated. Awareness and sensitivity toward differences are an asset, not a liability, which has bearing on the growth of the seed of the gospel. As Wes McAdams writes,

> *"Every congregation needs to strive to be as diverse as the community in which it is located, because diversity in the kingdom of God is a direct*

---

[144] Keep in mind that these families became mixed over time. Thus, attempting to find a "pure" descendant of each son of Noah is endless, totally speculative, and wholly futile (1 Timothy 1:3-4; Titus 3:9). Also, although one descendent of Ham was cursed, this does not mean that all were or that everyone in Canaan's bloodline in particular was inherently cursed. Ham's other descendants, e.g., Cush (i.e., Ethiopia) and Mizraim (i.e. Egypt), are not cursed like Canaan is. Canaan's descendants are condemned because of their choices, not because of inherited guilt (cf. Genesis 15:16). Each person dies for his own sins (cf. Ezekiel 18:4, 20). For a more detailed breakdown of the "Table of Nations," see: Parker, Eric. "God Made Every Nation from One Person." Listen Now: Sermons, 24 Mar. 2019, www.taylorsvillerdchurchofchrist.com/listen-now/sermons/2019/03/24/god-made-every-nation-from-one-person.

testimony to the Gospel's power. We must work hard to break down the dividing walls, bringing different ethnic and cultural groups together."[145]

Truly, God has created humanity in such a way that cultural differences can complement one another and bring out the best in who we are if they are embraced. For this reason, "color-blindness" (i.e., ignoring variations in appearance and culture) is not the solution. Rather, the solution is to see that every man, woman, and child on this planet is your blood relative and spiritual equal!

This subject takes on great importance in the New Testament as Paul shares the message of salvation to the Athenians in Acts 17:22-31. The historian Luke records,

> *"So, Paul stood in the midst of the Areopagus and said, 'Men of Athens, I observe that you are very religious in all respects. For while I was passing through and examining the objects of your worship, I also found an altar with this inscription, 'To an unknown God.' Therefore, what you worship in ignorance, this I proclaim to you. The God who made the world and all things in it, since He is Lord of heaven and earth, does not dwell in temples made with hands; nor is He served by human hands, as though He needed anything, since He Himself gives to all people life and breath and all things; and He made from one man every nation of mankind to live on all the face of the earth, having determined their appointed times and the boundaries of their habitation, that they would seek God, if perhaps they might grope for Him and find Him, though He is not far from each one of us; for in Him we live and move and exist, as even some of your own poets have said, 'For we also are His children.' Being then the children of God, we ought not to think that the Divine Nature is like gold or silver or stone, an image formed by the art and thought of man. Therefore, having overlooked the times of ignorance, God is now declaring to men that all people everywhere should repent, because He has fixed a day in which He will judge the world in righteousness through a Man whom He has appointed, having furnished proof to all men by raising Him from the dead.'"*

Much scientific research has validated the biblical fact that all humans have a common ancestry. Among the key areas in which research has verified common origin include linguistics, genetics, and genealogies.

Linguists repeatedly demonstrate that the diversity of languages we see to-

---

[145] McAdams, Wes. "Racism Is Still a Problem, but There Is a Solution." *Radically Christian,* 21 Mar. 2018, radicallychristian.com/racism-is-still-a-problem-but-there-is-a-solution.

day traces to a common root through primary language families dating back to around the time of ancient Babylon.[146] Language researchers describe these language origins:

"The Tower of Babel explains why everyone doesn't speak the same language today. There are over 6,900 spoken languages in the world today. Yet the number of languages emerging from Babel at the time of the dispersion would have been much less than this—likely less than 100 different language families...Both Vistawide World Languages *and* Cultures and Ethnologue, *companies that provide statistics on language, agree that only 94 language families have been so far ascertained. With further study in years to come, this may change, but this figure is well within the range of families that dispersed from Babel (Genesis 10)."*[147]

"The ancestral form of the language family that includes Greek is called Proto-Indo-European. We do not know what the people who spoke this form called their language, since they left no records. They probably lived in southeastern Europe more than five thousand years ago. Eventually groups of Proto-Indo-European speakers broke off from the main community in repeated migrations, gradually spreading throughout Europe and western Asia from India to Britain. Separated from one another, they developed mutually unintelligible varieties of the original tongue. Greek, Latin, Sanskrit, and Russian are varieties of Indo-European, as are English, French, and German. Although these languages may be related, the changes that took place in them are quite different."[148]

Geneticists have also traced human biology to a common ancestry. Researchers describe these findings:

"There is simplicity and all-inclusiveness to the number three – the triangle, the Holy Trinity, three peas in a pod. So, it's perhaps not surprising that the Family of Man is divided that way, too. All of Earth's people, ac-

---

[146] Easy to see examples from the Indo-European language family include: *father* (English), *pater* (Greek), *pater* (Latin), and *pitar* (Sanskrit); *is* (English), *esti* (Greek), *est* (Latin), and *asti* (Sanskrit); and *three* (English), *treis* (Greek), *tres* (Latin), and *trayas* (Sanskrit).

[147] Hodge, Bodie. "Was the Dispersion at Babel a Real Event?" *The New Answers Book 2: Over 30 Questions on Creation/Evolution and the Bible,* by Ken Ham, Master Books, 2008.

[148] Black, David Alan. *Linguistics for Students of New Testament Greek: A Survey of Basic Concepts and Applications* (Grand Rapids: Baker, 1995), 144.

cording to a new analysis of the genomes of 53 populations, fall into just three genetic groups . . . Population geneticists expected to find dramatic differences . . . [but] that's not what scientists have found. Dramatic genome variation among populations turns out to be extremely rare."[149]

"According to evolutionists, this [tripartite division originated when humans left Africa tens of thousands of years ago, splitting into African, Eurasian, and East Asian groups (the third of which includes Pacific Islander and Native American groups). For creationists, that division makes plain sense as reflective of the people groups that split off after Babel, all descendants of Shem, Ham, and Japheth."[150]

Genealogists have also linked back to Noah, affirming the biblical narrative regarding humanity's common origins.[151] They have discovered that genealogies worldwide trace back to Noah through Shem, Ham, and Japheth. Early Irish genealogies trace through Japheth to Noah. The 8th-century Roman historian Nennius traced various lineages of European groups through Japheth to Noah, particularly the Gauls, Goths, Bavarians, Saxons, and Romans. The Miautso people of China trace their people back to Nuah by three sons: Lo Han, Lo Shen, and Jahphu.

Sin, Interpersonal Issues, and Familial Antagonism

Despite the spiritual equality of humans and the common origin of all people, brothers and sisters throughout all time have overlooked, disregarded, or become ignorant of these God-given truths. Brothers and sisters, fathers and mothers, far-distant cousins, and every other relationship people share has incited treachery, animosity, and antagonism by means of war, murder, slavery, theft, and a host of other unholy and ungodly behaviors and actions.

---

[149] Brown, David. "Among Many Peoples, Little Genomic Variety." *The Washington Post,* WP Company, 22 June 2009, www.washingtonpost.com/wp-dyn/content/article/2009/06/21/AR2009062101726.html?sid=ST2009062200350.

[150] "Three Genetic Groupings." *Answers in Genesis,* 4 July 2009, https://www.answersingenesis.org/genetics/human-genome/three-genetic-groupings. See also: Thomas, Brian. "DNA Trends Confirm Noah's Family." *The Institute for Creation Research,* 20 June 2016, www.icr.org/article/dna-trends-confirm-noahs-family.

[151] Hodge, Bodie. "Extra-Biblical Tables of Nations and Genealogies That Go Back to Noah?" *Answers in Genesis,* 28 June 2019, answersingenesis.org/racism/what-about-extra-biblical-tables-nations-genealogies-that-go-back-noah/.

In many ways, this is one of the prevailing themes of Scripture. God frequently presents fraternal antagonism throughout the journey of humanity in such cases as Cain and Abel (Genesis 4; 1 John 3:12), Jacob and Esau (Genesis 25-33), Joseph and the patriarchs of Israel (Genesis 37-50), Moses, Aaron, and Miriam (Exodus 32; Numbers 12), Benjamin and the other eleven tribes of Israel (Judges 20-21), Amnon and Absalom (2 Samuel 13-18), Solomon and Adonijah (1 Kings 1-2), and even Jesus and His brothers (Mark 3:21; John 7:1-5). Prejudice is also well-attested by the frequent issues between Israel and other ethnic groups and nations (e.g., Egypt, Ethiopia/Cush, Babylon, Medo-Persian, Greece, Rome, etc.). Despite common origin and spiritual value, the frequency with which interpersonal conflict occurs is a sad testimony to the ongoing campaign of humanity against sin. Such hostilities are foolish! As the prophet Malachi concluded, *"Do we not all have one father? Has not one God created us? Why do we deal treacherously each against his brother so as to profane the covenant of our fathers?"* (Malachi 2:10)

Spiritual Oneness in Salvation

God provided another and superior bloodline to unite us in a way that transcends the effects of sin. God gave up His only begotten Son that we could become children of God (cf. John 1:12-13; 1 John 3:1-2). In and through Christ, all people can become fellow partakers in the divine nature (2 Peter 1:4). Because of Jesus, salvation is freely offered to all people, of every nation, of every minor variation. The gospel openly grants access to Jews, Gentiles, Scythians, and Barbarians (Colossians 3:5-11). Cultural distinctions do not prohibit or aid one's access to the saving blood of Jesus Christ. The Ethiopian eunuch from Africa, Lydia of Thyatira in Europe, and the Israelites from Asia were all saved in the same way, with the same conditions (Acts 15:11). This continues to be the case today!

In Christ, believers become the household of faith in which there is a standard of behavior expected of such privileged people (1 Timothy 3:15). Formerly aligned with the powers of darkness, we may now spiritually align as brothers and sisters in arms. That means we have responsibilities to one another, and if we do not meet these responsibilities, we forfeit that relationship. *"If someone says, 'I love God,' and hates his brother, he is a liar; for he who does not love his brother whom he has seen, how can he love God whom he has not seen? And this commandment we have from Him: that he who loves God must love his brother also"* (1 John 4:20-21; cf. 2:9-11; 3:10-17; 4:20-21; 5:16). Love cannot abide the sort of hatred expressed by racism (Romans 12:9-18; 13:9-10; 1 Corinthians 13:1-8).

Though His household of faith is full of people with ongoing issues, we are working together toward a time where all of those issues are eradicated, and our family can be at supreme peace and harmony. People in the church may at times remind you of the world's brokenness. They may sometimes do or say things they should not. They may hurt you. But through patience, cooperation, and love, we will overcome all of our issues and be exalted in Christ. Though faulted, the revitalized family gained in the church helps us to solve, or at the very least cope with, the problems we see in our nuclear family, extended family, and in our family of common descent in all of humanity. God help those who do not have the church!

God's Nature and His Decrees Against Partiality

God rejects partiality in all ways. His very nature is impartial. He is no respecter of persons and is repeatedly said to be without partiality (e.g., Acts 10:34-35; Galatians 2:6; James 2:1). His identity is antithetical to the partiality of prejudice, racism, and injustice. God looks beyond the outward appearance, overcoming a pitfall common to mankind (1 Samuel 16:7). His identity also necessitates precepts and principles to guide the behaviors, attitudes, and thoughts of mankind toward that same character. To better imbibe the gospel, people must learn not to judge according to appearance, but rather to examine character with righteous judgment (John 7:24). In the body of Christ, we are even given instructions about submitting to one another and how to handle cultural differences (Romans 14-15; 1 Corinthians 8; 10; Philippians 2:1-4; Ephesians 4:1-3). At times, it may even be evangelistically significant to engage in or expand one's cultural affiliations (e.g., Acts 21:17-26; 1 Corinthians 9:19-23). The caveat on this is that if a culturally unique element causes one to offend his brother or sister, or is itself impure, it should be laid aside. Such mores are condemnable on spiritual grounds and are not a mark of racism no matter how normative they have become for a people group. Jesus is the Savior of the world (Genesis 12:3; 22:18; Luke 24:47; John 3:16-17; Romans 1:16; 1 Timothy 2:3-4; 1 John 4:14). There is no room for partitions in the family of God (Galatians 3:28). All should show respect and love toward each other as a universal, golden rule (Matthew 7:12; cf. James 3:8-9). Any who seek to produce strife among brothers and sisters are an abomination to the Lord (Proverbs 6:16-19).

How Can Christians Effectively Address Racism?

The sin of racism is widespread throughout history and is present in the world today. Despite many fantastic advances since the days of colonial slavery, the Civil War, and Jim Crow, there is still much work to be done! To continue moving forward, Christians must overcome apathy, frustration, fear, and denial with passion, hope, love, and recognition. The gospel has this power and has demonstrated it since its inception. One believer explains:

"Sadly, many Christians believe the Gospel is powerless to disrupt the sinful social order of the world. I strongly disagree. When the Gospel is TRULY proclaimed and embraced, it begins to set the social order straight. Relationships between spouses, neighbors, parents and children, employers and employees all begin to be transformed and redeemed. Slaveowners are convicted about owning and oppressing their brothers and sisters. Sculptors who made a fortune crafting idols, change their business model. Mothers who disposed of babies they didn't want, adopt babies others don't want. Feuding families and tribes forgive injustices of the past and move forward without animosity. The Gospel has been exposing and disrupting societal evil for 2,000 years."[152]

Let's direct our attention to consider some of the steps that we can all take together to apply this transformative power in the real world.

We all need first to transform our philosophical and metaphysical views of humanity and conform them to the instruction of Christ.[153] The second greatest commandment is to love your neighbor as yourself (Matthew 22:39). The Parable of the Good Samaritan (Luke 10:25-37) illustrates that anyone and everyone is your neighbor, regardless of skin tone, culture, or any other worldly differences. Our neighbors are our family, and our family unit is bombarded by sin at each moment, especially by racism. The causes of these fractures in our family are self-interest, pride, egotism, and a whole slew of other issues. Our lack of love, forgiveness, and mercy toward our fellow man drives wedges into our family unit. While we see this when it happens in our nuclear family, might we sometimes fail to see it on this grand level? Here's a question for us all to consider: *"What would you do to protect your family?"* We need to see sin from this perspective. Sin attacks our family, and unless we defend against it, sin will destroy our family. We need vigilance! (1 Peter 5:8) We need to protect our family! And if we harbor racism in our hearts, we cannot be pleasing to God and must repent or else be eternally judged.

---

[152] McAdams, Wes. "3 Problems with Christian Defeatism." *Radically Christian,* 22 Oct. 2020, https://www.radicallychristian.com/3-problems-with-christian-defeatism.

[153] Great resources from the perspective of racism and Christianity abound, but two are especially helpful. *The Gospel in Black and White: Theological Resources for Racial Reconciliation.* Edited by Dennis L. Okholm. InterVarsity Press, 1997. Colley, Glenn, et al. *It's There in Black and White: Scriptural Answers to 37 Questions People Are Asking About Racial Tension in the Church.* PlainSimpleFaith, 2020.

ASPECTS & ASSUMPTIONS OF **WHITENESS** & **WHITE CULTURE** IN THE UNITED STATES

White dominant culture, or **whiteness,** refers to the ways white people and their traditions, attitudes and ways of life have been normalized over time and are now considered standard practices in the United states. And since white people still hold most of the institutional power in America, we have all internalized some aspects of white culture—including people of color.

Rugged Individualism
• The individual is the primary unit
• Self-reliance
• Independence & autonomy highly valued + rewarded
• Individuals assumed to be in control of their environment,

Family Structure
• The nuclear family; father, mother, 2.3 children is the ideal social unit
• Husband is breadwinner and head of household
• Wife is homemaker and subordinate to the husband
• Children should have own rooms, be independent

Emphasis on Scientific Method
• Objective, rational linear thinking
• Cause and effect relationships
• Quantitative emphasis

History
• Based on northern European immigrants' experience in the United States
• Heavy focus on the British Empire
• The primacy of Western (Greek, Roman) and Judeo–Christian tradition

Protestant Work Ethic
• Hard work is the key to success
• Work before play
• "If you didn't meet your goals, you didn't work hard enough"

Religion
• Christianity is the norm
• Anything other than Judeo–Christian tradition is foreign
• No tolerance for deviation from single god concept

Status, Power & Authority
• Wealth = worth
• Your job is who you are
• Respect authority
• Heavy value on ownership of goods, space, property

Future Orientation
- Plan for future
- Delayed gratification
- Progress is always best
- "Tomorrow will be better"

Time
- Follow rigid time schedules
- Time viewed as a commodity

Aesthetics
- Based on European culture
- Steak and potatoes; "bland is best"
- Woman's beauty based on blonde, thin – "Barbie"
- Man's attractiveness based on economic status, power, intellect

Holidays
- Based on Christian religions
- Based on white history & male leaders

Justice
- Based on English common law
- Protect property & entitlements
- Intent counts

Competition
- Be #1
- Win at all costs
- Winner/loser dichotomy
- Action Orientation
- Master and control nature
- Must always "do something" about a situation
- Aggressiveness and Extroversion
- Decision-making
- Majority rules (when Whites have power)

Communications
- "The King's English" rules
- Written tradition
- Avoid conflict, intimacy
- Don't show emotion
- Don't discuss personal life
- Be polite

"This informational chart was included in an online resource for the Smithsonian's National Museum of African American History and Culture. Several inclusions on this list provoked a media firestorm because of it's counterproductiveness in fighting racism. In response, the Smithsonian museum took the chart down and apologized for their failure. Chart recreated by Moonlight Graphics based on the chart included in: Watts, Marina. *In Smithsonian Race Guidelines, Rational Thinking and Hard Work Are White Values.* 17 July 2020, www.newsweek.com/smithsonian-race-guidelines-rational-thinking-hard-work-are-white-values-1518333."

Practical steps build on this worldview transformation. Looking at the history of racism in our country reveals many hurts and past pains that continue into the present. We should all learn to appreciate and share these burdens with our brothers and sisters. Education in and exposure to diverse cultures will destroy ignorance and apathy. We must also learn to move forward in the present, learning from the past and creating a better and more promising future, devoid of animosity. We need to get involved in zoning commissions and local governments to craft policies that combat or overcome racism. We need to fight against abortion, which preys upon and devours minority families. We need to fight human trafficking, which disproportionately affects emerging majorities. We need to fight economic disenfranchisement in businesses, as Martin Luther King Jr. did when he was assassinated in Memphis in 1968. We need to encourage and build devout families who positively impact every facet of society.

Finally, all Christians must continually have healing, helpful, and holistic discussions regarding racism. To accomplish this, common pitfalls must be avoided! In order to overcome these trouble spots, we must all thoroughly commit to focusing on objective biblical truths, resisting race-baiting and gaslighting by means of misinformation and manipulation, especially in the realm of statistics ("Figures lie and liars figure!"), and loving all people because we are all created in the beautiful image of God.

Closing Thoughts

What is the cure for inequalities, inequities, prejudice, and racism? Laws? Education? Fines and penalties? All of these initiatives have been put to work and have helped, but they have imperfections that make them all only partial solutions. What Christians ultimately need to do is transform how we all see each other as human beings. We need to change our vision and the value that we attribute to others, raising our estimations to mimic heavenly values. We can and should do this by taking a look at our history to see humanity as we truly are. Nothing accomplishes this goal better than understanding mankind's creation and value in Christ. We close with a quote from Wes McAdams:

"Whole books could be written on how Gospel proclamation confronts and defeats racism. Sadly, books could also be written on how Christians have oversimplified, compromised, and failed to proclaim the Gospel, and thus fallen victim themselves to the snares of racism. Even so, nothing else can challenge and overcome racism like the Gospel.

On a theological level, the Good News about Jesus' reign is the foundation of our multiethnic, multinational, multilingual community in which the Spirit of God dwells (Ephesians 2). And on a practical level, the preaching of the Gospel helps us understand that people from other social and ethnic groups often have different cultures, perspectives, and even burdens to bear (Romans 14-15). When we embrace the Gospel, we embrace our responsibility and privilege to leverage our own wealth, status, and even our very lives for the good of one another (Philippians 2:1-11; 1 John 3:16).

I will say once again: Nothing is more central to the Gospel message than unity, and nothing is more contrary to the Gospel than racism. I know of no other way to deal with racism than preach and live out the Good News of Jesus' reign."[154]

---

[154] McAdams, Wes. "Is Preaching the Gospel Enough to Defeat Racism?" *Radically Christian*, 23 July 2020, https://www.radicallychristian.com/is-preaching-the-gospel-enough-to-defeat-racism.

Thought Questions

1) What emotions arose as you read this chapter and how did this information affect you?

_____

_____

_____

2) What issues may arise when using the oversimplistic terms "black" and "white"?

_____

_____

_____

3) What are some commonly cited examples of systemic racism?

_____

_____

_____

4) How important is strong biblical teaching on the origin of mankind?

_____

_____

_____

5) What is God's view on partiality? What are some challenging biblical examples that Christians should be prepared to respond to with respect to partiality?

_____

_____

_____

6) In what areas do you believe the church has been effective at fighting racism? In what areas do you believe it has not been as effective?

_____

_____

_____

7) What will you do this week to positively impact the problem of racism?

_____

_____

CHAPTER 12

Homelessness

In June 2013, Willie Lyle, the newly appointed minister for the Sango United Methodist Church in Clarksville, Tennessee, spent four-and-a-half days living on the streets in the semblance of a homeless man. After doing this, he lay under a tree on the church lawn covered by a large overcoat to see how many congregants would acknowledge him, approach him, and offer any form of assistance to him. Some did, but many did not. Once their worship services started, he transformed his visage and preached a message on the least parts of the body from 1 Corinthians 12. He said, *"Too many of us only want to serve God one hour each week. That doesn't cut it. That is not God's plan."*[155]

In November 2013, David Musselman posed as a homeless man and interacted with congregants outside of a Taylorsville, Utah Mormon church before services one Sunday. Some gave him money, most were indifferent, and five people asked him to leave the property. He describes the experience: *"Many actually went out of their way to purposefully ignore me, and they wouldn't even make eye contact. I'd approach them and say 'Happy Thanksgiving.' Many of them I wouldn't even ask for any food or any kind of money, and their inability to even acknowledge me being there was surprising."*[156]

---

[155] Parrish, Tim. "Pastor Goes Undercover for 5 Days as Homeless Man." *USA Today,* Gannett Satellite Information Network, 24 July 2013, www.usatoday.com/story/news/nation/2013/07/24/pastor-homeless-experience/2583241/.

[156] Stevens, Abby. *Mormon Bishop Disguises Himself as Homeless Man to Teach Congregation about Compassion.* Deseret News, 27 Nov. 2013, www.deseret.com/2013/11/27/20530459/mormon-bishop-disguises-himself-as-homeless-man-to-teach-congregation-about-compassion.

Now, be honest. What is your response to these two real-life news stories? Do these social experiments shock you? Or did you immediately begin justifying the actions of the congregants? Maybe it was a mixture of both? These examples are certainly not unique, and they teach us that evil perceptions, lack of compassion, maltreatment, and superficial judgment are prevalent among issues connected with homelessness.

Homelessness as a Psychosocial Issue

I have always been puzzled by the existence of homelessness, considering we live in a land of such exceeding bounty. I have lived in very rural areas of the country as well as metropolises, and have consistently seen it to varying degrees. I currently live in one of the largest cities in the country, Louisville, Kentucky, and the homeless population here, especially in wintertime, is quite large and conspicuous. I grew up in a little town called Lecanto, Florida, and while homelessness was nowhere near as prevalent as it is in Louisville, I still remember passing homeless people on the streets. Maybe you can sympathize based on your experience. If you live in a major city, homelessness tends to be more visible and prevalent. If you live in a rural area, homelessness may be less visible and prevalent. There are many factors impacting this disparity, but let's consider some baseline data to better comprehend how rampant homelessness is in the United States and what trends are taking place in efforts to address the underprivileged.

Recent homelessness data comes from Point-in-Time (PIT) and Housing-Inventory-Count (HIC) statistics gathered by the US Department of Housing and Urban Development (HUD), as well as the US Census Bureau's 2018 American Community Survey Single Year Estimates.[157] These numbers come from census data, research in homeless communities, and estimates made on the available data from homelessness assistance programs. The statistics are

---

[157] "PIT and HIC Data Since 2007." *HUD Exchange*, Jan. 2020, www.hudexchange.info/resource/3031/pit-and-hic-data-since-2007/. "2018 American Community Survey Single-Year Estimates." *The United States Census Bureau*, 26 Sept. 2019, www.census.gov/newsroom/press-kits/2019/acs-1year.html.

not without fault, but they generally gauge the issue.[158] According to this data:

- *Approximately 17 out of every 10,000 people in the US experienced homelessness on a single night in January 2019. This amounts to 567,715 human beings, and these numbers represent a cross-section of America, including every region of the country, family status, gender, and racial/ ethnic group.*
- *Of these 567,715 people, nearly 70% are individuals living on their own or in the company of other adults, while 30% are families with children.*
- *Males are disproportionately at higher risk of homelessness. Amongst homeless individuals, nearly 70% are males and unaccompanied male youth. This is the difference between 343,187 men and 219,911 women (the remaining 4,617 identify as transgender and gender non-conforming).*
- *37% of the total homeless population, or about 200,000 people, are unsheltered. This rate rises to 50% among homeless individuals due to greater resource availability for homeless families.*
- *By total number, Caucasians make up the largest portion of the homeless (approximately 270,607). Proportionately, Pacific Islanders and Native Americans are most likely to be homeless (160 out of every 10,000, almost 10x the national average).*
- *17% of the homeless population are disabled, 7% are veterans, and 6% are unaccompanied youth (<25 years old).*
- *National homelessness rates increased for three consecutive years between 2017 and 2019. Despite these recent increases, primarily among individuals, homelessness has had an overall decrease of 12% since 2007.*
- *Overall decreases in homelessness since 2007 have been highest among: veterans, whose rates are down 50%; families, whose rates are down*

---

[158] One source highlights the difficulty of gathering accurate statistics: *"Part of the difficulty is that there are different definitions of homelessness now in use. For example, the US Department of Housing and Urban development (HUD) uses a narrow definition largely limited to people living in shelters, in transitional housing and in public places. The US Department of Education (DoE) uses a broader definition that includes families who are doubled-up with others due to economic necessity. Another difficulty concerns methodology. HUD reports annual 'Point-in-Time' counts of the 'unsheltered' homeless population; however, the methodology used to collect those numbers varies by community and is often deeply flawed. HUD also reports annual counts of the sheltered population; this number varies with shelter capacity, which depends on variables such as available funding."* (*Homelessness in America: Overview of Data and Causes.* National Law Center on Homelessness & Poverty, Jan. 2015, nlchp.org/ wp-content/uploads/2018/10/Homeless_Stats_Fact_Sheet.pdf)

29%; people experiencing unsheltered homelessness, whose rates are down 10%; and chronically homeless individuals, whose rates are down 9%. These decreases are attributed to prioritization in policy and practice, specifically in funding decisions.

- *Among individual states, 37 have seen decreases in homelessness since 2007. Michigan, Kentucky, and New Jersey have seen the most substantial reductions.*
- *Homelessness rates have consistently been highest in California, Florida, New York, Texas, and Washington, D.C. 56% of people experiencing homelessness are in the five states with the largest homeless counts. Rates are lowest in Louisiana and Mississippi. This difference is typically explained in light of differences in housing costs and rent burdens.*
- *Temporary housing availability (e.g., Emergency Shelter, Safe Haven, and Transitional Housing) has decreased 9% since 2014. Temporary housing for families has been in surplus, while temporary housing for homeless individuals has met a 49% shortfall. Permanent housing availability (e.g., Permanent Supportive Housing (PSH), Rapid Re-Housing, and Other) has increased by 20% since 2014. These changes reflect shifts in policy priorities.*

Contributing Factors to Homelessness[159]

Homelessness results from an assortment of factors, some within the control of the homeless and others outside of their control. Let's consider a few of the major catalysts.

A large portion of homelessness results from the United States currently facing one of the most severe affordable housing crises in history. Prior to the mid-1980s, affordable housing was common and plenteous. Since then, however, the supply of low-cost housing has shrunk significantly. Compounding this dearth, rents have continually risen, and income disparities have grown. Currently, eight million extremely low-income households pay greater than half of their income toward housing! One controllable factor that plays a role in this problem is materialistic ambitions within the hearts of the poor, middle-class, and the wealthy. Living outside of one's means has become a hallmark of American society. "Keeping up with the Joneses" can play a poisonous role in homelessness. Materialism drives the poor to become poorer and the rich to strive more than ever for greater gains. Likewise, individualism and

---

[159] This section relies on the helpful information provided at: "Housing." *National Alliance to End Homelessness*, 27 Jan. 2020, endhomelessness.org/homelessness-in-america/what-causes-homelessness/.

pride are controllable factors that inhibit those in need from seeking assistance and those in a position to assist from providing aid. More selfishness, less collectivism, more profits, fewer investments, and housing issues exponentially rise as a result. Two additional elements that can compound the overall situation even further include a lack of ambition to better one's position in life by multiplying skills, and widespread abuse of available welfare and supplemental programs. Two less controllable factors include aging properties and population growth.

Homelessness also has strong connections to health issues and debts. This includes medical, dental, and mental health, but especially the latter. Of course, health issues become exacerbated by homelessness, so this only intensifies problems among the homeless. Data from the US Department of Housing and Urban Development consistently shows higher rates of acute and chronic health issues among the homeless. Their data reveals that people living in shelters are more than twice as likely to have a disability than the general population and are more than six times as likely to have diabetes, heart disease, and HIV/AIDS. Their data also shows 20% of the homeless population have a debilitating mental illness, 16% have conditions related to chronic substance abuse, and more than 10,000 have HIV/AIDS. These connections are compounded by the PTSD experienced by veterans and survivors of domestic violence, who are statistically far more likely to end up being homeless. For these two demographics, approximately 1 in 156 veterans become chronically homeless, and domestic abuse survivors make up 15% of all homeless adults.

For various reasons, some may willingly choose homelessness as a lifestyle.[160] The pressures of work, marriage, parenting, and other sources leads a person to seek escape. For many, the prospect of not going to a sixty-hour-a-week job, paying an overwhelming mortgage, being tied down to a place, etc., offers a seemingly welcome release. Some may even choose homelessness as a self-imposed punishment for shameful choices they have made. On the other hand, some suggest that the only type of people who choose homelessness are those with compromised mental faculties. These individuals argue that nobody of sound mind chooses homelessness. Still others believe that some choose to be in the open rather than staying at a shelter because they prefer freedom

[160] "Why Would A Homeless Person Not Want to Go to A Shelter?" *Bowery Residents' Committee,* www.brc.org/why-would-homeless-person-not-want-go-shelter. Shapiro, Ari. "Why Some Homeless Choose the Streets Over Shelters." NPR, 6 Dec. 2012, www.npr.org/2012/12/06/166666265/why-some-homeless-choose-the-streets-over-shelters. "The Reason Some Choose to Be Homeless." *Shelter Outfitters | Shelter Furniture,* www.shelteroutfitters.com/smartblog/5_the-reason-some-choose-to-be-homeless.html. Hanes, Kristin. *I Became Homeless on Purpose.* Marie Claire, 12 Oct. 2017, www.marieclaire.com/culture/a27792/homeless-on-purpose/.

from the rules that shelters often have, or are fearful of theft and abuse. To a degree, sympathy for any of these justifications for choosing homelessness is not hard to come by, but healthy choices, knowing the Lord, and having a relationship with Him and His people can surely help one cope with the stresses of life and offer far more wonderful freedoms than homelessness offers.

What Does the Bible Say About Homelessness?

The Bible deals with several facets of the issue of homelessness. The Parable of the Good Samaritan sheds perhaps the greatest light on the disciple's role toward the destitute. In fact, the whole point of this parable is to expose religious claims with no practical expression toward the afflicted (cf. James 2:14-26). Luke 10:25-37 records:

"And a lawyer stood up and put Him to the test, saying, 'Teacher, what shall I do to inherit eternal life?' And He said to him, 'What is written in the Law? How does it read to you?' And he answered, 'You shall love the Lord your God with all your heart, and with all your soul, and with all your strength, and with all your mind; and your neighbor as yourself.' And He said to him, 'You have answered correctly; do this and you will live.' But wishing to justify himself, he said to Jesus, 'And who is my neighbor?'

Jesus replied and said, 'A man was going down from Jerusalem to Jericho, and fell among robbers, and they stripped him and beat him, and went away leaving him half dead. And by chance a priest was going down on that road, and when he saw him, he passed by on the other side. Likewise, a Levite also, when he came to the place and saw him, passed by on the other side. But a Samaritan, who was on a journey, came upon him; and when he saw him, he felt compassion, and came to him and bandaged up his wounds, pouring oil and wine on them; and he put him on his own beast, and brought him to an inn and took care of him. On the next day he took out two denarii and gave them to the innkeeper and said, 'Take care of him; and whatever more you spend, when I return I will repay you.' Which of these three do you think proved to be a neighbor to the man who fell into the robbers' hands?' And he said, 'The one who showed mercy toward him.' Then Jesus said to him, 'Go and do the same.'"

As shown in this parable, true religion is expressed in deeds of mercy and love. God uses this paradigm in many other places:

"Is this not the fast which I choose,

To loosen the bonds of wickedness,
To undo the bands of the yoke,
And to let the oppressed go free
And break every yoke?
Is it not to divide your bread with the hungry
And bring the homeless poor into the house;
When you see the naked, to cover him;
And not to hide yourself from your own flesh?
Then your light will break out like the dawn,
And your recovery will speedily spring forth;
And your righteousness will go before you;
The glory of the Lord will be your rear guard." (Isaiah 58:6-8)

"Pure and undefiled religion in the sight of our God and Father is this: to visit orphans and widows in their distress, and to keep oneself unstained by the world." (James 1:27)

"But whoever has the world's goods, and sees his brother in need and closes his heart against him, how does the love of God abide in him? Little children, let us not love with word or with tongue, but in deed and truth." (1 John 3:17-18; cf. 4:19-20)

There are also significant theological reasons to aid the homeless. Though God is no respecter of persons, He often expresses a particular love and compassion toward the despised of society (e.g., Psalms 35:10; 112:9; 132:15; 140:12; Isaiah 25:4; Ezekiel 18:7; et al.). This aspect of God's nature often serves as the motivation clause for charitable deeds towards those people in need within His precepts (e.g., Leviticus 19) and also functions as a summary description of those to whom the gospel is given (e.g., James 2:5; Isaiah 61:1-3// Luke 4:18-19). Indeed, God has an incredibly unique ability to understand and empathize with homelessness in a way that may easily go unrecognized. Consider this theological truth in light of these verses:

"Jesus said to him, 'The foxes have holes and the birds of the air have nests, but the Son of Man has nowhere to lay His head.'" (Matthew 8:20)

"For you know the grace of our Lord Jesus Christ, that though He was rich, yet for your sake He became poor, so that you through His poverty might become rich." (2 Corinthians 8:9)

"Have this attitude in yourselves which was also in Christ Jesus, who, although He existed in the form of God, did not regard equality with God a thing to be grasped, but emptied Himself, taking the form of a bond-servant, and being made in the likeness of men. Being found in appearance as a man, He humbled Himself by becoming obedient to the point of death, even death on a cross. For this reason also, God highly exalted Him, and bestowed on Him the name which is above every name, so that at the name of Jesus every knee will bow, of those who are in heaven and on earth and under the earth, and that every tongue will confess that Jesus Christ is Lord, to the glory of God the Father." (Philippians 2:5-11; exemplified also in the apostolic ministry—1 Corinthians 4:11)

In light of Who God is and what Jesus has done for the church, who could refuse to show love and compassion to the world's afflicted? In truth, that is entirely in agreement with the spirit of Scripture as reflected in just a sampling of Old Testament and New Testament passages which teach God's people the virtue of caring for the poor and the needy (e.g., Leviticus 25:35-26; Psalm 82:3; Proverbs 29:7; 31:8-9, 20; Matthew 5:42; Luke 3:10-11; Acts 20:35; Galatians 2:10; Philippians 2:4; 1 Timothy 6:17-19; Hebrews 13:16). Imitating God's love stores up treasure in heaven and promises reward both now and in eternity (Proverbs 19:17; 22:9; 28:27; Isaiah 58:10; Matthew 6:19-20; 19:11; Luke 6:38; 14:13-14). The Scriptures also make a point of condemning apathetic oversight and/or exploitation of the poor and needy (Proverbs 14:31; 17:5; 21:13; 22:22-23; 30:14; Jeremiah 22:1-17; Ezekiel 16:49; 22:29).

Though such stipulations of God's followers are manifest, some believe that Jesus' teaching of the ever-present needs of the poor (cf. Matthew 26:11) in some way suggests that focus there is irrelevant or misguided. This runs aground on one of the most extensive passages focusing on care for the poor—Deuteronomy 15:1-11. Verse 11 says that it is precisely because the poor never cease from the land that God's people have a responsibility to attend to them! To misuse Jesus' words to justify apathy and disinterest is irreverent and profane, engaging in the same wresting of Scriptures that Satan exhibits (cf. Matthew 4:1-11; 2 Peter 3:16). But what of those who have contributed to their own downfall through their actions? All have fallen, including you and me. Would you not like a hand up even when you tripped yourself? Even so, tough love may at times be necessary as is most certainly the case for those with no interest in working (2 Thessalonians 3:10). In the instance of those whose nefarious activities led to their own homelessness, they are to turn from their ways, making a concerted effort to change their circumstances, in turn enabling them to help others (Ephesians 4:28).

How Can Christians Effectively Address Homelessness?

Helping the homeless sounds good in theory, but how does theory become a practical reality? The National Alliance to End Homelessness provides some general logistical direction for assisting people to exit homelessness quickly.[161] They state: *"The goals of an effective crisis response system are to identify those experiencing homelessness, prevent homelessness when possible, connect people with housing quickly and provide services when needed."* They proceed to describe the necessary elements to achieve these goals as:

- *Outreach: Outreach workers connect people at risk of or experiencing homelessness to coordinated entry, emergency services, and shelter. They work with other programs in the system to connect people to stable, permanent housing.*
- *Coordinated entry: Coordinated entry is a process designed to quickly identify, assess, refer and connect people in crisis to housing, assistance, and services.*
- *Diversion and prevention: Prevention and diversion are important components of a community's crisis response and can help it reduce the size of its homeless population. Prevention assistance can aid households in preserving their current housing situation, while diversion prevents homelessness for people seeking shelter by helping them identify immediate alternate housing arrangements and, if necessary, connecting them with services.*
- *Emergency shelters and interim housing: People experiencing a housing crisis or fleeing an unsafe situation need to quickly find a place to stay. Emergency shelter and interim housing can fill this role in a crisis response system. These interventions should be low-barrier and align their goals and program activities with the larger system's goals.*
- *Permanent housing: A crisis response system must have the capacity to connect people experiencing homelessness with permanent housing programs, such as rapid re-housing, permanent supportive housing, and other stable housing options.*

While these logistical elements are vital and advantageous, Christians also need some practical guidance on how the spiritual intersects with the psychosocial issue of homelessness. As noted above, homelessness springs from a variety of factors. These factors can have individual and/or collective com-

---

[161] "Crisis Response." *National Alliance to End Homelessness*, 25 Jan. 2019, https://www.endhomelessness.org/ending-homelessness/solutions/crisis-response/.

ponents as well as controllable and/or unforeseeable considerations. Because of this multiplicity of factors, many options are available in order to spiritually engage the issues that arise with homelessness. With these options, compassion, creativity, and dedication can help both churches and the individual Christian play a part in addressing the homeless or soon-to-be homeless who are so often neglected.

Collectively, churches can serve a primary role in shaping people's worldview and driving philosophical change as a spiritual consequence of the gospel of Jesus Christ. This may be done by steadfastly instilling cornerstone spiritual values: the sanctity of all human life; the mercy of God upon the helpless and destitute; the importance of labor and diligence; the value of family and home; the responsibilities of God's people towards family, friends, and neighbors; the dangers of substance addictions; sound financial stewardship; etc. Christians can extend healing and freedom to veterans, domestic abuse survivors, and the ailing. Christians can offer grace, mercy, and forgiveness to the pimps, prostitutes, drug dealers, and sinners of the world upon the condition of repentance. In so doing, this will strategically minimize those who fall into homelessness and limit reoccurrence. Conscientiously performed, this would all be entirely within the realm of the church's spiritual focus, the authorizations of the New Testament, and the preeminence of the spiritual man, without apathetically marginalizing the afflicted in the real world.

In the individual realm, the scriptural shaping of the spiritual man and woman would lead to the type of zeal for good deeds for which God's people are remade (cf. Ephesians 2:8-10; Titus 2:11-14). Simple, immediate, and practical actions might include: collecting and delivering tents, blankets, hot drinks, gloves, and extra socks during cooler seasons; providing cool water and drinks during hot seasons; and keeping quick meal kits or handout bags in your car. When preparing and while engaged in these works, keep in mind that a homeless person may not have everything needed to prepare these meals. Canned foods without pop-tops need a can opener, macaroni and cheese needs butter and milk, Rice-a-Roni requires oil, Hamburger Helper needs ground beef, cleansing requires clean water, shampoo, and body wash, etc. Also keep in mind that certain items are a luxury for the homeless (e.g., feminine hygiene products, sugar and flour, cake, sandwich bread, a haircut, quarters and laundry detergent for clothes, pillows and blankets, etc.). Other commitments might include job and skills training, resume development and production, hygiene treatments, medical and dental treatments, mental health counseling, transportation, and a host of other possibilities. These can be pursued in proportion to one's personal talents and opportunities, as a mediator for or supporter of the government and non-profit agencies who may have greater information, assets, and resources at their disposal.[162] Please keep in mind that while the work of the collective church is to focus on benevolence for its members, edification, and evangelism, the work of Christians individually is not so limited (Galatians 6:10). In full harmony with the Scriptures, Christians may develop groups outside of the spiritual collective of the church to organize such benevolent efforts.

Closing Thoughts

Is our faith as radical as it needs to be? Are we willing to go the extra mile for those created in the image of God? Is our faith consequential? Famed writer David Platt shares two examples challenging our often words-only level of dedication. He writes:

"One Christian in India, while being skinned alive, looked at his persecutors and said, 'I thank you for this. Tear off my old garment, for I will soon put on Christ's garment of righteousness.'

As he prepared to head to his execution, Christopher Love wrote a note to his wife, saying, 'Today they will sever me from my physical head, but they cannot sever me from my spiritual head, Christ.' As he walked to his death, his wife applauded while he sang of glory."[163]

The next time you see a homeless person, see them through the eyes of Jesus. While the sad reality of this world is that you cannot help each and every circumstance related to a person's homelessness, and you may not be able to provide deliverance for everyone, you can consistently show compassion, make a concerted effort, and do all that you can to inhibit people's descent into homelessness.

Let's close this chapter and indeed this entire book with one last consider-

---

[162] Groups that assist with everything from healthcare to job skills training include the National Health Care for the Homeless Council (https://nhchc.org) and Understanding Homelessness (http://www.understandhomelessness.com). The latter has a fantastic tool that categorizes opportunities to help the homeless based on the benefactor's situation in life (http://www.understandhomelessness.com/strategies/).

[163] Platt, David. *Radical: Taking Back Your Faith from the American Dream.* Multnomah Books, 2010, 35. Another one of Platt's resources that is helpful for the entire subject matter of this book, though imperfect, is: Platt, David. *A Compassionate Call to Counter Culture In a World of Poverty, Same-Sex Marriage, Racism, Sex Slavery, Immigration, Persecution, Abortion, Orphans, Pornography.* Tyndale House Publishers, 2015.

ation of the Final Judgment scene in Matthew 25:31-46:

> *"But when the Son of Man comes in His glory, and all the angels with Him, then He will sit on His glorious throne. All the nations will be gathered before Him; and He will separate them from one another, as the shepherd separates the sheep from the goats; and He will put the sheep on His right, and the goats on the left.*
>
> *Then the King will say to those on His right, 'Come, you who are blessed of My Father, inherit the kingdom prepared for you from the foundation of the world. For I was hungry, and you gave Me something to eat; I was thirsty, and you gave Me something to drink; I was a stranger, and you invited Me in; naked, and you clothed Me; I was sick, and you visited Me; I was in prison, and you came to Me.' Then the righteous will answer Him, 'Lord, when did we see You hungry, and feed You, or thirsty, and give You something to drink? And when did we see You a stranger, and invite You in, or naked, and clothe You? When did we see You sick, or in prison, and come to You?' The King will answer and say to them, 'Truly I say to you, to the extent that you did it to one of these brothers of Mine, even the least of them, you did it to Me.'*
>
> *Then He will also say to those on His left, 'Depart from Me, accursed ones, into the eternal fire which has been prepared for the devil and his angels; for I was hungry, and you gave Me nothing to eat; I was thirsty, and you gave Me nothing to drink; I was a stranger, and you did not invite Me in; naked, and you did not clothe Me; sick, and in prison, and you did not visit Me.' Then they themselves also will answer, 'Lord, when did we see You hungry, or thirsty, or a stranger, or naked, or sick, or in prison, and did not take care of You?' Then He will answer them, 'Truly I say to you, to the extent that you did not do it to one of the least of these, you did not do it to Me.' These will go away into eternal punishment, but the righteous into eternal life."*

Thought Questions

1) What emotions arose as you read this chapter and how did this information affect you?

_____

_____

2) What was your response to the two news stories that opened the chapter?

_____

_____

3) Is homelessness equally seen in urban and rural areas? Why or why not?

_____

_____

4) What are two contributing factors to homelessness and what does the Bible have to say about these factors?

_____

_____

5) What biblical people faced homelessness and what can we learn from their experiences?

_____

_____

6) How might developing a standard operating procedure with your local congregational leadership more effectively address homeless attendees?

_____

_____

7) What will you do this week to positively impact those struggling with homelessness?

_____

_____

Made in USA - North Chelmsford, MA
1313933_9781941422595
05.11.2022 0825